MW01053165

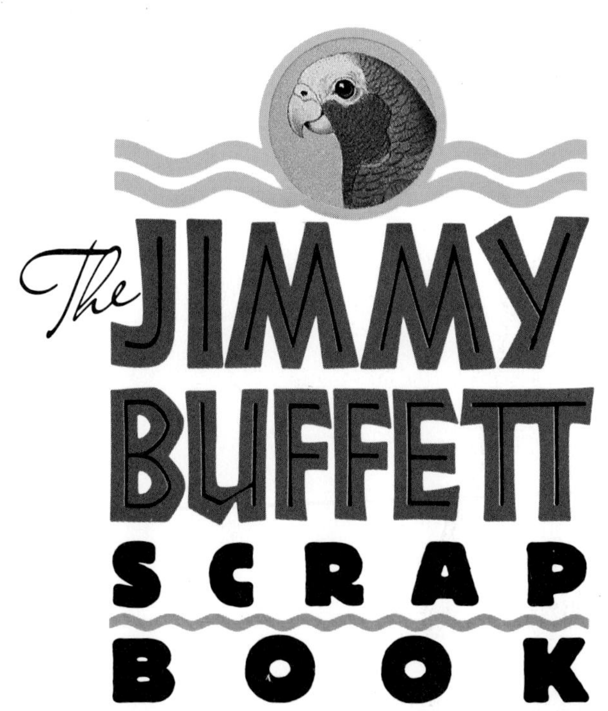
The JIMMY BUFFETT SCRAP BOOK

Terry Brykczynski Collection

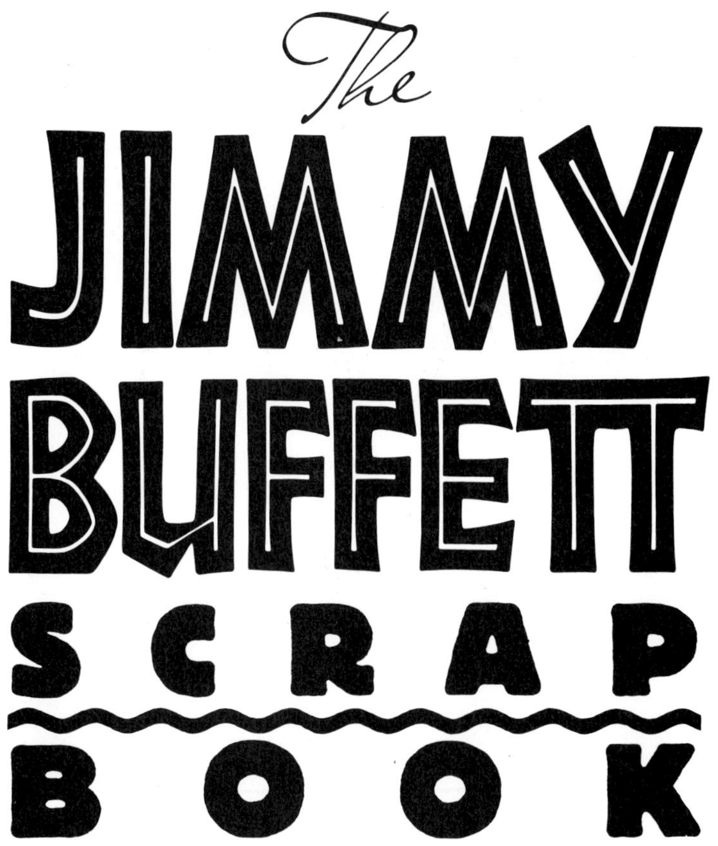

MARK HUMPHREY
WITH HARRIS LEWINE

A Citadel Press Book
Published by Carol Publishing Group

A Citadel Press Book
Published by Carol Publishing Group
Citadel Press is a registered trademark of Carol Communications, Inc.

Editorial Offices: 600 Madison Avenue, New York, N.Y. 10022
Sales and Distribution Offices: 120 Enterprise Avenue, Secaucus, N.J. 07094
In Canada: Canadian Manda Group, P.O. Box 920, Station U, Toronto, Ontario M8Z 5P9

Queries regarding rights and permissions should be addressed to: Carol Publishing Group, 600 Madison Avenue, New York, N.Y. 10022

Carol Publishing Group books are available at special discounts for bulk purchases, for sales promotion, fund-raising, or educational purposes. Special editions can be created to specifications. For details, contact: Special Sales Department, Carol Publishing Group, 120 Enterprise Avenue, Secaucus, N.J. 07094

Produced, Edited, and Art Directed by Harris Lewine

Manufactured in the United States of America
10 9 8 7 6 5 4 3 2 1

Library of Congress Cataloging-in-Publication Data

Humphrey, Mark.
The Jimmy Buffett scrapbook / by Mark Humphrey with Harris Lewine.
p. cm.
"A Citadel Press book."
ISBN 0-8065-1461-2
1. Buffett, Jimmy—Portraits. 2. Rock musicians—United States—Portraits. I. Lewine, Harris. II. Title.
ML88.B79H8 1993
782.42164'092—dc20
[B] 93-26115
CIP
MN

CONTENTS

ACKNOWLEDGMENTS

Along with some preferring anonymity, the following individuals and research facilities provided invaluable information and resource materials for preparation of this book, and the authors wish to extend deeply felt thanks to them. *Akron:* Mark Faris. *Atlanta:* Russ DeVault. *Chicago:* Susie Philipson. *Key West:* Dink Bruce, Joyce Carpenter, Tom Hambright, Historical Director, Monroe County Library; John Hellen, Bud Jacobson, Wright Langley, Vic Latham, Tina Lutz, Shelly Malone, Bobby Mayo, Paulie Raymond, Chris Robinson, Carol Shaughnessy, Phil Tenney, Sharon Wells, and Freddie, a Full Moon Saloon customer. *Los Angeles:* Mary Katherine Aldin, Larry Cohn, Bob Kingsley, Barry Hansen (Dr. Demento), Music Library, UCLA; Santa Monica Public Library. *Memphis:* Larry Nager. *Mobile:* Carol Cain. *Nashville:* Peyton Hoge, Paul Kingsbury, Reggie Young. *New Orleans:* Syndey Byrd. *New York:* Michael Abramson, Phil Ahrens, Gotham Book Mart; The American Dust Company, Paul Bacon, The Bettmann Archive, Bookleaves, Steven Brower, Carol Publishing; Terry Brykczynski, Culver Pictures, Frank Driggs Collection, Paul Gamarello, Eyetooth Design; The Golden Disc, Illustration House, Stan King Collection, Harris Lewine Collection, Lawson Little, Margaret Miller, Mitch Miller, Music Division, NYPL for the Performing Arts; Photofest, Retna, Ltd., Geoff Rizzo, Dave Rosetti, Strider Records, Skyline Books & Records, George Waltman, Wide World Photos. *Pascagoula:* Curtis Rockwell. *St. Petersburg: Florida Trend* magazine.

And finally, special thanks to Key Wester Scotty Hillman of the houseboat *Pink Cloud*—the benign friend of a quarter century whose knowledge of that land's-end milieu enhanced this book immeasurably—and cat John Ballouz ("me, me, me").

Every effort has been made to identify the copyright owners of the pictures used in this publication; we aplogize for any omissions.

Introduction

Hail to you, Dionysos, son of fair Semele.
He who forgets you can never fashion sweet song.
—From the Homeric hymn *Dionysos and the Pirates*
circa seventh century B.C., translated by Penelope Proddow

Long ago in ancient Greece, otherwise respectable women ran naked through the woods with a goat god, Dionysos, who lured them with music, plied them with wine, and gamboled with them in frankly goatlike fashion. The day after an ecstatic night on the woods, the women returned to their mundane business of weaving, herding, and housewifery. But for the night, at least, they had been consorts of a god.

Across America for generations, college football games have been an accepted opportunity for young scholars to blow off steam. Blow they do, though their antics pale alongside the bloodcurdling (and often alcohol-induced) whooping of the alumni. Come Monday, they'll be tied to their jobs and families again, but for Saturday afternoon at least, they are once again nineteen, free, and fearless.

As humans we have a need for something like this. It's a need understood and expressed variously by Pentecostal preachers, rock singers, coaches, and female mud wrestlers. With time we are increasingly fettered by responsibilities and an inevitable awareness of our own mortality. We yearn for the abandon of youth and some ritual forum for reliving it, if only briefly and symbolically. Such forums often offer alcohol as a depressant to inhibitions. Happily buzzed, we proclaim our oneness with other supplicants by wearing an identifying uniform—a team sweatshirt for some rituals, Hawaiian shirts and shark-fin hats for others. We deeply need such a community of abandon. "My songs," Jimmy Buffett told *USA Weekend* in 1986, "touch on people's desire to have controlled insanity." In an America increasingly committed to abstemiousness and caution, the popularity of Buffett's concerts has mushroomed in recent years.

Mushroomed, even as this singer-celebrity has visibly aged. He does not kid us that he is a kid. Can one be a middle-aged Dionysos? Jimmy Buffett teases us with the question. He flaunts his adventures in seaplanes, his fabulous wealth and extravagant lifestyle, his travels to exotic climes. He beams a beatific bright smile and seems to say, "Yes, I've got it *all,* and through me, you, too."

If that sounds too messianic, consider that Buffett was born on Christmas and raised Catholic. Along with volumes by Mark Twain, Faulkner, and Hemingway, one of this voracious reader's favorite books is Joseph Campbell's The Power of Myth. More than the average pop music or sports star, Buffett clearly understands exactly the kind of dance in which he and his fans are engaged.

It's a pretty straightforward one, really. Buffett has never been one for mercurial image-lifts or cryptic poses. He has always called his songs "90 percent autobiographical," and proudly points to his influences in everything from literature to movies to music to his family. Bluntly honest about his appetities and enthusiasms, he is a man who clearly likes being liked. Buffett is as apt to haul out his closet's skeleton for your admiration as he is to lock the closet door when company comes.

His life, more than that of many performers, is an open book, one whose theme obviously is the enjoyment of life. We have rewarded his enthusiasm by making Buffett wealthy, a man with many toys. The more he feeds our fantasy—"Growing Older but Not Up"—the richer we make him. The richer we make him, the more Buffett beams his beatific smile our way. In Memphis, a band called Armed Voices performs a song they've written called "I Wish I Was Jimmy Buffett for Just One Night." For those of us who can't be, but wish, may this book be a pleasant diversion. For just one night.

Spring 1993

CHAPTER ONE

Tripping on the Three-Masted Cadillac

We're the closest thing to the fucking circus you'll ever see.
–Jimmy Buffett describes himself and
his Coral Reefers to a concert audience

Sing we for love and idleness,
Naught else is worth the having.
–Ezra Pound, *An Immortality*

"Isn't this just the *coolest,* Lorraine?" says one woman in shorts and a bright tropical blouse to another. They are walking through a parking lot loose with revelers wearing pink flamingo-shaped balloons on their heads, or shark-fin hats, or papier-mâché parrots, or pirate caps, or straw hats crowned with fruit and drink glasses. Beer bottles and plastic cups in hand, the partiers weave among vehicles topped by shark fins. A Toyota four-wheeler displays the license plate PARUT HD. From the door of one RV spills a group of college-age kids, male and female, wearing grass skirts. Atop another, a bearded dad and his tiny pirate-hatted daughter scan the horizon with binoculars as Jolly Rogers fly from their craft. Footballs are tossed; passersby are playfully doused by high-pressure water guns. Tailgaters drinking strong spirits sing along with tape decks playing Jimmy Buffett. You are never out of earshot of his music, be it on tape or a boozy parking lot sing-along.

It is the first Friday of June, the first post-Memorial Day weekend of summer. In a couple of hours Jimmy Buffett will take the stage at California's Irvine Meadows to play the second of thirty-six performances in his 1993 Chameleon Caravan Tour. At the outset of 1992's Recession Recess Tour, Buffett announced, "A lot of people don't believe it, but this will be the last summer for a while." There was good reason to disbelieve it, especially considering the size and loyalty of Buffett's following and the money generated by his appearances. "He made a million bucks last year for

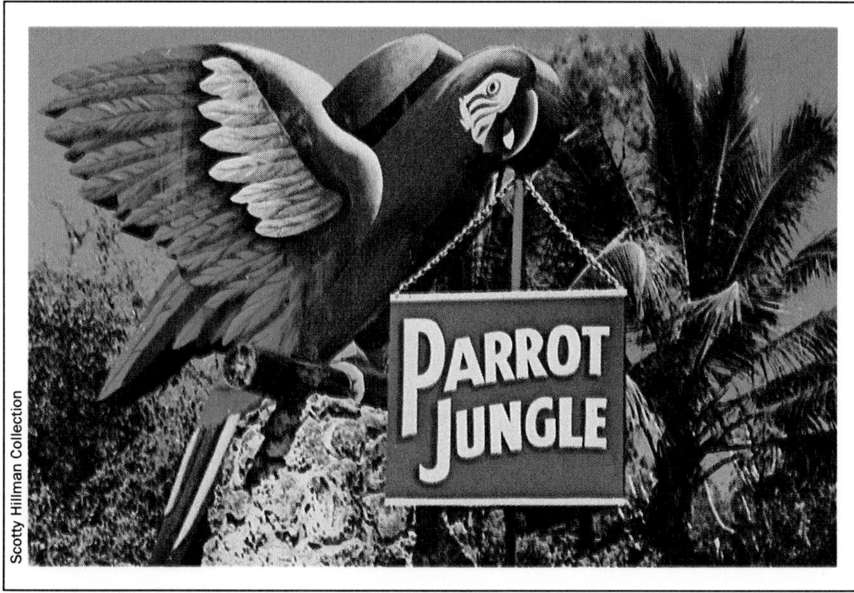

Scotty Hillman Collection

IMA0604 LOGE 4 AA 410 ADULT
37.25 $35.00+ $2.25SUR 37.25
4.00 CORONA EXTRA PRESENTS
LOGE 4 JIMMY BUFFETT
SECTION/AISLE
CA 21X PROD. BY AVALON
AA 410 IRV.MEAD.AMPH.*RAIN/SHINE
ROW/BOX SEAT
OPL1452 MLT.FLT. MAY CAUSE PSTPNM
A28APR3 FRI JUN 4, 1993 8:00 PM

Author's Collection

four nights," former *Cincinnati Post* pop critic Larry Nager marveled in recalling Buffett's 1992 stint at Cincinnati's Riverbend Amphitheater. The Chameleon Caravan pitched its tent for *six* nights at Riverbend in 1993, meaning that, at a single venue, nearly a hundred thousand tickets were sold.

Tickets to the Chameleon Caravan do not come cheap—a loge seat at Irvine Meadows costs $35—and tickets are only a part of Buffett's concert revenue. He has a lucrative endorsement deal with Corona beer; his opening act, The Iguanas, is a band signed to his own label, Margaritaville Records; T-shirts and sweatshirts on sale at concert concessions, ranging from $25 to $45, are another important revenue source. Buy a ticket, guzzle a beer, take home a souvenir T-shirt: One can easily contribute $100 to maintaining Buffett's yachts, seaplanes, and multiple homes.

Making no apologies for being rich, Buffett is uncommunicative about the extent of his financial empire. Even by not factoring in his two Margaritaville nightclubs/restaurants/souvenir shops in Key West and New Orleans, earnings from the best-selling novel *Where Is Joe Merchant?* and other writings, and sales of recordings or threads via his Caribbean Soul apparel line, or income from any less public business ventures, simple arithmetic suggests why Buffett is still willing in his forty-sixth summer to clown and croon from Memorial Day to Labor Day.

If he plays 36 annual dates at venues such as Irvine Meadows, seating 15,000 customers (some

Photo: Syndey Byrd

"Another opening , another show." Chameleon Caravan Tour, 1993.

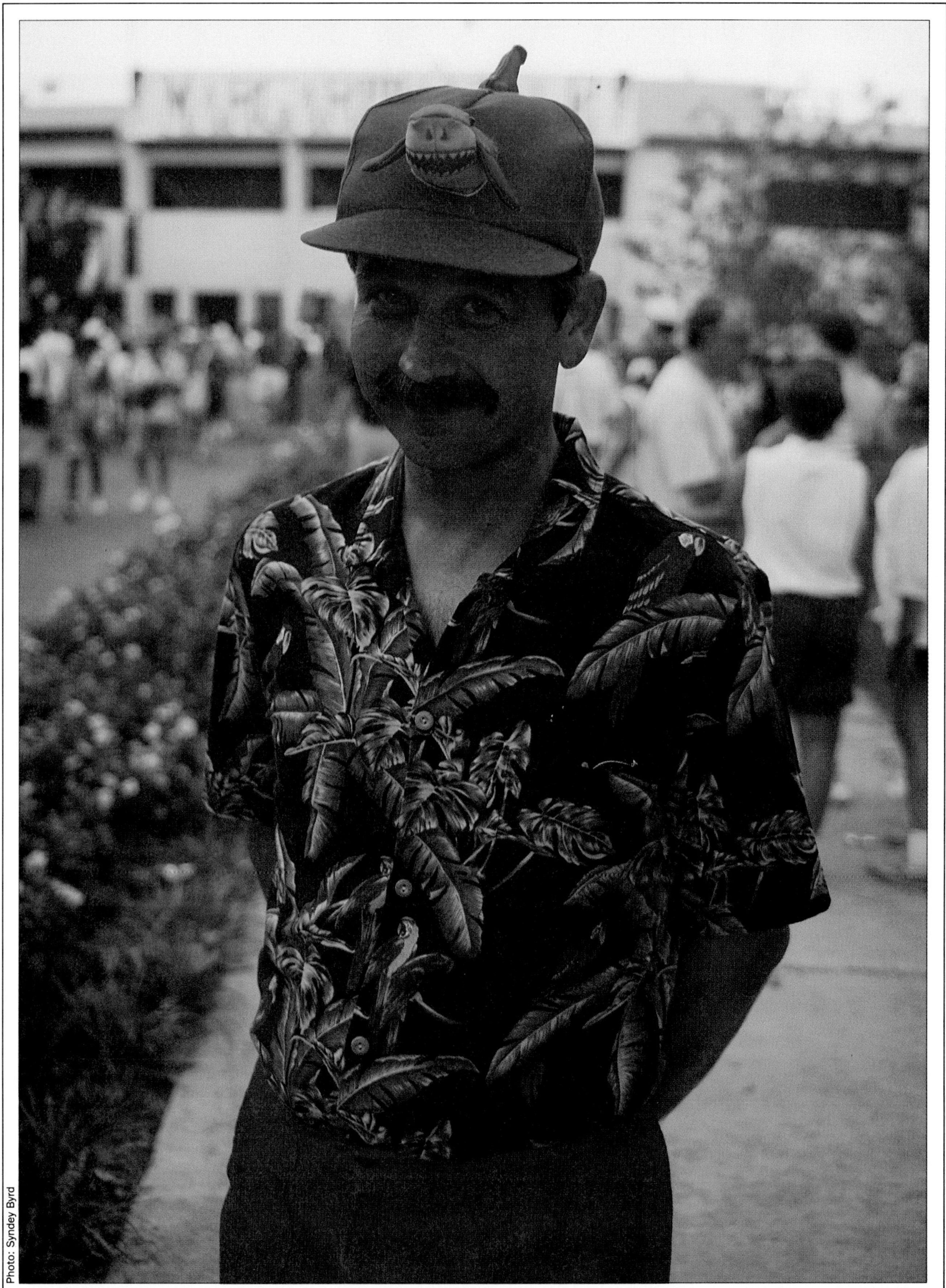

Photo: Syndey Byrd

"Oh, the shark has pretty teeth, dear."—Bertolt Brecht. Primo Parrothead Partier expresses oneness with Buffett's world.

seat twice that many), that's 540,000 tickets. As an arbitrary figure, let's say the average fan spends $50 (ticket included) at a Buffett concert. Multiply that by 540,000, and you enjoy a gross profit of $27 million. Buffett, of course, won't pocket that much from touring. For one thing, he has to pay a 50-person entourage, ranging from band members to bus drivers. But if he were to clear even somewhat less than a quarter of that hypothetical figure, say around $5 million, then he's had what many of us would call a remarkable summer vacation. And he may do far better.

His record sales always zoom during his tour season, so with nothing fresh to ship this year Buffett dusted off some twenty-three-year-old recordings and released them as *Before the Beach.* Regardless of the anachronism of this Vietnam-era folk rock, Buffett knows his fans will eagerly snap up the album. For the same reason, a sampler album of acts who have played his Margaritaville Cafe called *Late Night Menu* is stickered to emphasize that it contains three otherwise unavailable Buffett performances. Both *Before the Beach* and *Late Night Menu* were shipped to stores the week before the Chameleon Caravan Tour began, a marketing strategy tied to Buffett's presence on the road and his fans' eagerness to scoop up his every recording as a part of their summer "feeding frenzy." Given the secrecy with which such information is guarded, there's no telling how much this upped Buffett's summer take. It seems ironic now that he once penned a piece for his *Coconut Telegraph* fan newsletter grousing about the cost of *laundry* on the road!

Walking through an Orange County parking lot, Lorraine and her friend will soon become as one with a mass of 15,000 happy drunks baying under a full moon. These women in floral print blouses are not young—they are easily Buffett's age—but he assures them (and us) that aging doesn't mean abandoning the party. Nor does it mean pretending to be young when you obviously aren't. "I'm the spokesman for the bald-spot generation," Buffett once bragged to *USA Today.* He jokes about getting older onstage ("That was when we still had *hair,*" he says after a vintage video clip), and is cheerfully self-deprecating in a way that demeans neither himself nor his audience. Yet he isn't an "oldies" act, not in the usual sense anyway, and many of the partiers at his concerts weren't even born when Buffett first came to national attention twenty summers before his Chameleon Caravan Tour.

"Who wants to do a beer bong?" shouts a young man in shorts and a pirate hat as he lopes across the parking lot, funnel in hand. "I've *got* to find a bathroom," says one girl to another as they weave toward the amphitheater. Neither was born when Buffett waxed "Why Don't We Get Drunk (and Screw)" in 1973. To her friend, but really for the benefit of a guy walking past, the full-bladdered young lady announces, "I got *laid* today." No response. Louder, in case he missed it: "I got *laid* today. Did *you?*"

"*That* looks like a good place to piss!" The absence of port-a-potties in the parking lot prior to Buffett's concert is a strategical disaster. Puddles alongside cars suggest some partiers simply take the path of least resistance. When the gates to the outdoor amphitheater finally open, a pack of young men desperately survey the landscape for a place to disgorge their beer-swollen bladders. Their leader has spotted some bushes at the top of a ridge, and they gallop toward them like a pack of hounds pursuing the sole fire hydrant in the Sahara. Had they waited to stand in endless restroom lines, they would have witnessed their fellows swilling the source of their discomfort even as they hunkered over the urinals. Drinking at a Buffett concert is a serious sport.

Tailgate partiers in the parking lot are at least half the show at a Buffett concert. Many have found imaginative ways to achieve oneness with the world that Buffett's songs describe for them. Merely getting drunk isn't enough. *Atmosphere* is essential. One group at Irvine mingled around a bamboo-thatched bar that they had set up for the evening. Alongside it, an oil lamp on a pole flamed from a wicker basket. Behind the bar, a truck tailgate supported an impressively tall potted palm. There, in the middle of an Orange County parking lot, was a replica of a 1950s tiki bar. "Heh, heh, yeah," said a bearded man enjoying a libation there. "A *scotch* tiki bar."

Oneness expressed itself, too, by apparel and headgear. "Isn't this just the *coolest?*" is an odd question here, since the faithful at a Buffett concert, the fans he calls his Parrot Heads, aren't trying to be cool. Not the least bit. Everyone is dressed up to get messed up. One man strolls through the crowd in a full-face parrot mask, complete with feathers. He adjusts the mask to get the eyeholes centered, though his vision may be askew for other reasons. A burly guy wears a T-shirt proclaiming erection specialists—WE ALWAYS GET IT UP. It provokes the admiration of a young lady who introduces herself by pawing his back in a slow-motion stupor. A bald man has what looks from a distance like a scar or birthmark running down the top of his skull. It isn't. Tattooed atop his chrome dome is a bright red parrot. Buffett inspires exceptionally devoted fans.

Perhaps no greater symbol of that devotion appeared among the parking-lot pre-concert revelers than the vehicle Buffett himself christened "the three-masted Cadillac." He had the number of masts right, though not the make of car. It is really a white Oldsmobile Fiesta Super 88 station wagon from the 1960s. It is a great drunken apparition, Mom's station wagon become a pirate ship crewed by naked Barbie dolls. The Barbies stand watch in crow's nests on the ship's three masts, waving to the world as they pass. In the center of the car's hood is a pirate's treasure chest containing not doubloons or pieces of eight but cheeseburgers—plastic painted cheeseburgers! Jutting from the grill of this Fiesta Super 88 is a prow, and tied on the prow is another naked Barbie, and on the breasts of *this* naked Barbie have been painted bright red nipples. No, the nipples aren't simply an additional crudity lavished on the last Barbie rigged to the vessel, a drunken afterthought. As with everything else in his fans' fantasy world, they are careful references to the iconography of Buffett's work. In this case, the reference is not to a song but to a passage in *Where Is Joe Merchant?* Desdemona, the hippie backup singer turned would-be starship traveler, says: "All the ships of the great adventurers adorned the bows of their vessels with bare-breasted women. Legend has it that a bare-breasted woman can calm a raging storm."

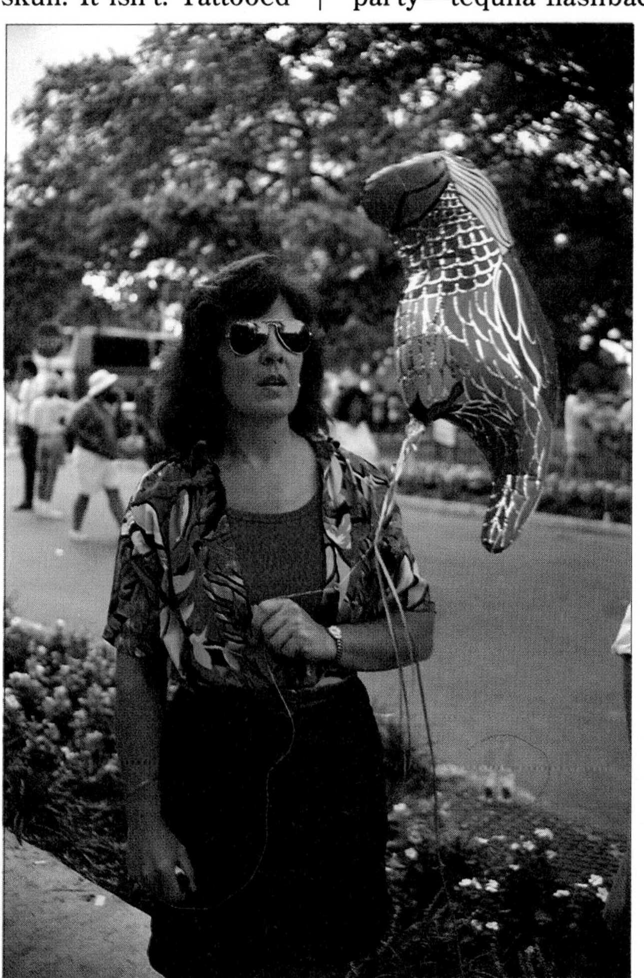

Photo: Syndey Byrd

"Walking my parrot back home." Primo Parrothead Party, June 12, City Park, New Orleans.

Before the show, the video screens on either side of the stage replay some of the parking lot party—tequila flashbacks for the participants—and, of course, the Fiesta Super 88 is prominently displayed. After his third song, Buffett can't help mentioning what he calls "the three-masted Cadillac. Could be a *song* title! Can you imagine going down the 405 [freeway] at 2:30 in the morning hoping not to be noticed in *that* son-of-a-bitch?" The crowd roars in empathy with the driver/navigator's plight. Buffett adds, "You better have a designated driver!"

The creator of the "three-masted Cadillac" had more ideas than room on his station wagon. He brought a *second* vehicle with a volcano erupting on its roof, thanks to dry ice. On the rear windshield were the words, I DON'T KNOW WHERE I'M GONNA GO, from Buffett's song, "Volcano." Elsewhere in the parking lot, a smoky inferno was spewing from a tentlike paper volcano. Volcanoes evoke island paradises like Montserrat, where Buffett and Keith Sykes wrote the song. They evoke, too, our culture's image of "blowing off steam," for which Buffett's concerts can be a safety valve. Last but not least, volcanoes, as evidenced in the love/lava verse of Buffett's song, are phallic symbols.

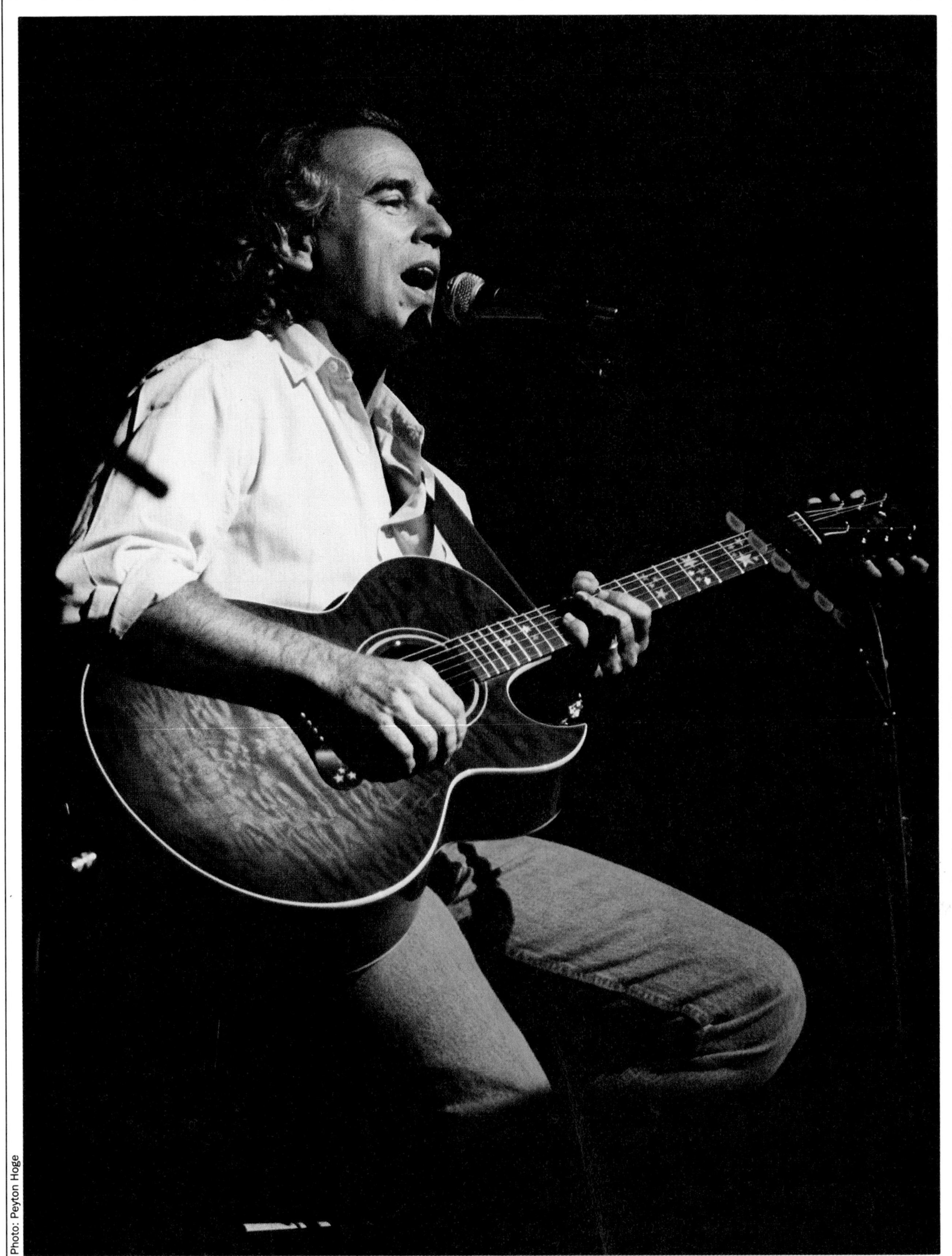
Photo: Peyton Hoge

"Jimmy's like a kid in a lot of ways. He has tremendous enthusiasms. He comes into a room and lights up the room, just because he lives with the enthusiasm of a child. Most of us have lost that by the time we're about ten. Jimmy never lost it."—Carol Shaughnessy. (Opposite) Primo Parrothead enthusiasm with a little help from Corona Extra.

Photo: Syndey Byrd

Photo: Syndey Byrd

Confessions of a Parrot Head: Curtis Rockwell

I'm the assistant sports editor at the *Pascagoula Press Register.* When somebody mentions Pascagoula in a song or a book, you say, 'Hey, that's my home; that's where I'm from.' You have that kind of kinship with him. Today there are so many people who get big and famous and go and trash their old hometown. Buffett's somebody who's never done anything like that. Although he may not live here, may not get back here that much, everytime you hear him talk about it, he pays homage to it. He says how big a part Pascagoula and the Gulf Coast played in his life, and really gave him a lot of the ideas that made him what he is today.

"You never hear a cross word about him here. A lot of people realize the things he brought to Pascagoula by songs such as 'The Pascagoula Run' (also the title of a short story in *Tales From Margaritaville*), and there's a song, 'It's Midnight and I'm Not Famous Yet,' which is on *Somewhere Over China,* where he sings, 'Off to Pascagoula in a few more days....' He's definitely mentioned Pascagoula. You feel a kinship, knowing that a lot of the things you grew up with, he grew up with down here—like sitting out on the pier at the beach point, the sun's coming up and the island's out there and stuff. You know that this may be something he did at one time, and brought all these songs to life.

"I'm probably as big a fan as anybody I know. You can be having the worst day of your life, but you might get a call: 'Hey, I heard that Buffett's coming here,' and it has a way of brightening your whole day up.

"I was a fan before he dubbed 'em Parrot Heads. I was a Buffett fan when he wasn't selling out every concert. I remember the first concert I saw in New Orleans, and Jerry Jeff Walker opened up. That was when I was thirteen years old; my brother took me. There were probably two thousand people there. It's amazing to me, since I have followed him since I was thirteen years old, the way that it's picked up in the last few years. At his concerts you see people from fifteen to fifty-five. Last year when he was at the New Orleans Jazz & Heritage Festival, [Margaritaville Records act] Evangeline was on, and he came on and sang a duet with them. There's probably ten or twelve sixteen-year-old girls standing there, and he comes on, and they're screamin' 'n' hollerin'. One of 'em turns to me and goes, 'Do you know which one he is?'

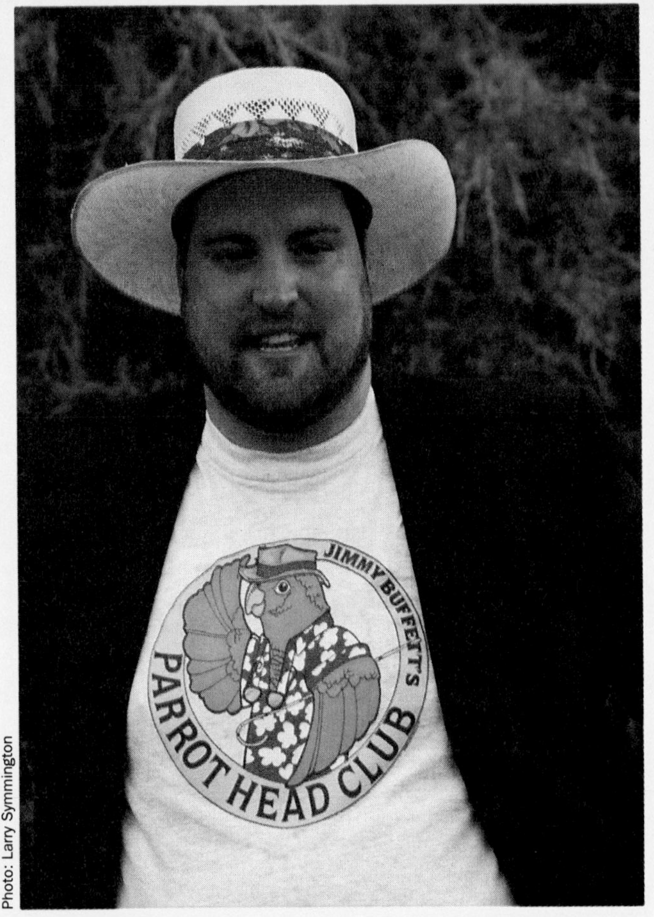

Photo: Larry Symmington

"I wrote the last article the *Press Register* did on him. The headline is 'A Parrot Head Speaks.' We have a Friday feature about a local person or somebody from here who made it. If you don't mind, I'll just read you a part of my article: 'I guess I was about thirteen years old when I first discovered the music of Jimmy Buffett. That's not to say that I hadn't heard some of his songs before that time, but when I purchased my first Buffett album in 1977 and my brother later took me to my first Buffett concert that year, I quickly became engulfed in the mystique of Jimmy Buffett. Now, some fifteen years and twenty-eight concerts later, I consider myself the epitome of a Parrot Head, the moniker given by Buffett himself to describe his vast legion of fans. By the time you read this, I will have taken my twenty-ninth and thirtieth voyages aboard the Margaritaville Clipper. In other words, if all goes according to plan, I will attend my twenty-ninth Buffett concert in Biloxi tonight before traveling to Baton Rouge for number thirty Saturday.

"'Buffett dubs his followers Parrot Heads after enjoying their antics at his concerts year after year. At any given show you're likely to see a banker or a lawyer wearing a shark fin on their head or dressed up in Hawaiian shirts and surfer jams. You're just as likely to see your next-door neighbor wearing a full-size foam rubber Gumby suit or blowing up a six-foot-tall Godzilla rubber doll and tossing it around.'

"It's almost like being a fan of a sports team. Everybody knows that you're there for one reason: to have a good time. I don't think I've ever seen a fight at a Jimmy Buffett concert. The ones I go to, we carry ten or twelve people with us and get there early and picnic and tailgate and things like that. The group that I've seen the most besides Buffett is ZZ Top. These guys come onstage and there's three of 'em, and they make this incredible sound for just having three people there. But they probably might not say ten words to the crowd. Buffett, he comes on and talks and gets the crowd involved. He could sing the wrong words and laugh about it, and people would still laugh, too."

Photo: Larry Symmington

Sacher Nature Collection

Parrot Heads have another favorite phallic symbol, the shark fin. Many of their vehicles have shark fins sprouting from the roofs, a reference to "Fins," a song about horny guys hitting on a girl from that hotbed of Parrot hedonism, Cincinnati. And it is the apex of Parrot Head High Mass when Buffett leads the faithful in the fin dance: thousands of happy drunks with steepled hands overhead, swaying from leeward to windward. It's just one of those things that came about on the road," Buffett told *Rolling Stone*'s Chet Flippo in 1979. "'Fins' was an in-thing with the band, just a term for checking out chicks. A 1979 version of 'Girlwatchers.' But I think it has a little more class. It's really about land sharks who live in bars and feed right after dark. My audiences picked up on it and started 'finning.'" Flippo describes Buffett "finning" by "taking his hands . . . and wagging them above his head: *'Fins up!* Or'—he lets one hand wilt like a limp penis—'fins *down*. Finettes. Fin soup. Fin pie. Fins everywhere."

Fins were also a phallic symbol for Buffett's parents' generation, and a status symbol, too, when Cadillacs and other top-of-the-line GM "cruiser crafts" of the late 1950s and early 1960s sported tumescent tailfins. Is it just coincidence that so many Parrot Heads have "recycled" this Eisenhower-era design by adding shark fins to the roofs of Jeeps and other vehicles? Much of Buffett's imagery draws from the popular culture of his childhood, recycling bits of old movies and TV shows and other alluring collective kitsch. His fans, even those too young to recognize references such as "Sky King's Penny" from an early 1950s TV adventure series, instinctively pick up his beat and follow right along.

He teases our memory of Looney Tunes cartoons, appearing on giant video screens in the soft-edged concentric circles which once told movie audiences a new Looney Tune was about to start. Instead of Porky Pig, a big-screen-video Buffett tells us before the flesh-and-blood Buffett comes onstage: "This evening's show comes to you in Parrot Vision." The video Buffett turns into a bright red cartoon of a showbiz parrot with vaudevillian straw boater and cane, a transformation effected by computer graphics. That's typical Buffett razzmatazz: he's spun a couple of layers of puns in just a few seconds, calling up childhood cartoon memories, lampooning Hollywood's self-promoting 1950s technomania of VistaVision, PanaVision, and the like, and finally expressed his oneness with his Parrot Heads by turning—*abracadabra, presto chango!*—into a parrot before their very eyes.

"Jimmy loves being onstage," says Carol Shaughnessy, who edited and wrote the early editions of Buffett's *Coconut Telegraph* newsletter when it debuted in 1985. "The energy that he puts forth onstage, it's not a sham, that's really Jimmy. The laughter and the goofing and the spontaneity is really Jimmy. The people are important to him. How can you not love an auditorium full of people loving you?"

After singing "Volcano" with his fans at Irvine Meadows, Buffett takes a moment to bask in the waves of applause and generous good vibes rushing his way. He beams that cheery "Ain't life grand" grin of his, and says, "I don't have a snowball's chance in hell of ever retiring!" For this tour at least, he won't even tease the crowd with the notion that this may be his last. No reason they can't all do this again (and again, and again) well into the twenty-first century!

"There are few concert experiences as downright fun as being in the midst of the Parrot Head brotherhood," wrote Robert K. Oermann of a 1987 Buffett appearance for the *Nashville Tennessean*. "For there is simply no audience as devoted, as involved, as loving as the one that comes to party along with the coconut-flavored, rum-soaked, rhythm-crazed Buffett."

"There is a full moon tonight," Buffett cautions his fans at Irvine Meadows. "I know a lot of you people are going, 'boo'gie'! This is a song for all you people who are Michael and my ages [a reference to long-time keyboardist Michael Utley] who want to slow dance. We can't get too aerobic, can we?" He then sings "Come Monday," which did well on both country and "easy listening" charts in 1974. (It was Buffet's first hit.) As if to foil Buffett's ageist remarks, two young ladies who may not have been conceived when "Come Monday" charted sway hand in hand to the song. They seem to know it, too.

"You see grandparents who were Parrot Heads back in the early seventies, when he first started," says Geoff Rizzo of Middletown, New

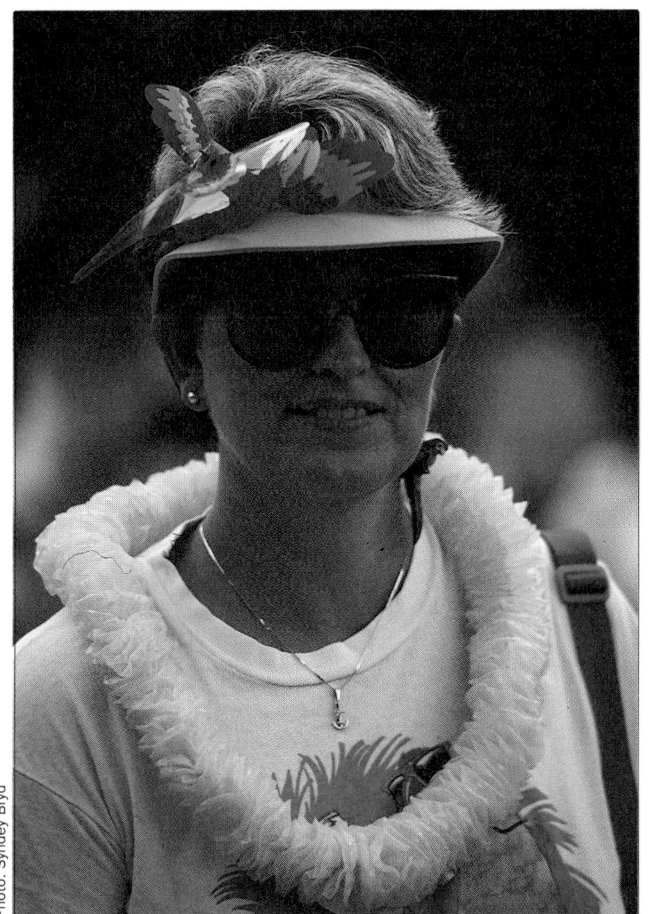

Photo: Syndey Bryd

". . . growing older but not up . . ."—Jimmy Buffett

York, a fan and veteran of many Buffett concerts. "They had kids, and now their kids are bringing *their* kids. It's a whole range of people, from little kids running around in diapers up to probably fifty, sixty years old."

Back in pop music prehistory, Pete Seeger and similar banjo-strumming folkniks used to exhort their crowds to sing along. As if in a classroom, they would carefully teach their audience the chorus before beginning a new song. At Buffett's concerts, the crowds sing along spontaneously, uninvited. Buffett couldn't stop them if he wanted to, though he clearly doesn't. For a guy who mentions Mitch Miller as an early inspiration, this must be heaven! The crowds know the words to every song, and eagerly join him without any obnoxious "Put your hands together now and *sing*" pleas from the star. They sing because the songs are important to them, and getting to sing them in public *with* Buffett is especially important to them.

This is a ritual into which everyone is cheerfully initiated, a game in which everyone gets to play. The only time Buffett lets his fans down is when he sings a new song, because they can't know the words yet, and Parrot Heads seem a bit hurt or at the very least distracted when Buffett steps outside the perimeters of their well-practiced ritual dance and solos. "We are doing a new record this year," Buffett announces to the faithful at Irvine Meadows. "Yeah, I know. It's been too long." He sings what he says will be the title song of his new album, "Quietly Making Noise." Before the song, he tells a story about British playwright Oscar Wilde complaining to the management of a Paris hotel (one at which Buffett has since stayed) that either the wallpaper in his room goes, or he goes. "The next day," said Buffett, "he went." The song had something to do with Oscar Wilde, famous turn-of-the-century gay "decadent" and a highly unlikely Parrot Head hero. No one but Buffett knew the words, anyway, so the song becomes an excuse for a massive bar and bathroom break.

Parrot Heads are much happier when Buffett performs one of their favorite songs, one he has

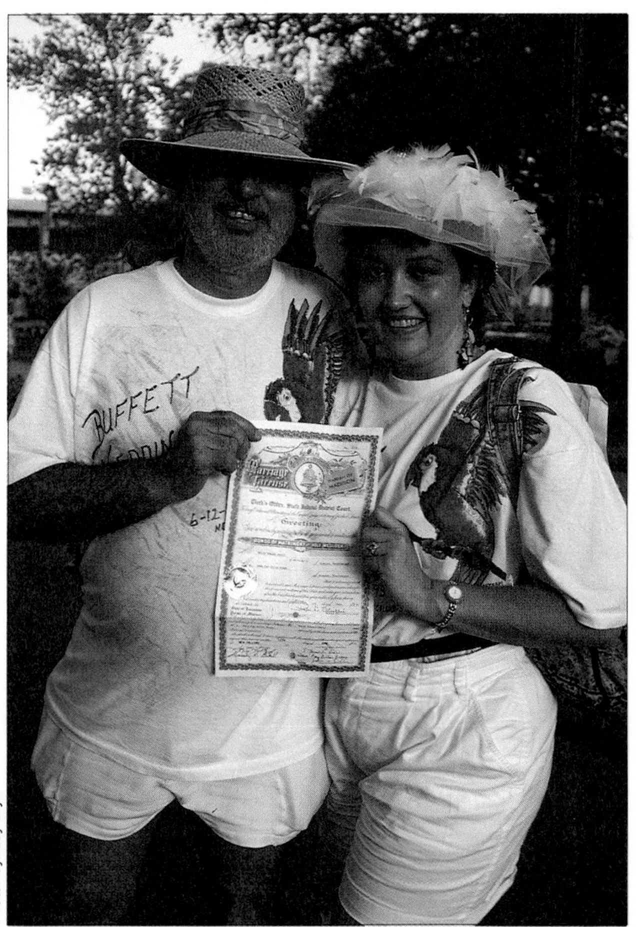

Photo: Syndey Bryd

Parrot love: Macon and Kay Davis embark on the road to nuptial bliss after tying the knot in a ceremony attended by several thousand revelers at the Summer '93 New Orleans Primo Parrothead Party. (Following spread) Double the nuptial bliss.

Photo: Syndey Byrd

Greeting

presented in many ways over the years, including mock clergy garb to tweak Jerry Falwell's Moral Majority. "I tried to think of a new way to do it this year," he says, "and decided, 'Hell, why don't *you* sing it?' You don't win anything. Maybe a trip on the three-masted Cadillac." A black female violinist sings "Why Don't We Get Drunk and Screw." (If her teachers at the Juilliard could only see her now!) Buffett prowls the front rows and dances with female admirers. The words of the chorus flash on the giant video screens and a bouncing ball leads us in song. There are shots, too, of a brass bedstead and female hands reaching up to grasp the posts; of obelisks being raised and rockets being launched.

Phoom! Beach balls are slammed, tossed, and jostled around the crowd. So are inflatable sharks, one of which wears an inflatable bra. A happy drunk dances with a giant cutout palm tree strapped to his back. Buffett congratulates his fans on their creative foolishness: "You haven't given up your childish ways." He encourages them, too, in their pursuit of "Margaritaville," the biggest sing-along fave of all. "There's a new Parrot Head disease out," he says. "It's called CRS. Can't Remember Shit." Fifteen thousand happy drunks roar in self-recognition.

Photo: Peyton Hoge

"... when you're up on stage, your adrenaline is flowing. It's a buzz when you get up there. That may be the best high there is." —Jimmy Buffett, interviewed in *High Times*, December 1976.

"I've gotten letters from people blaming me for their kids getting killed," Buffett told Robert Hilburn of the *Los Angeles Times*, "and I've written back. I understand their grief, but I feel I bring a hell of a lot more joy than pain to people. I know in my heart that the people at our shows are normal people 364 days a year. We come to town and some of them get blasted, but that may help them get through the other 364."

Russ DeVault used to see Buffett at an Atlanta club called the Bistro, sometimes playing for audiences of only one or two people. That was twenty years ago. Now Buffett sells out Atlanta's Grant Field, which holds around 40,000. His audiences certainly have expanded, but the *Atlanta Journal-Constitution* writer sees Buffett's message as little changed: "Smoke dope, drink beer, have a good time," says Devault. "It ain't brain surgery! As long as it keeps him on his boats, moving about, and from time to time helping young acts, he's happy."

Buffett certainly looks happy onstage. He beams at the fans who love him, the ones who enable him to live the "Margaritaville" fantasy of adventure and escape which he offers them through his songs. That he isn't a great singer doesn't bother them: Great singers don't like being upstaged by their audience, but Buffett doesn't mind. That he isn't a sex symbol enables him to "grow older but not up" along with his audience without sacrificing stud status. Buffett is gently rowdy but not sexy, so he can joke self-effacingly about bald spots and the like without really putting himself down. All he's selling, he says, is "a little bit of humor and a little escapism." Judging from the success of his tours, those are commodities for which there is a hungry market. "In concert," Buffett told *USA Weekend* reporter Craig Modderno in 1986, "I try to convince people that if they can't go to paradise I can bring it to them."

His personal "adventures in paradise" started at an early age, growing from an active imagination and a remarkable family background that steered Buffett on his course. As his song told us, he was truly a "Son of a Son of a Sailor."

Confessions of a Parrot Head II: Dave Rosetti

I'm a principal in Marathon, New York, just south of Syracuse. It's a nice little town. I think if my students saw me at a Buffett concert right now, they'd shoot me! They'd think I was nuts. His concerts are really active! I've been in crowds with kids who have been fifteen, sixteen years old, and doctors and lawyers, and all kinds of craziness. Once we start comparing what we are, we're real happy that nobody catches us out!

"I've been listening to Buffett since the mid-seventies. My sister lives in Miami, and she and my brother-in-law got me hooked on Jimmy Buffett. I used to go to parties with them. We'd go to somebody's house in Miami Shores where they live, and there'd be doctors and bankers and lawyers there. Then somebody'd throw on a Jimmy Buffett tape, and they'd all go nuts. I'd see them all jumping around like a bunch of *nuts*. I'd be kind of taken aback, you know, 'What is this?' But now I'm one of the nuts!

"Normally my vacations are somewhere in the South. Once I pack up the family, and once I get past Richmond, I feel like I'm away from work. I kick in a Buffett tape, and they're asleep, and I can drive forever. Tapes just keep flying in and out of the tape deck, and I'm perfectly content. I have a sound system in my office at work, and during the quiet times when I get a moment I'll slip a tape in and turn it down real low.

"I can put one of his tapes on and just get lost in the song. He's got a lot of different songs that remind me of different people I've known in my life. I just lost a good friend of mine that I taught with for ten years. He was my physics teacher when I was in high school, and he was one of those crusty old out-on-the-sailboat-all-summer kind of guys. One of Buffett's songs, 'A Pirate Looks at Forty,' reminds me of him—it's

Courtesy Geoff Rizzo

him to a T. He was definitely two hundred years too late, no doubt about it, for the type of lifestyle that he liked to live. I guess there are a lot of other songs that make connections for other people like that, too. There are a couple of songs that I don't like at all that my sister loves. So he's got enough different songs and a cross section of topics that he can appeal to just about anybody.

"I have two boys, one of 'em's four-and-a-half and the other's two-and-a-half, and my four-and-a-half-year-old, T.J., everytime I put music on, he asks me if it's Jimmy Buffett. A year and a half ago, he recognized him in a music video on TV, turned to me and goes, 'Dad, that's Jimmy Buffett!' So he's already got the disease. I gotta make sure they appreciate him while he's still alive.

"The group I hang out with are friends I know from when I was teaching. When we all get together, there's no question about throwing on a Jimmy Buffett tape, and, depending on the song, we'll start talking about different things we did. We've done some pretty wild things. Tom and I, when Geoff [Rizzo] was living in Florida, we worked at a bar together [in New York], and somebody would go and play one of those goofy songs on the damn jukebox. Before I knew it we'd be at the airport on one of those damn People Express flights, and we'd be at Rizzo's doorstep in the morning for breakfast. We'd go out, spend a week drinking and going crazy, then come home, dry out again, and go to work. It was *his* fault! We used to blame it on Jimmy Buffett! Every time somebody played that damn song, we ended up on an airplane!

Courtesy Geoff Rizzo

Courtesy Geoff Rizzo

Geoff Rizzo, book salesman and Parrot Head, at a 1992 book signing of ***Where Is Joe Merchant?,*** Jones Beach: "He's a nice guy, real down to earth. I'm glad he wasn't a jerk. His concerts are just like giant parties. We all dress up in stupid hats, drink beer, and just have a good ol' time, dancing on the seats."

CHAPTER TWO

SON OF THE SOUTH AND "SON OF A SON OF A SAILOR"

Did you ever hear of Captain Wattle?
He was all for love, and a little for the bottle.
—Charles Dibdin, *Captain Wattle and Miss Rose*

I grew up in a seaport town with a rough waterfront and all of my family were seamen. So I was into that whole existence as a kid. Jean Lafitte was my hero.
—Jimmy Buffett to Helen Bransford, *Interview*, 1986

W.C. Fields died the day Jimmy Buffett was born. The sixty-six-year-old comic sourpuss checked out on Christmas Day, 1946, and it was perfectly in character that he'd poop the holiday party with his exit. It was also in character that James Delaney Buffett III should arrive on a day he knew would forever be one of celebration.

Christmas 1946 was only the second peacetime Christmas since 1941 for most Americans. It had been longer yet for much of the world, still gripped by the agonies of rebuilding and continued struggles. In Palestine, British troops searched worshipers at the Grotto of the Nativity for arms as they entered. It was not the cheeriest Christmas on record, and while holiday "messages of hope" were decreed by Pope Pius XII, President Truman, and King George VI of England, playwright George Bernard Shaw grumbled to England's *Reynolds News:* "Christmas is for me simply a nuisance. The mob supports it as a carnival of mendacity, gluttony, and drunkenness. Fifty years ago I invented a society for the abolition of Christmas. So far I am the only member."

Harris Lewine Collection

Pirate, patriot, and Parrot Head hero, Jean Lafitte helped Andrew Jackson defeat the British at the Battle of New Orleans, 1815.

Shaw's cynicism was leavened by the "uplift" of Frank Capra's *It's a Wonderful Life,* playing for the first time that Christmas season in American theaters. The "holiday classic" film wasn't a smash on its first run, which tells us much about the cautious optimism of the time. Competition, too, played a role in its limited success, what with John Ford's *My Darling Clementine* and Walt Disney's animated *Song of the South* coming out at the same time. December 1946 yielded a bumper crop of "classic" Hollywood films.

To the union of James D. Buffett, Jr., and Mary Loraine Peets Buffett, it yielded a son. James Delaney Buffett III first saw light in the Jackson County Memorial Hospital in Pascagoula, Mississippi. Pascagoula's shipyards boomed during the war years, but it was on wartime's brink that James and Mary were wed in Pascagoula's Our Lady of Victory Rectory on May 6, 1942. With America's entry into the global war many couples opted for a brief season of married life before the fates might deal them separation, even annihilation. Those marriages that endured World War II celebrated survival, victory, and reunion through an extraordinary production of offspring—the "baby boom." Jimmy Buffett would later refer to his contemporaries among his fans as "war babies."

Nineteen forty-six was not a time when astrology was widely regarded, but followers of the stars will note that Buffett was born under the sign of Capricorn, whose children are noted for their drive and determination. "Jesus was a Capricorn," Kris Kristofferson sang some decades later, and sharing His birthday may have been a weighty responsibility for a child trained in the mysteries of the One True Church at St. Ignatius Elementary School in Mobile. "I spent eighteen years in the Catholic School systems," Buffett told a 1979 concert audience. "After I finished school I had to bust out and taste the many things that had been denied me while I was growing up."

He went to New Orleans for that taste (it turned into a lengthy banquet), a place where you can still buy a classic Depression-era numerology book called the *Kansas City Kitty Dream Book,* for "playing policy." Along with the lucky numbers and birthstones (Buffett's is turquoise) are descriptions of the characteristics of persons born on particular days. *Kansas City Kitty* offers this profile of those born between December 19 and 25: "You are shrewd and determined, desirous of your own way in everything. Love your home, but like to move and find change of scene and environment, but take your home with you. Lay much stress on outward appearance and have some love of show. Love to study and live in the mysterious. Are a great reader, and have a retentive memory." Miss Kitty sure had Jimmy Buffett's number.

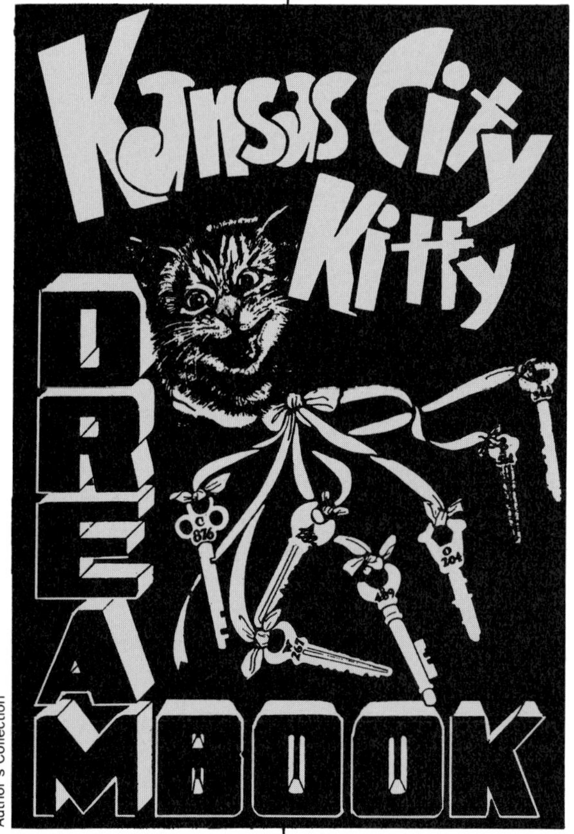

Author's Collection

A naval architect by trade, James D. Buffett, Jr., moved his family from Pascagoula to Mobile, where he would retire from doing cost analyses for building ships at the Alabama State Docks in 1987. Jimmy, his parents, and his sisters, Laurie and Lucy, often returned to Pascagoula to visit his grandparents and other relations. His grandfather especially made a deep impression, and Buffett memorialized him in the song, "The Captain and the Kid." It was to Captain James Buffett that his grandson attributes his storytelling abilities. "As a kid, I'd go down and get all these stories from him," Buffett told Whoopi Goldberg on her short-lived television talk show. "When he would come back from his trips, it was a big family event. He always brought things for all the kids back from his exotic travels. Here I am, sitting in Pascagoula, Mississippi, with a teak chest from India going, 'What the hell is *this* all about? What's going on out there?' I wanted to know about it. So from a very early age, I was destined to be gypsy."

Capt. James Buffett was certainly a persuasive role model for an aspiring gypsy. He first put to sea at age eleven, and prided himself on keeping his captain's license current even after his retirement. He died in his eighty-first year on January 2, 1970, not long after poor eyesight caused him to fail the exam to renew his license. It so shook him that Captain Buffett dispiritedly hocked his sextant.

In the summer of 1969, he took a final trip back to his native Nova Scotia, an event reported by Harry McDonnell for the *Mobile Press Register* beneath the headline, ADVENTUROUS MARINER FLYING TOWARD REUNION. "A Gulf Coast master mariner with an adventurous career at sea behind him flew back Monday to his native Nova Scotia and a reunion with a sister he has not seen for sixty-five years.

"Capt. James Buffett, eighty-one, retired, of Pascagoula, Miss., and his wife, the former Hilda Seymour, boarded an airliner at Bates Field late Monday for a trip to his boyhood home, which he has not seen since 1904.

"A spry man who looks at least twenty years younger than his eighty-one years, Captain Buffett confided he and his wife planned to stop off in Boston Monday night for a lobster supper before going on to Grace Bay near Sidney, Canada, to visit his sister, Mrs. Mabel Stratton.

"His blue eyes twinkling, Captain Buffett recalled a career that included fur sealing in both the Arctic and Antarctic, sailing the last four-masted schooner, the *Chiquimula,* that visited the Port of Mobile, and years later entering the port as master of the *General Howze,* the largest steamship at that time to have visited here. He also served as a Navy commander in World War II in the Pacific theater.

"The charred remains of Captain Buffett's schooner command, the *Chiquimula,* may still be seen at the foot of Spanish Fort Hill off Battleship Causeway in Baldwin County. After her retirement the vessel was purchased by a contractor who used it as a workman's dormitory and construction headquarters during the building of the causeway. She lay there for many years, graceful, even as a rotting old hulk—until one night a pyromaniac touched a match to the dry timbers just to see flames leap into the sky....

"Captain Buffett is among a few old-timers who can boast of having held a master's mariner's license for sail, steam and motor vehicles."

"My grandfather was quite a character," Jimmy Buffett told an interviewer for Mississippi television station WLOX. "He was a sailing ship captain who migrated from Nova Scotia to Pascagoula, where my grandmother was from. He was a great storyteller, and made quite an impression on my life. It was he that first instilled in me the idea of traveling around the world. He helped me imagine that, by following the little bayou from behind his house on Parsley Street, you could leave there and reach the Mississippi Sound and trace your way around the entire world, if you were only brave enough and had a little imagination."

Young Jimmy's imagination was surely piqued by Captain Buffett's strange tale of the Polynesian Buffetts. "The older I got," Buffett told Whoopi, "I thought, 'Well, is there really a string of Buffetts out in Polynesia, or was it just the old man sort of fooling around during the Big War?'" He started scouting for answers once when he was playing in Hawaii. "I just sort of looked in the phone book," he recalled, "'cause it's an odd name. And sure enough, there are a lot of Buffetts there. I called one of them, and he said, 'We come from Tahiti.'" *Tahiti?*

Buffett wasn't exactly a superstar in French Polynesia, but he conned an agreeable Hawaiian promoter into booking his first Tahitian tour. "I spoke a little French," Buffett told Whoopi, "and we would go to the harbor and take billboards for the show and paste them on palm trees in front of boats with American home ports."

Along with his grass-roots promotion efforts, Buffett probed into his grandfather's Polynesian Buffett story, and learned that it wasn't fabricated for his boyhood amusement. If anything, the story he unearthed was more fabulous than any of the exotic baubles the Captain "gifted" on young Jimmy. He learned that his distant cousins in Polynesia were descendants of a man who played

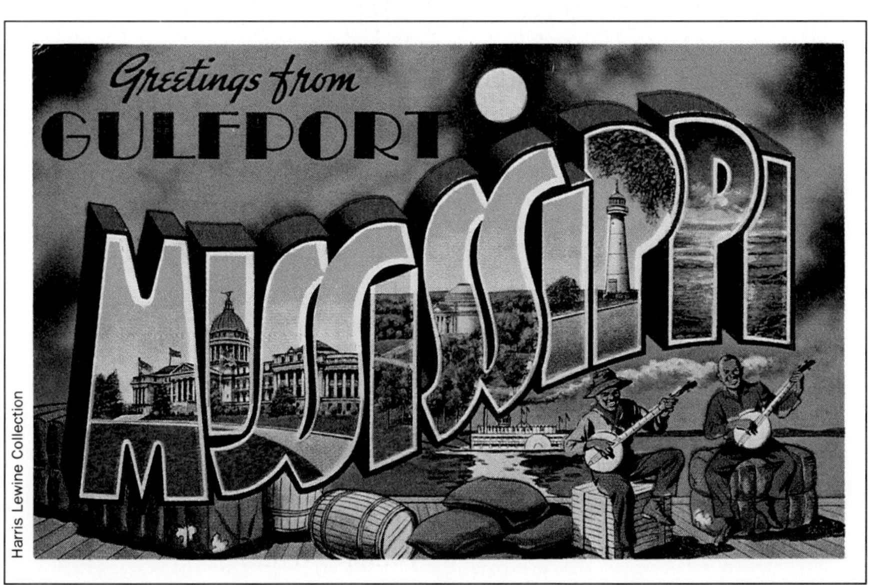

Harris Lewine Collection

a key role in the aftermath of the infamous 1789 mutiny aboard His Majesty's Ship *Bounty.*

John Buffett was born in Bristol, England, in 1797. He was apprenticed to a cabinetmaker, but quit the trade to join the Royal Navy. He had a rare knack for shipping out on vessels which wrecked, surviving calamities ranging from a Cape Cod blizzard to a Manila typhoon.

In 1823, Buffett shipped out of California on a London-based whaler. Loaded with 1,700 barrels of sperm oil, the whaleship *Cyrus* stopped for refreshments at Pitcairn's Island on December 10, 1823. Buffett would later write: "The inhabitants being in want of some person to teach them to read, and write, the Captain asked me if I should like to remain there. I told him I should, and was discharged and went on shore." Joined by his friend, John Evans, the English whalers enjoyed the distinction of being Pitcairn's first European settlers since the mutineers.

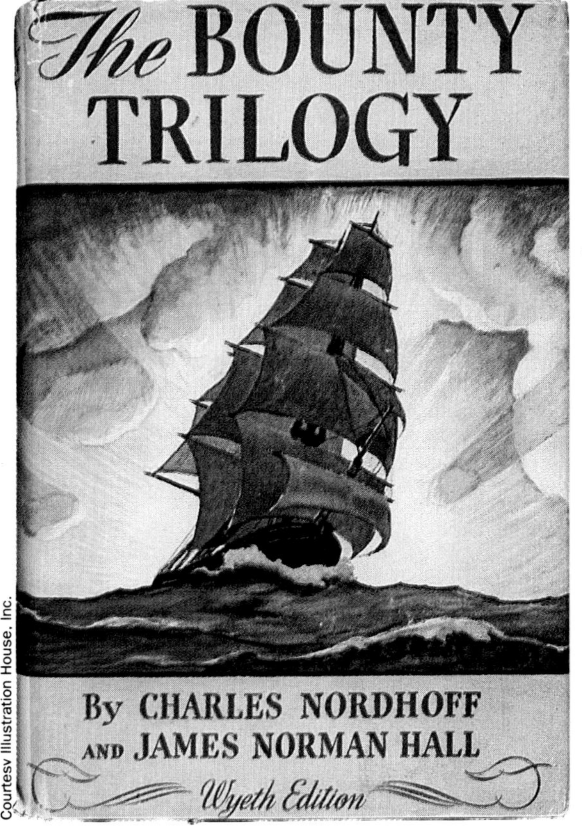

The BOUNTY
TRILOGY
By CHARLES NORDHOFF
AND JAMES NORMAN HALL
Wyeth Edition
Courtesy Illustration House, Inc.

N. C. Wyeth's evocative cover for *The Bounty Trilogy* of Charles Nordhoff and James Norman Hall was a Depression-era hint of America's fixation on South Seas "exotica." Buffett can claim a distant kinship with *Bounty* mutineer Fletcher Christian, whose granddaughter bore two children by seafaring John Buffett, dropped from a whaler on Pitcairn's Island in 1823.

Only nine weeks after his arrival, twenty-six-year-old John Buffett had wed one of their daughters, Dolly Young. She bore Buffett four sons, offspring he noted, among those of other islanders, in the register of "Births, Deaths, Marriages and Remarkable Family Events" which he kept. Perhaps it was in the "Remarkable Family Events" category that Buffett's son and daughter by Mary Christian were entered. Buffett was conducting religious services as well as teaching at the time the seventeen-year-old granddaughter of chief mutineer Fletcher Christian bore him a daughter. A son followed four years later, and this indiscretion was one of the excuses a tyrant, Joshua Hill, used for Buffett's public flogging in 1833. He was sentenced to "three dozen lashes with a cat, upon the bare back and breach, together with a fine of three barrels of yams or potatoes, to be paid within one month, or in default thereof, an extra barrel will be required for this reiterated contempt of court."

Hill's tyranny was short-lived, and while Buffett was often embroiled in power plays and disputes of the small-town politics sort, he thrived—to the extent one does in a yam economy—and was generally respected. He was fifty-nine when he and his family joined the majority of Pitcairn's nearly two hundred residents in a three-thousand-mile oceanic exodus to a former penal colony, Norfolk Island. The people had simply outgrown tiny Pitcairn. A year before the 1856 exodus (thirty-four residents declined to go), a census noted 18 Buffetts on Pitcairn. The first non-mutineer European to sow his seed on Pitcairn lived to the ripe old age of ninety-three. Like Capt. James D. Buffett, he would make a final voyage home to visit in 1868. For John Buffett, home no longer meant England but Pitcairn.

"We were on our way to Australia for a tour," Buffett told Whoopi 125 years after John Buffett last saw home, "and I had to just go check it out." He invited James D. Buffett, Jr., and Mary Loraine Peets Buffett—Mom and Dad—to join him on his improbable odyssey. "We left Auckland," Buffett recalled, "and Norfolk Island is way out there—we flew a *long way!* And we got to the airport, and they were all there! There were like two hundred people. So there indeed was this huge clan of Buffetts on Norfolk Island."

The Buffett clan, says its most famous member, was originally Welsh. The Welsh reputedly sing and play the harp beautifully and spin stories as they do so. These singers/pickers/spinners are called Bards, and take their business pretty seriously, having annual contests for Boss Bard. So Buffett's story-songs really just move his "family tradition" out of Wales and into the Gulf Stream. No Bards ever sang about dope smugglers, maybe, but they *did* wail about border brigands, and howled loudly off-key when they had a snootful of hops, so there's a definite DNA chain link somewhere.

Given their seafaring ways, there surely was a Buffett or two among the stouthearted Welshmen led by Prince Madoc, who dropped anchor in Mobile Bay sometime in the twelfth century (or so says local legend). Even if you don't buy the Madoc legend, Mobile is a fitting port for the Buffetts. "The Gulf Coast is sort of keyed to New Orleans," Buffett told *Stereo Review* reporter Noel Coppage in 1974. "It's a Catholic-based culture, Creole and Cajun influences and all that, you know, not a redneck culture at all." When the Federal Writers' Project of the Works Progress Administration (WPA) sized up Mobile in its American Guide Series during the Roosevelt years, it observed: "Mobile, though it likes to call itself the City of Five Flags—French, Spanish, English, Confederate, and United States—shows surprisingly few traces of its French and Spanish past. [Nonetheless,] the city's long history and maritime contact with the outside world give to Mobile an indefinable cosmopolitan atmosphere that sets it apart from Alabama's other large cities."

Phil Ahrens, Gotham Book Mart

Mobile celebrated the first Mardi Gras in the Americas. "As early as 1830 masked members of Mobile's Cowbellian de Rakin Society paraded, danced, and feasted on New Year's Eve," wrote Virginia Van der Veer Hamilton in *Alabama: A History* (W. W. Norton, 1977). "The Cowbellians were succeeded in 1841 by the Striker's Club whose members travelled en masse to New Orleans the following year to attend the first ball of that city's Mystic Krewe of Comus." It was in Mobile in 1835 that an astonished English gentleman named George Featherstonhaugh "came upon a group of joyous Spanish Creoles performing the bolero in broad daylight." Horseracing, cockfighting, and prodigious drinking were the constant delight of antebellum Mobilians. "Its citizens continue to indulge a lusty appetite and quench a boundless thirst," wrote Hamilton. "Sober-minded hinterlanders, drawn to Mobile for conventions, experience a strange giddiness at the sight of such open and unashamed self-indulgence. Mobile's blithe Mediterranean spirit still lifts the heart and tempts the flesh."

Despite Catholic school repression, then, Buffett grew up in a culture which wasn't really anathema to his mythic Margaritaville. Imagine little Jimmy daydreaming while a priest drones on about a heaven populated by pretty sexless angels. Restless, Buffett stares beyond the stained glass windows to a vision of an earthier, more American paradise. He imagines its inhabitants gorge on the manna of cheeseburgers and gulp sacramental margaritas till they sway and stagger from cloud to billowy cloud. They sing, wear Hawaiian shirts, and sport halos of festive headgear Jimmy himself has sold to them. *"That's heaven,"* thinks young Buffett. "A paradise I can take to the bank...."

Buffett's imagination was nurtured early by books. "I was a reader as a youngster," he told Robert Hilburn of the *Los Angeles Times,* "thanks to my mother. Robert Louis Stevenson and Mark Twain were my first favorites . . . *Treasure Island* and *Huckleberry Finn.*" Literature, naturally, to reinforce the inherited Buffett traits of wanderlust and watery adventure. His imagination was further fired by the Catholic Theater Guild of

Parrot Heads and City Slickers: Spike Jones

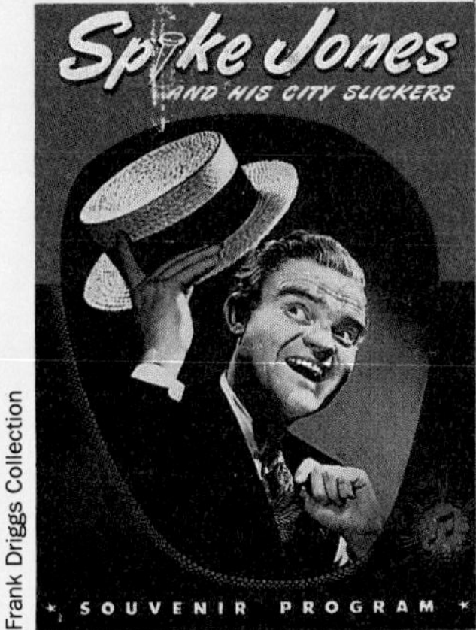

Frank Driggs Collection

Frank Driggs Collection

Frank Driggs Collection

Younger Parrot Heads may be forgiven if they draw a blank at the name Spike Jones. Jones had already peaked commercially by the time Buffett was teething, and was only a half-remembered relic of the World War II era when he died in 1965. Yet he continued to tour incessantly with his City Slickers and even enjoyed sporadic television stardom between 1954 and 1961. Via tube or train, Jones's pistol-shot-and-noisemaker-riddled parodies of classics (the opera *Carmen*) and pop ballads ("Cocktails for Two") crashed into the consciousness of the Howdy Doody generation. "I remember going to see Spike Jones as a kid and loving it," Buffett told Robert Hilburn of the *Los Angeles Times,* "the way he had fun with an audience." Jones proudly described his raspberry burlesque sound as *Makes You Want to Blow Your Brains Out Music.*

Jones understood the Lord Buckley axiom Buffett likes to quote: "Terror is the absence of humor and humor the absence of terror." In 1942, young American men were being shipped to uncertain warrior fates in Europe and the Pacific. Terror and anxiety tensed beneath America's fighting resolve. Spike Jones and his City Slickers blew the Bronx cheer at Hitler and gave Americans a therapeutic collective laugh with "Der Fuehrer's Face." The record instantly propelled a thirty-year-old percussionist/bandleader from the West Coast to stardom. When Spike entertained American troops in Europe, even a German prisoner of war clamored for his autograph.

Like Buffett, Spike Jones had grown up near the water (Long Beach, California) and developed a boyhood penchant for hamburgers. He was likewise crazy for New Orleans music, though for Jones it was jazz, not rhythm and blues, which still brewed uncooked in the era of "Der Fuehrer's" popularity. A fine drummer, Jones cut his chops in Depression-era dance halls, where he once used what the English call his "wedding tackle" as a xylophone mallet to get the attention of a bored crowd. His novelty-oriented City Slickers band, heavy on car horns and live sound effects, evolved from Jones's penchant for collecting anything that would make a noise: He once ripped a pair of telephones off the wall at the Biltmore Hotel and snuck them out under his overcoat. Jones sought out like-minded souls, and founded the City Slickers in 1939 with Del Porter, whose genius was manifested by a bagpipe made of a tin whistle hooked to a douche bag by a rubber hose.

And like Buffett, Jones was a tireless self-promoter: He lacked a *Coconut Telegraph* or merchandising line, but he understood publicity and would ask associates, "What can I do to get sued?" Lawsuits, he knew, drew press notices, as did the letters he constantly wrote to columnists and stunts such as driving down Sunset Boulevard with a kangaroo in his convertible. He sent disc jockeys birthday cards and copies of his latest release via memorable couriers, some of whom were female and nude.

Business for Jones was a pleasure, and he actually relished grueling road tours: He once did 139 consecutive one-nighters in 139 different cities! His fans included President Truman and Chester Gould, who wrote Jones into his Dick Tracy cartoon strip thinly disguised as "Spike Dyke and His Musical Nuts."

Jones toured with ankle-biting midgets, buxom blondes, and vaudeville-seasoned musicians who could sneeze and belch on cue. Life Buffett, Jones drew a fanatical following, especially in the Midwest, and they relished becoming a part of his *Musical Depreciation Revue.* During "The Hawaiian War Chant," the lights would go down and the drummer (Spike mostly played novelty percussion and emceed) would furiously pound the skins with fluorescent sticks. At a 1948 performance in Wichita, Kansas, thirty-some bobby-soxed cuties took that cue to switch on batteried twinkle lights in their bras.

Life Buffett, Jones was seen as a mite risqué and often ran afoul of censors. A 1946 recording of the World War I-era "By the Beautiful Sea" was yanked when complaints were received by Victor Records that the singer allegedly yowled, "Over and under and then *up her ass.*" Such lyrics would likely have given even Buffett pause, but "Why Don't We Get Drunk (and Screw)" would not have shocked the salty Jones. In 1952, Jones and his City Slickers cut "I Saw Mommy Kissing Santa Claus"—saccharine kid stuff whose sweet taste they quickly dispelled with a never-released alternate take, "I Saw Mommy Screwing Santa Claus."

A five-pack-a-day habit finally got the best of Jones, but not before he fractured the national funny bone with what his forties-era manager, Dick Webster, called "organized bedlam." Nearly half a century later, Buffett would call the shows "controlled insanity," and no doubt Jones played a role in shaping them as Parrot Head Prophet.

Frank Driggs Collection

Spike Jones and *all* the City Slickers.

Mobile's production of *South Pacific.* Buffett was especially impressed by his piano teacher singing "Bali Ha'i" in an Alabama drawl. "She hooked me on the myth and planted the seeds of discovery that eventually led me to the South Pacific," Buffett wrote in *Tales From Margaritaville* (Harcourt Brace Jovanovich, 1989).

The myth of the South Pacific was deeply encoded in America's consciousness by Rodgers and Hammerstein's 1949 musical based on James A. Michener's *Tales of the South Pacific.* Set on a Pacific island during World War II, *South Pacific* wove a love story between an American nurse with the comic-awful name of Nellie Forbush and a worldly-wise older French planter, Emile de Becque, who has fathered two children by a native woman. (Shades of John Buffett!) It was Ezio Pinza who caressed and crooned "Some Enchanted Evening" to Mary Martin in the original Broadway production, which boasted the biggest advance sales of any Broadway show on its debut in 1949. Despite changes in the lead

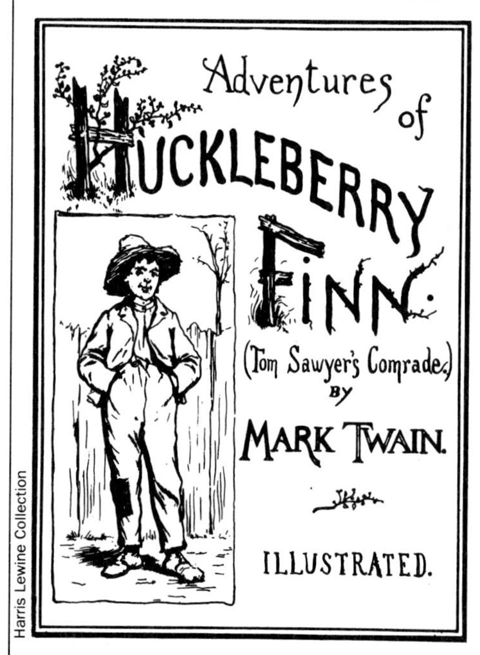

One of Buffett's favorite books, Mark Twain's 1885 classic was also praised by Ernest Hemingway: "All modern American literature comes from one book, *Huckleberry Finn.*"

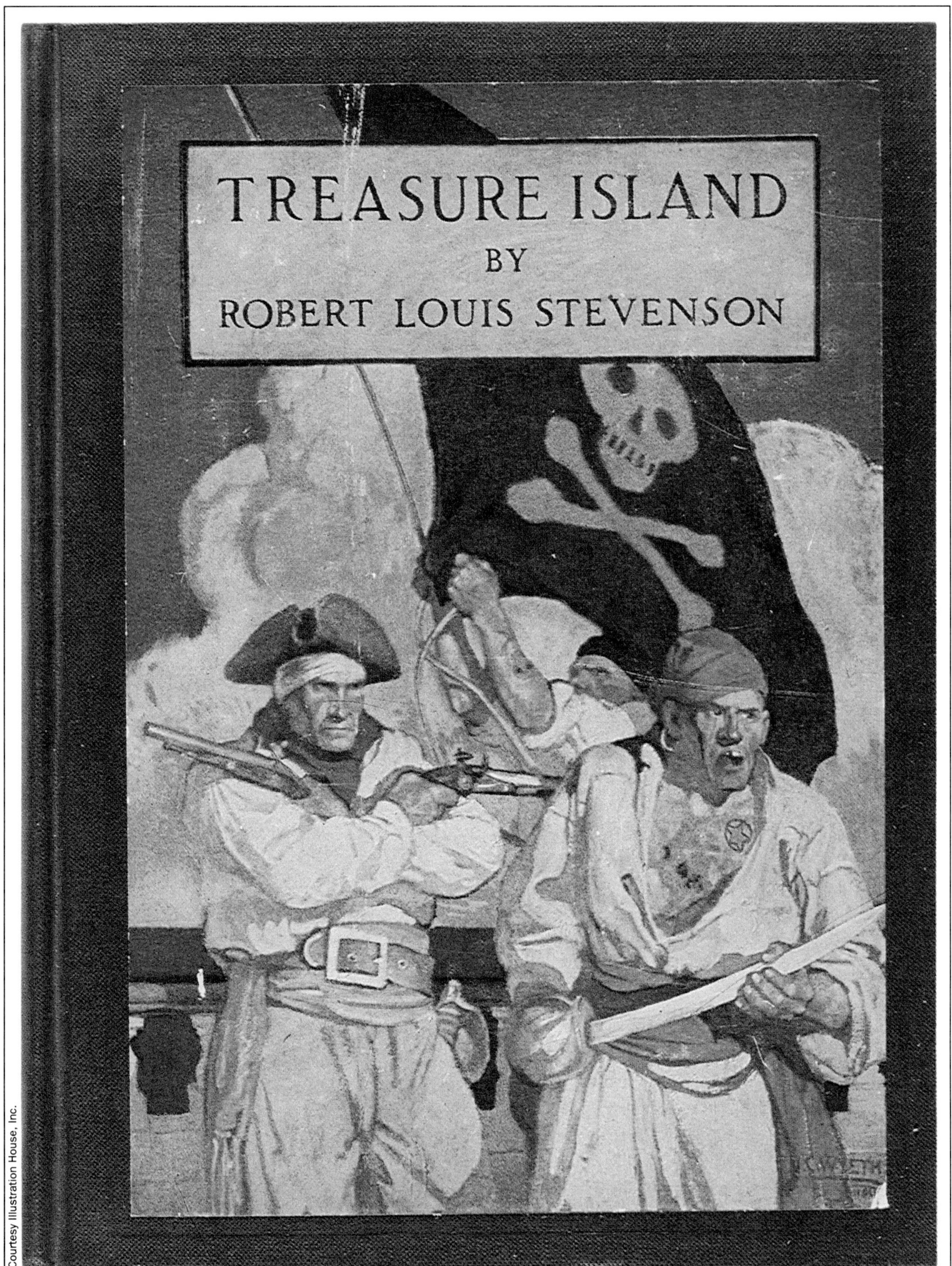

Courtesy Illustration House, Inc.

An Old Boy's book and a New Boy's book: Robert Louis Stevenson's *Treasure Island,* illustrated throughout by N. C. Wyeth.

Goatees and Glow Worms: Mitch Miller and the Mills Brothers

Buffett may have grown up on what locals affectionately call "the redneck Riviera," but he denies ever listening to country music. That's a little like growing up in Jamaica and denying you've heard reggae, but there it is. No, for Buffett it was that "nostalgic rage" he praised in "Pencil Thin Mustache." Where other singer-songwriters of the seventies would cite Bob Dylan and the Beatles as primary influences, Buffett, who relished his role as self-proclaimed "professional misfit," looked back to Mom and Dad's day. An early ABC Records press release says "he managed to avoid the country music permeating the radio waves to remember the Mills Brothers and Mitch Miller as early influences."

And why not? The four Mills Brothers hailed from Piqua, Ohio, and, as teenagers, got their first break performing on radio station WLW in that future birthplace of the Parrot Head nation, Cincinnati. They blended creamy-smooth crooner harmonies with uncanny imitations of horns, saxes, and string bass. It was a gimmick, of course, but the kind of gimmick that transcends gimmickry. Jazz was basically dialogues among instruments imitating conversations among human voices. The Mills Brothers were superb vocalists who returned the compliment. Lester Young, saxophonist supreme, said his favorite sax section was the four Mills Brothers, and he wasn't kidding.

The Mills Brothers recorded extensively ("Paper Doll" was their biggest hit in 1943), appeared on network radio broadcasts, and could be heard alongside such slick-sidewalled stars as Dick Powell in Hollywood musicals like 1934's *Twenty Million Sweethearts.* Their father, John

Frank Driggs Collection

Frank Driggs Collection

Sr., took over bass vocal and guitarist duties in 1935 when John Jr. died, and the group was otherwise stable well into the time of Buffett's rise in the 1970s. How many groups of *any* kind last more than forty years?

The Mills Brothers' satin a cappella ensemble sound has attracted disparate admirers: Hank Thompson, a honky-tonk bandleader best known for "The Wild Side of Life" and "A Six Pack to Go," recorded a tribute album of Mills Brothers standards in the seventies. Lux Interior, lead vocalist for the cult "shockabilly" band, the Cramps, praised the Mills Brothers in an interview with V. Vale for *Incredibly Strange Music* (Re/Search Publications, San Francisco, 1993). "Those all-voice arrangements have such a beautiful effect," said Interior, "so eerie. That's the way the Mills Brothers started out. They all imitated instruments and did the weirdest things you've ever heard. It's unbelievable; you'd swear you were listening to an orchestra, but it's just these four guys with their mouths."

Courtesy Mitch Miller

Mitch Miller was something else entirely. A celebrated symphonic oboist featured with Andre Kostelanetz on CBS radio in the early 1940s, Miller diligently worked his way from highbrow to lowbrow via stints as artist-and-repertoire man, arranger, and producer at Keynote, Mercury, and, finally and most influentially, at Columbia. Miller had an ear for songs and a formula that worked: "Keep it simple, keep it sexy, keep it sad." He produced hits for Tony Bennett, Doris Day ("Qué Será, Será"), Patti Page, and Johnny Mathis. With Frank Sinatra he had less success, and Sinatra would vehemently claim Miller ruined his career in the early 1950s with "Mama Will Bark," a novelty duet with dumb-blonde Dagmar featuring canine woofs (shades of Spike Jones!). "Before Mr. Miller's advent on the scene, I had a successful recording career which quickly went into decline," moaned Blue Eyes, who demanded a Congressional investigation into the matter. (Strangely, Congress declined.)

Miller entered Buffett's world via hi-fi and television. Remembering the "follow the bouncing ball" device popularized in Depression-era short subjects (check out some *Betty Boop* videos if you wonder what this was), the master oboist and musical dog trainer concluded that your average American would love hearing some standards that would inspire folks to *sing along* in an average kind of way. Mitch was right. In September 1958, *Sing Along With Mitch* was America's number 1 pop LP. Miller made a series of such albums, and in 1962 *Sing Along With Mitch* came to NBC television for two years. Seen today, the program might not inspire those whose notion of music video is rooted in MTV. The avuncular Miller conducted a chorus of middle-aged men in such stirring chestnuts as "In the Good Ol' Summertime" while the lyrics rolled across the bottom of the TV screen. *Sing along!* Buffett was fourteen when the show had its debut, and he loved it. It probably was aimed at people his grandpa's age, but Buffett liked any excuse to sing. Three decades later, his own shows are big boozy sing-a-longs, and Mitch Miller's son-in-law is a Parrot Head. "I'm more of an emcee on stage than a singer," Buffett once remarked of his "Sing-along With Jimmy" shows.

roles (Martha Wright replaced Mary Martin in June 1951), *South Pacific's* New York run exceeded 1,900 performances! A 1951 *New York Herald Tribune* headline read: "SOUTH PACIFIC" FEAT: TWO YEARS WITHOUT A SEAT IN HOUSE EMPTY.

South Pacific tapped a deep well of longing for a sensual paradise in the alternately drab and paranoid America of the Truman years, and that well did not dry up as the avuncular Eisenhower and adolescent rock 'n' roll merely changed the national decor. No, the well of longing just grew deeper. Twentieth Century-Fox brought *South Pacific* to the big screen in 1958, and America's appetite for it was greater than ever. *Time* said the atmospheric film offered "some of the smoothest Technicolor that has ever creamed a moviegoer's eyeballs...." The movie, with Rossano Brazzi and Mitzi Gaynor in the leads, easily fulfilled *Variety's* prediction—"It should mop up ... can't be anything but boffo"—while its soundtrack did better still. *South Pacific* became one of the bestselling albums of the LP era: It was on the *Billboard* charts a phenomenal 262 weeks, number 1 for 31 of those weeks! If a family owned a hi-fi in 1958, it had the *South Pacific* soundtrack.

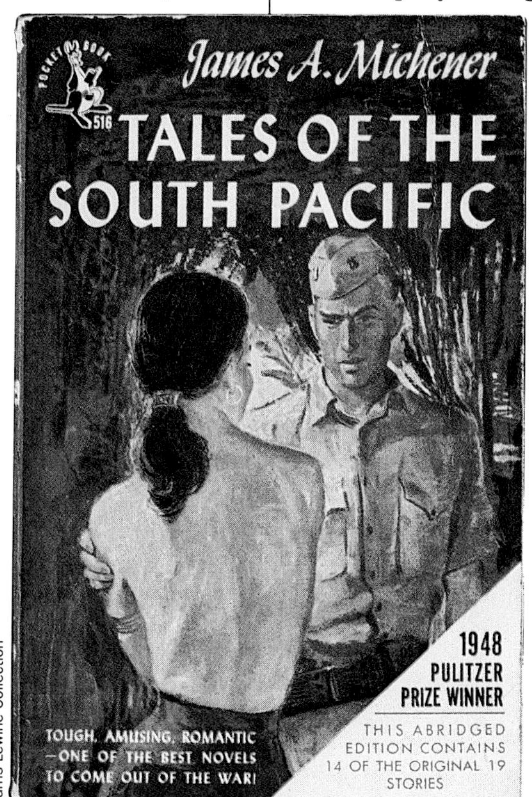

Harris Lewine Collection

On the album's cover, a virile yet gray-at-the-temples guy embraces an attractive younger blonde in a red halter top. She gazes up at him in compliant adoration. If you were a World War II veteran turned suburbanite in the late 1950s, living the American good life but working damn hard for it and losing a battle with time and midriff bulge and bratty kids and a receding hairline, wouldn't this be your fantasy? Your Margaritaville?

South Pacific produced some interesting fallout. Tiki bars with Polynesian decor and Hawaiian music sprouted across America, serving fruity topical drinks. The night sky across suburban backyards was suddenly ablaze with torches illuminating Styrofoam replicas of Hawaiian gods (tikis) impaled in lawns. Housewives did the hula in grass skirts while their husbands, some wistfully remembering the Pacific, the Big War, and their youth, enjoyed a rare opportunity to get drunk, grab ass, and howl. For the kids' amusement, there were hula hoops.

The view that popular music in the late 1950s was *only* rock 'n' roll is revisionist history, a lie. Rock tickled adolescent hormones, sure, but pirates looking at forty were otherwise aroused. Teenagers bought 45s, adults LPs. Because of extended playing time, the LP didn't require as many back-and-forth trips to the hi-fi. You could relax, fix a drink, and, if the company was agreeable, indulge in some "heavy petting" abetted by mood-enhancing music. To this end, Martin Denny's *Exotica* arrived from Hawaii itself!

Denny was a pianist who hit on a unique sound combining Latin rhythms with, in his words, "the feeling of the South Pacific, the languor, a relaxed sound." He replaced the steel guitar common to Hawaiian music with vibes and other mallet instruments. The result was an unabashed adult audio aphrodisiac: "A lot of people told me ... that when they heard that music, they had some wonderful 'matinees,'" Denny told Stuart Swezey and Brian King in 1990.

Exotica was strictly instrumental, except for some jungle birdcalls mimicked by percussionist Augie Colon. The sound that made a 1957 hit of Denny's "Quiet Village" was inspired in a rare moment of cross-species musical communion: "We had a very exotic setting in this room that I played in," Denny told Swezey and King. "It was called the Shell Bar, and there was a little pool of water right outside the bandstand, and rocks and palm trees growing around ... very tropical, very relaxed. One night, we were playing this tune and suddenly I became aware that these bullfrogs started to croak—*ribbet, ribbet, ribbet, ribbet*—and when we finished the

Frank Driggs Collection

James Michener's short story collection, *Tales of the South Pacific,* won the Pulitzer Prize in 1948 and inspired Rodgers and Hammerstein's most successful musical. Buffett's South Seas fantasies were inflamed by a Mobile music teacher's rendition of "Bali Ha'i," first sung on Broadway by Juanita Hall.

Harris Lewine Collection

Mary Martin's elegant energy was a key component in making *South Pacific* Broadway's biggest smash in 1949. As nurse Nellie Forbush, she wowed thousands singing "Honey Bun" and "I'm Gonna Wash That Man Right Outa My Hair."

Bookleaves, NYC

America's favorite romantic fantasy couple was played by Mitzi Gaynor and Rossano Brazzi in the 1958 Big Screen version of the Broadway musical. What woman could resist "Some Enchanted Evening"? The soundtrack album was on *Billboard's Top 40* charts for over three years. Only *West Side Story* was more successful.

song, they stopped croaking! I thought, well, that's a coincidence. I thought a little later on we would try it again. And sure enough, the frogs came in again! But this time, as a gag, the guys started doing these birdcalls, like a 'meanwhile back in the jungle' type thing. And everybody cracked up about it—it was just a spoof. The following day, somebody came up to me and said, 'Mr. Denny, would you do that arrangement you did with the birds and the frogs?'"

Minus the frogs but with plenty of evocative birdcalls amid the vibes and bongos, Martin Denny's first *Exotica* album was America's number one pop LP for four consecutive weeks during the summer of 1959. Also firing adult libidos was an "exotica" movie, *The Naked Maja,* depicting the life of the Spanish painter Goya, with Tony Franciosa as the painter and Ava Gardner in the title role. Jimmy Buffett was twelve that summer and grappling with the awkward itch of puberty and all its myriad implications. While his parents' generation necked and swilled mai tais to Martin Denny, interesting news was breaking far from Mobile in June: Wladziu Valentino Liberace, the popular American pianist and television entertainer, was awarded $22,400 damages for libel in London after a trial against the *London Daily Mirror* which had implied the pianist was homosexual. Using a bulldozer and tear gas, prison guards broke into a barricaded wing of the U.S. Prison Bureau Medical Center at Springfield, Missouri, on June 23 and subdued 106 mentally unstable inmates. The prisoners had taken five guards hostage and demanded more time to watch TV.

Jimmy Buffett was just teething when *Howdy Doody* debuted in 1947. As a member of the original video generation, Buffett nevertheless harbors mixed emotions about the medium, evidenced by his comments about music videos ("Music should enter the ears first, not the eyeballs") and the corrupting influence of satellite dishes on Caribbean culture in *Where Is Joe Merchant?* But he fondly recalls such video icons as Ricky Ricardo (almost a character in Joe Merchant), and points to a largely forgotten series called *Adventures in Paradise* as a personal crossroads. "That series changed my life," Buffett wrote in *The Parrot Head Handbook.* "It made me want to get the hell away from Mobile, Alabama; it got me started on my search for Margaritaville."

Adventures in Paradise had its debut on ABC-TV in October 1959 and ran for eighty-one episodes through April 1, 1962. It was an hour-long drama about Korean War veteran Adam Troy, played by Gardner McKay. Troy is captain of an eighty-five-

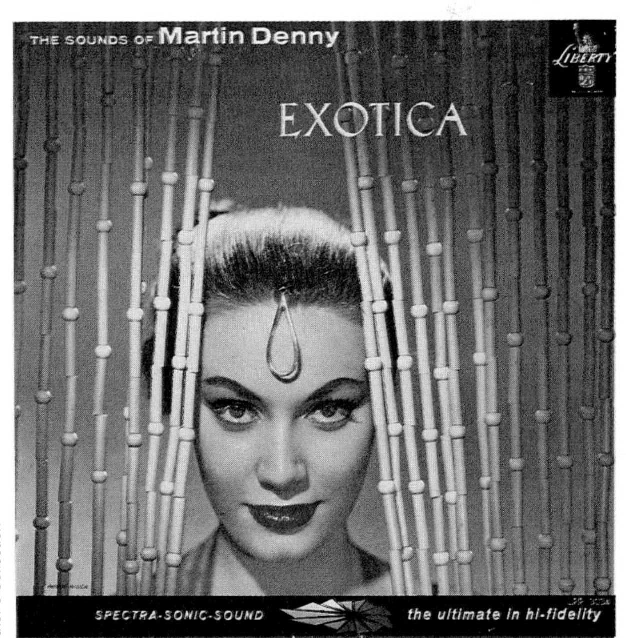

Author's Collection

Hawaii's Martin Denny mixed escape and aphrodisia in thirty-seven mood-enhancing albums (". . . the hook was these exotic bird calls."). Model Sandy Warner was the "Exotica girl" on Denny's most memorable album covers.

foot schooner he sails through the South Pacific, on the lookout for cargo, passengers, and adventure. The schooner is named the *Tiki.* He often drops anchor in Tahiti and marks time with the lovely proprietor of Renee's Bar, played by Linda Lawson. Warm waters, warm women, and a schooner named *Tiki*—Buffett endured the trials of puberty with this fantasy, and it has served him well since. Sons of men who envied Adam Troy's life thirty-plus years ago now stand in their fathers' place, sharing a variation on Dad's tropical fantasy, dimly remembered from the days of hula hoops. Jimmy Buffett helps provide it.

The end of *Adventures in Paradise* in the spring of 1962 must have been a blow to young Buffett, but there were other titillating tropicana to savor that year. MGM's epic remake of *Mutiny on the Bounty* was released. It starred Marlon Brando, a pirate looking at forty (he was thirty-seven) when he and the crew anchored in Tahiti for the filming. Brando's alleged petulance, coupled with production bungling (no fault of his), ballooned the film's cost from the $10 million budgeted for it to twice that amount when it was finished. Rumors of debauchery were rife; it was said that the cast and native women re-created the conditions that had made Bligh's crew restive in 1789. The Technicolor curves of Tahitian lovelies compensated for Brando's mincing take on Fletcher Christian and the production bloat evident in this *Bounty.* Many of these women were topless save for dark tresses and leis strategically positioned (and, apparently, somehow stuck) so that their nipples were covered but little more. Buffett's fifteen-year-old pulse surely quickened at such sights, and he wanted nothing so much as to be out of McGill Institute with its Catholic school pedantry, out of Mobile and plowing the waves of the South Pacific aboard his schooner toward beaches of willing women wearing little more than flowers and a smile.

It took some time, but he would come closer to having his Adam Troy fantasy than most of us. Thirty-one summers after Brando's *Bounty,* Buffett shows a brief onstage video clip during his Chameleon Caravan Tour at the end of the song, "One Particular Harbor." Parrot Heads briefly view two apparently topless Tahitian girls, breasts

Gauguin, eat your heart out! Tarita shows just what Bligh's men mutinied for (it wasn't breadfruit) in the 1962 version of *Mutiny on the Bounty.*

Harris Lewine Collection

Harris Lewine Collection

Harris Lewine Collection

Marlon Brando's star-crossed relationship with Tahiti began in 1961 on the *Bounty* location. Cast as Fletcher Christian, he took a public flogging for allegedly pouting on the set of the troubled production. Young Jimmy Buffett probably just admired the company Brando kept, and followed his path to Tahiti a couple of decades later.

Hillbillies in Paradise

Tropical Fever has insinuated itself into Southern popular culture via sundry routes, not the least of them the country music which Buffett claims was never gentle on his mind. Yet Buffett wasn't the first of his countrymen to, musically speaking, don the flowered shirt and sip the spiked punch of paradise. That honor goes to the man dubbed the Father of Country Music, a tubercular railroad brakeman from Meridian, Mississippi, named Jimmie Rodgers (1897-1933).

Rodgers had an ear for everything afloat in American music in the 1920s, from Victorian relics ("Mother Was a Lady") to rural blues ("Let Me Be Your Sidetrack") to jaunty pop tunes ("Any Old Time"). He even made a record with Louis Armstrong, "Blue Yodel No. 9 (Standing on the Corner)." Like Buffett, Rodgers was likably eclectic and, if the pigeonholes into which pop music is slotted had been firmly set then, he would have been hard to peg. Whatever else he was, listeners heard in Rodgers's lazy drawl the rural South, and his most ardent fans were its residents. They had no objections to his recording with black jazz and jugbands, and they especially liked it when he was accompanied by dreamy Hawaiian guitars, as he was on some of his finest recordings.

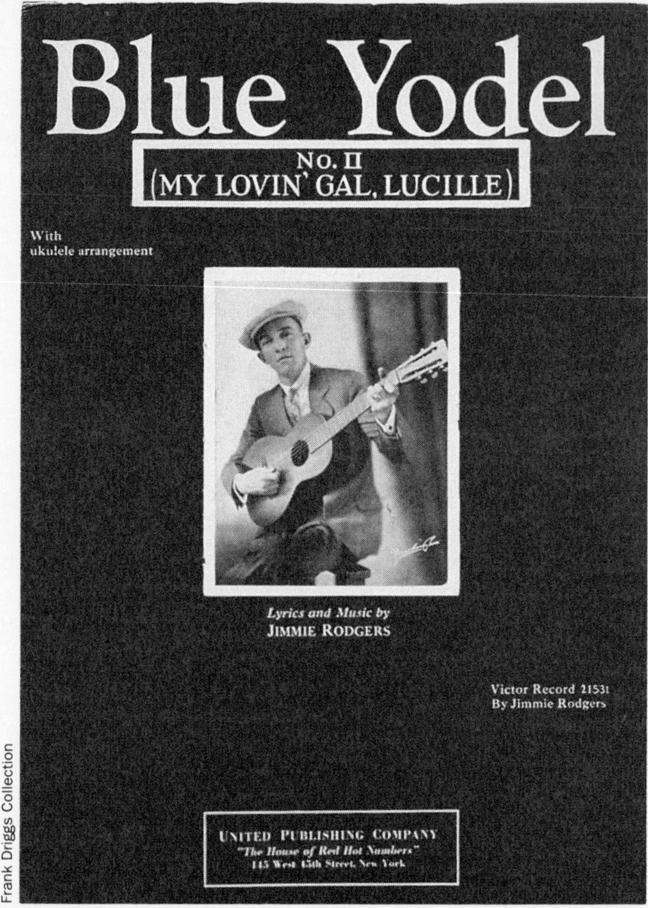

Frank Driggs Collection

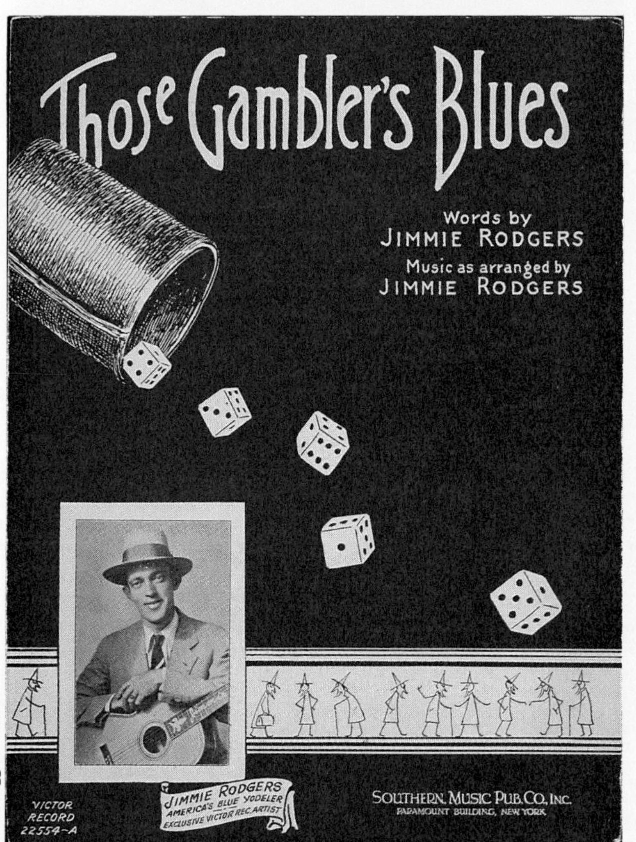

Frank Driggs Collection

In 1929, Jimmie Rodgers, hailed as America's Blue Yodeler and one of the top stars of the Victor Talking Machine Company, recorded a perfect Parrot Head fantasy about a randy rube in paradise called "Everybody Does It in Hawaii." To the accompaniment of Hawaiian guitarist Joe Kaipo, Rodgers drawled of his island voyage: "I picked me out a hula-hula girl before my boat could land." And the Father of Country Music went on the praise her finer qualities:

> She's got it here, and she's got it there,
> Her lips are red and her feet are bare.
> She's shy on clothes, but I don't care,
> 'Cause everybody does it in Hawaii.

Frank Driggs Collection

Frank Driggs Collection

CH at BALI-BALI
ALOHA OE
(HAWAIIAN FAREWELL SONG)
by
QUEEN LYDIA LILUOKALNI
ON A COCONUT ISLAND
79
Words and music by R. ALEX ANDERSON
With additional Chorus for PIANO ACCORDION arranged by PIETRO DEIRO
Chant
HONOLULU BLUES
by M. J. GUNSKY AND NAT GOLDSTEIN
SOUTH SEA ISLAND MAGIC
lyric by LYSLE TOMERLIN music by
Y OF 1921
ies
Select

On the Isle of
Wicki Wacki Woo
Song
WORDS BY
GUS KAHN
MUSIC BY
WALTER DONALDSON
Composers of "CAROLINA IN THE MORNING" and "MY BUDDY"
Jerome H. Remick & Co.
NEW YORK DETROIT
MADE IN U.S.A.

Skyline Books, NYC

Harris Lewine Collection

By the 1920s, "it" had already become a euphemism for sex (Hollywood's sexy Clara Bow was dubbed the "It" Girl). While not exactly "Why Don't We Get Drunk (and Screw)," Rodgers's record was racy enough to prompt show-biz trade paper *Variety* to caution: "[Record] dealers should use discrimination and not sell 'Everybody Does It in Hawaii' to polite families or for juvenile consumption."

Following its Father, country music's next notable proto-Parrot Head was Hank Snow, whose 78s are mentioned in Buffett's "The Wino and I Know." Chances are Buffett's seafaring grandfather may have been the true Hank Snow fan of Jimmy's acquaintance, since Snow, too, hailed from Nova Scotia. He idolized Rodgers and was himself "Blue for Old Hawaii" on a 1937 recording, the first of many recorded island junkets by Snow. But his greatest contribution to pre-Buffett country tropicana came in the form of such Caribbean-flavored kickers as 1951's "Rhumba Boogie" and 1954's "That Crazy Mambo Thing." These records combined Latin island rhythms with Snow's clipped guitar and a northern nasal twang spewing loopy lyrics about "Madam Lazonga teachin' the conga in her little cabana down in ol' Havana...." Snow started a minor craze for country records with Caribbean rhythms, and while Buffett protests that he neither liked nor listened to country as a kid, there are echoes of Hank Snow's camp Caribbean country in Buffett's very different arrangement of some of the same elements.

Finally, no survey of hillbilly tropicana would be complete without mention of the man whose "White Sports Coat" Buffett stained in vain, Marty Robbins. Robbins's Hispanic-tinged hits like "El Paso" are well-known, and were widely influential. He also recorded at least two albums' worth of Hawaiiana, songs like "Sweet Leilani," delivered sweet and dreamy and even with an islander's falsetto. Robbins was one of country's great eclectics, a man who could (and did) sing almost anything, and sing it damn well. Even if only as an "oldies" hit-maker, Buffett gave him a nod as an influence.

Skyline Books, NYC

Harris Lewine Collection

CHAPTER THREE

Changes in Latitudes, Changes in Attitudes

New Orleans...a courtesan whose hold is strong on the mature, to whose charm the young must respond. And all who leave her, seeking the virgin's unbrown, ungold hair and her blanched and icy breast where no lover has died, return to her when she smiles across her languid fan...New Orleans.
—William Faulkner, "New Orleans," *The Double Dealer,* 1925

"Oh, God! I don't want to die in Nashville in a rented Gremlin!"
—Jimmy Buffett to Noel Coppage, *Stereo Review,* 1974

Wanderlust got the better of Buffett early. "I used to go jump boxcars and ride them from my mom's house to my grandmother's," Buffett told *Interview's* Helen Bransford, "forty-three miles away in Pascagoula. And when I was twelve, I'd jump on the freights and ride with the hobos." Boys will be boys, and Buffett came from unorthodox stock anyway. "Aunt Coo was just nuts," he told an audience back in 1974. "She died of some incurable brain disease, and my uncle, he was an alcoholic. When she died he sold this elegant old antebellum mansion, columns and everything, for, like, four cases of Budweiser and a fifth of wine."

Buffett hasn't mentioned Aunt Coo much lately, but he still pays tribute to Uncle Billy Buffett, who wasn't Aunt Coo's ex but Capt. James Delaney's youngest son and the Buffett clan's favorite black sheep. Introducing "The Pascagoula Run," a song from his last studio album, 1989's *Off to See the Lizard,* Buffett tells his fans at Irvine Meadows that this one's for "my old Uncle Billy Buffett, who passed away last year." Smiling, Buffett adds, "It's okay! He was *full throttle* while he was here."

If we believe Buffett's autobiographical story, "The Pascagoula Run" from his *Tales from Margaritaville,* then Uncle Billy was indeed "a wonderful bad influence on my life," as Buffett said elsewhere. "He went to sea most of his life and would always bring me exotic gifts. He lived out on the edge, and even though I didn't see him enough,

Scotty Hillman Collection

Frank Driggs Collection

The "folk boom" that coincided with Buffett's discovery of girls and guitars drew inspiration from Woody Guthrie, the wandering Oklahoman who sang for the downtrodden and wrote of his life on the road in *Bound for Glory.*

you always knew when Uncle Billy was in town."

Uncle Billy had been a fighter, a football player, and a World War II naval hero (in the Pacific, naturally, where he "married a Tahitian princess for five days") before serving twenty-five years as first mate of a Hong Kong steamship company. A 1986 press release for the *Floridays* album presented a Buffett chronology in which Uncle Billy cameoed. "1955: Jimmy's uncle buys him his first tropical shirt. Little Jimmy refused to wear it. His taste will change drastically over the years." Later, we read, "*1975:* By now, Jimmy has added the fifty-seventh tropical shirt to his private collection. His uncle claims responsibility for Jimmy's good taste."

In Buffett's short story, he takes a drive on the wild side in his uncle's red Jaguar XKE convertible and drinks and dances at a honky-tonk called the Oasis. On the way, "Jim Delaney" and Uncle Billy pause briefly at Spanish Fort: "They both looked out at the rotting frame of the old ship that lay dying in the tidal pool." Buffett doesn't say so in his story, but this was his grandfather's schooner, the *Chiquimula,* docked off Spanish Fort Hill "for many years," as the *Mobile Press Register* had reported, "graceful, even as a rotting old hulk—until one night a pyromaniac touched a match to the dry timbers just to see flames leap into the sky."

Since "Jim Delaney" has a driver's license in "The Pascagoula Run," he is evidently at least sixteen but not yet in college.Buffett graduated from Mobile's McGill Institute in 1964 and spent much of the following five years halfheartedly pursuing higher education and wholeheartedly pursuing the lessons Uncle Billy had taught him (and a few more besides).

His first stop was Auburn University, where Buffett picked up the guitar and little else. "I was at a pledge swap at Auburn University," Buffett told Helen Bransford, "and I was a very shy young altar boy, into skin diving and outdoor things." (Sounds like a "personals" ad, Jimmy.) "You know how awful pledge swaps were, especially if you weren't very good at talking to girls. We just sat in a corner and scratched our asses and the girls sat

Courtesy Milton Glaser

Bob Dylan blended Guthrie's grit with Allen Ginsberg's beat poetry in electric folk-rock exemplified by Milton Glaser's popular 1966 poster.

in a corner and straightened their bras, and only a few people talked. But this one guy, he had a guitar and played it and the women loved him! Later, I went to his room and asked, 'How'd you do that, man?' He told me, 'You see all those chicks? It only takes three chords.' And I said, 'Teach me those chords.'"

Buffett eagerly drank in the Secret to Meeting Girls, folkstyle 1964. It was a time when Peter, Paul, and Mary were hammerless but heavy, when girls wore their hair long (and ironed) in admiration of Joan Baez, and guys wore work shirts to look like Bob Dylan trying to look like Woody Guthrie. The electric Dylan and the first rumblings of psychedelia were still at least a year away, and the innocent idealism of the Kennedy era was still an afterglow. It was a good time to be an aspiring folknik, even if one's highest aspirations were to coeds' knickers.

Aside from learning the three magic chords of folkdom, Buffett's academic career at Auburn was singularly undistinguished. It was also short-lived, due to an unspecified transgression. Buffett was, by his own admission, "banished to Poplarville," the Mississippi hometown of Pearl River Junior College. After a semester there, he transferred to the University of Southern Mississippi at Hattiesburg. USM graduate Curtis Rockwell describes it as a campus supporting roughly thirteen thousand students, "your typical Southern school—thousands of pretty girls, the Southern belle kind of thing. The athletic program is important." But for Buffett, the most important thing was Hattiesburg's proximity to New Orleans, eighty miles to the south. "I went to class in Hattiesburg," Buffett told *Offbeat* reporter Keith Spera, "but I sort of lived in the French Quarter."

"The French Quarter in those days would eat a young man alive," recalls Vic Latham, proprietor of Key West's landmark Full Moon Saloon who knew Buffett during his Big Easy days in the 1960s. "That was definitely Jimmy's first introduction to the fast lane." But not, as it turns out, to New Orleans itself. "My personal history goes back to New Orleans when I was a kid," Buffett told the New Orleans music publication *Offbeat,* "because my grandfather was a captain for the Delta Steamship Company. I remember coming over to meet his ships. When I decided to go out on my own, New Orleans was just, to me, the haven of lunatics from the South, and I fit right into that category.... I'm a firm believer in the reason that I've been able to maintain my success and popularity is that I came off of Bourbon Street and I learned to be a performer on those streets."

Latham doesn't recall Buffett ever singing on the streets for tips, as Jerry Jeff Walker did. He does remember him playing steadily on Bourbon Street at the Bayou Room. "The Bayou Room was right next door to a strip joint," recalls Latham. "Consequently, we had strippers and hookers in and out of there all the time." Quick, Jimmy, strum those three magic chords! "I was thrown into the spotlight of being the leader of the band 'cause I was the only guy that had credit at Werlein's to

Harris Lewine Collection

Harris Lewine Collection

Harris Lewine Collection

Harris Lewine Collection

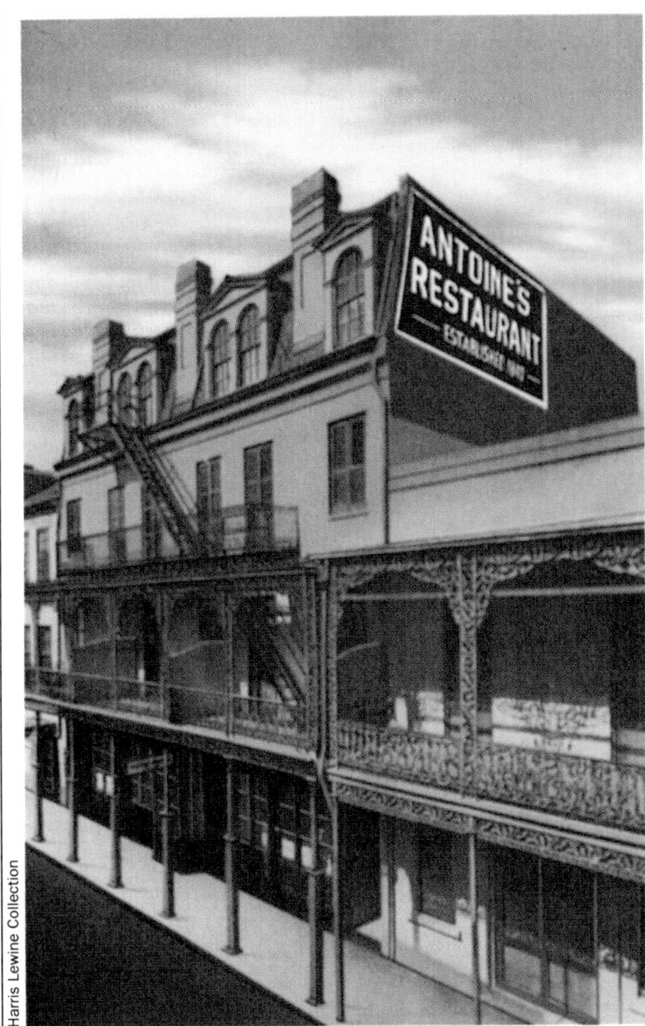

Harris Lewine Collection

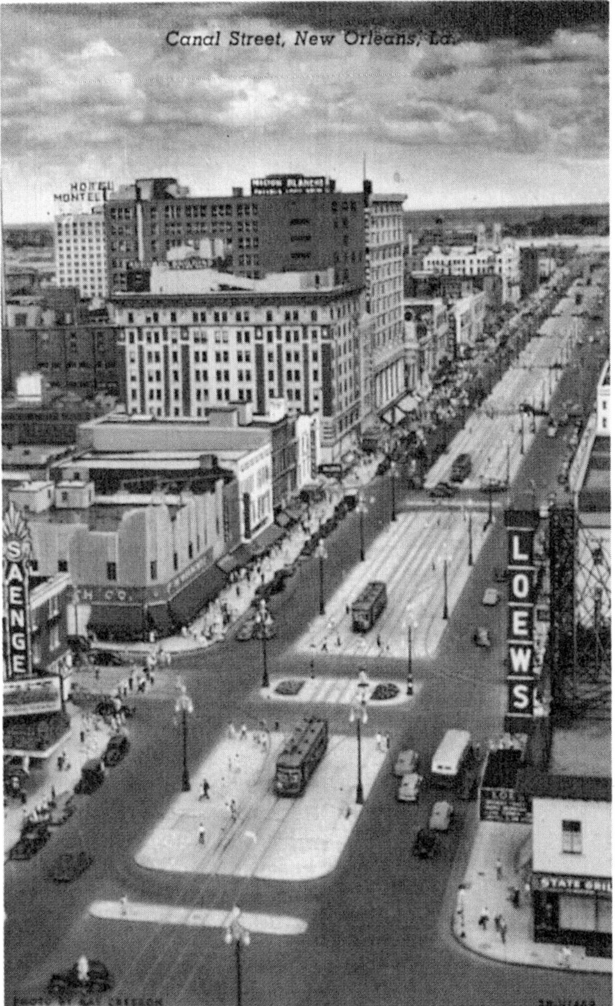

Harris Lewine Collection

Harris Lewine Collection

The 1940s New Orleans of Blanche DuBois and Stanley Kowalski was still tangible to Buffett when he came there to make music in the mid-six-ties. He loves the city's music, and New Orleans tourists love his Margaritaville.

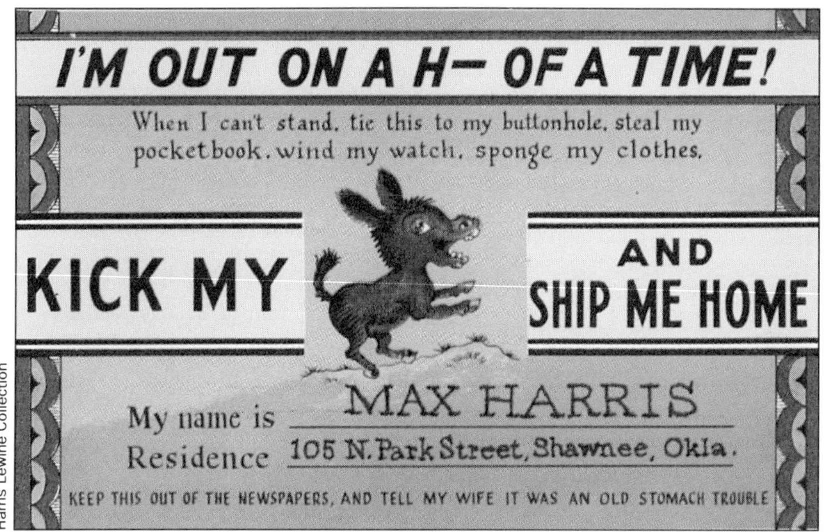

I'M OUT ON A H— OF A TIME!
When I can't stand, tie this to my buttonhole, steal my pocketbook, wind my watch, sponge my clothes.
KICK MY
AND
SHIP ME HOME
My name is MAX HARRIS
Residence 105 N. Park Street, Shawnee, Okla.
KEEP THIS OUT OF THE NEWSPAPERS, AND TELL MY WIFE IT WAS AN OLD STOMACH TROUBLE

Harris Lewine Collection

buy the sound system," Buffett told *Offbeat.* "All I wanted to do was be a background-singing bass player, but then I had no choice."

Buffett once described his Bourbon Street band as "a hard-core Jefferson Airplane cover band," which seems out of character. Latham, who sometimes sat in with the group and played blues harmonica, remembers it more as a folk band which may have covered everything from Dylan songs to sea chanteys. "He's always loved the water," says Latham, "so he's always had that element even in other people's songs that he did." He doesn't recall Buffett doing many original songs back in the sixties.

In 1992, Buffett told *Los Angeles Times* critic Robert Hilburn: "I went to New Orleans and I lived in the French Quarter when I was eighteen years old, and it was *amazing.* Here I was a Catholic altar boy and I was in the middle of the most decadent, wonderful place, and it was filled with this sense of literature—and I've been thinking about writing a book ever since then, but music just took over."

While still in college, Buffett began playing other gigs around the Gulf Coast. Trader Jon's, a Biloxi beach roadhouse, was one of the first important ones. Buffett mentions it (and its destruction by Hurricane Camille) in his comments on the Jesse Winchester song, "Biloxi," in his *Parrot Head Handbook.* Perhaps just as important was a lesson in crowd control learned at a piano bar in Hattiesburg. "Camp Shelby is right outside Hattiesburg," says Curtis Rockwell, who heard Buffett tell this sixties vintage story. "That's a mili-

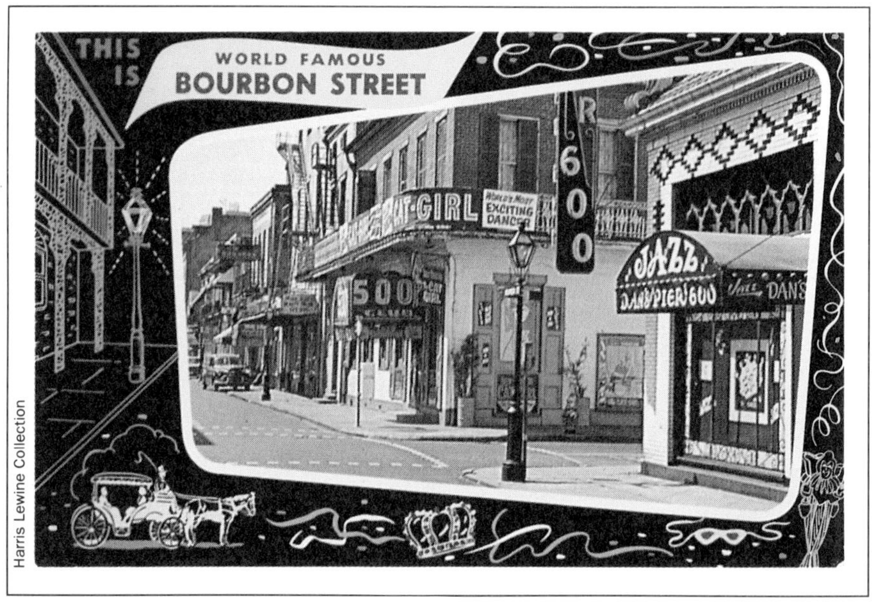

Harris Lewine Collection

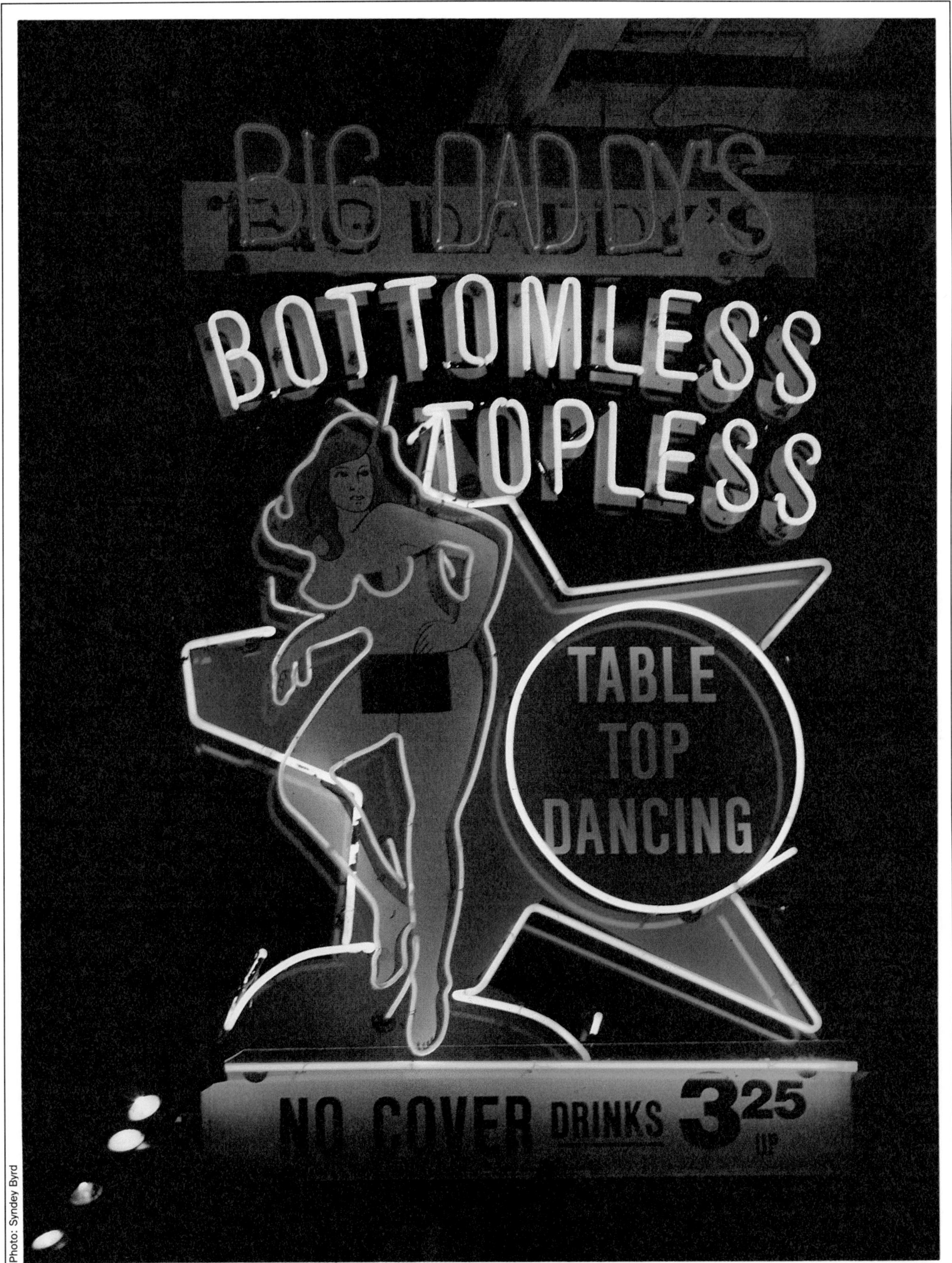

Photo: Syndey Byrd

The timeless sleaze of the French Quarter was a major element in Buffett's world when he played the Bayou Room in the sixties. His dues-paying days there made a performer of Buffett, who survived in part (according to his "Peanut Butter Conspiracy") by shoplifting.

"What a delight, what a roaring, rollicking, footstomping wonder this book is! I laughed until my sides ached, and then I laughed on."
—Henry Kisor, Chicago Sun-Times
A CONFEDERACY OF
DUNCES
THE PULITZER PRIZE-WINNING NOVEL BY
JOHN KENNEDY TOOLE

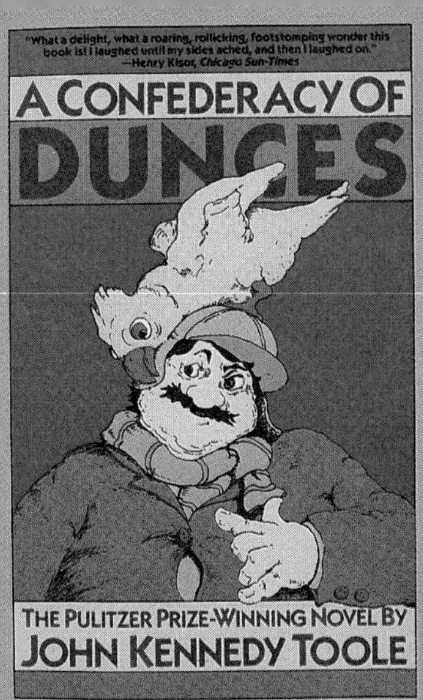

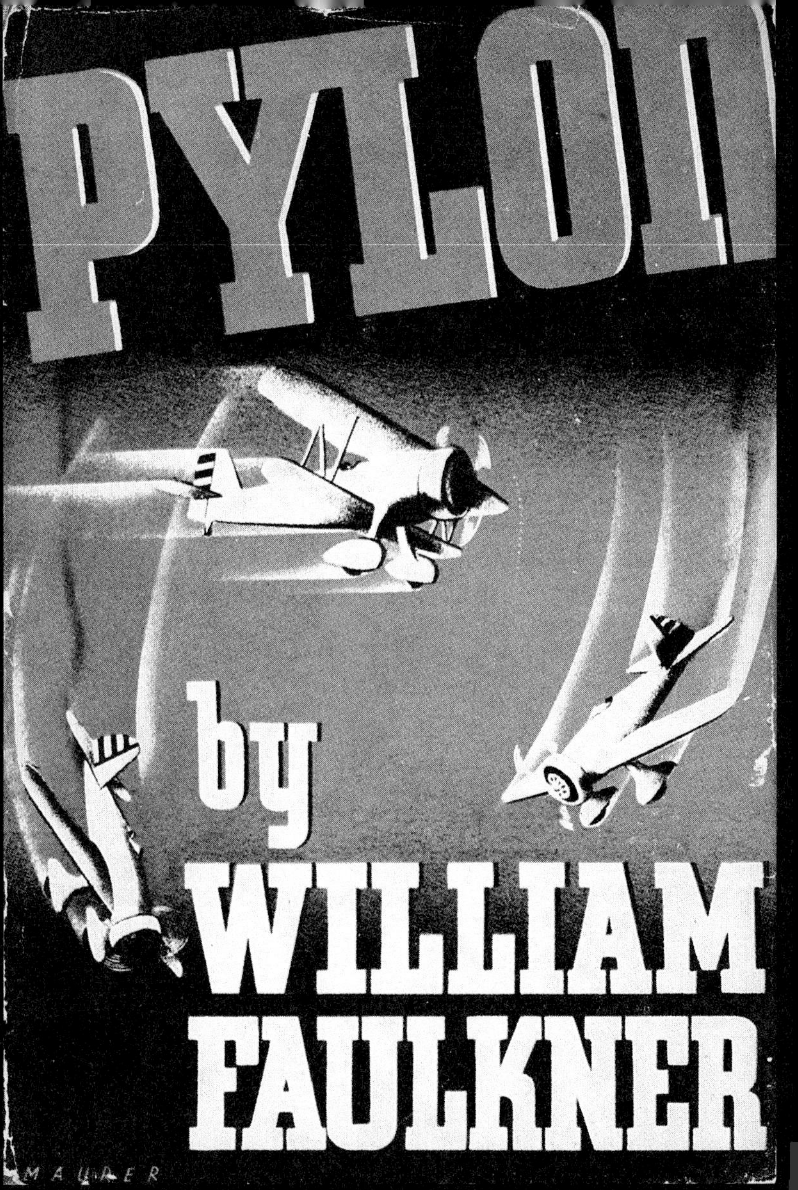

PYLON
by
WILLIAM
FAULKNER
MAURER

A Hall of Mirrors
A Houghton Mifflin Literary Fellowship Award Novel
Robert Stone

COUNT
ROLLER
SKATES
By Thomas Sancton
AN UNUSUAL NOVEL ABOUT NEW ORLEANS

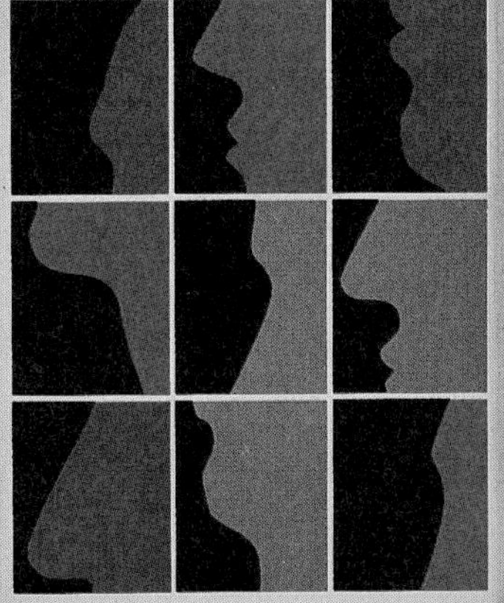

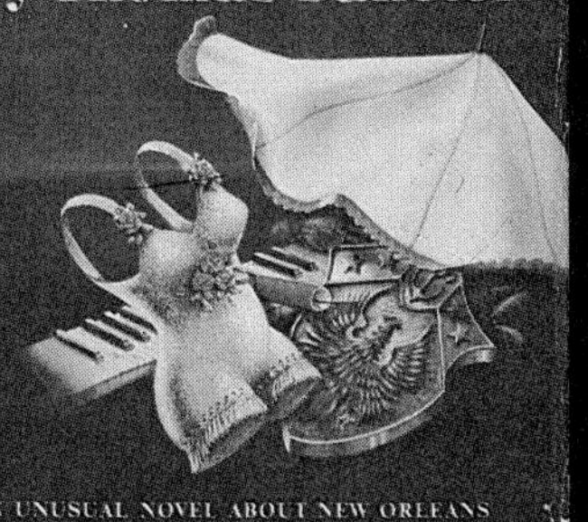

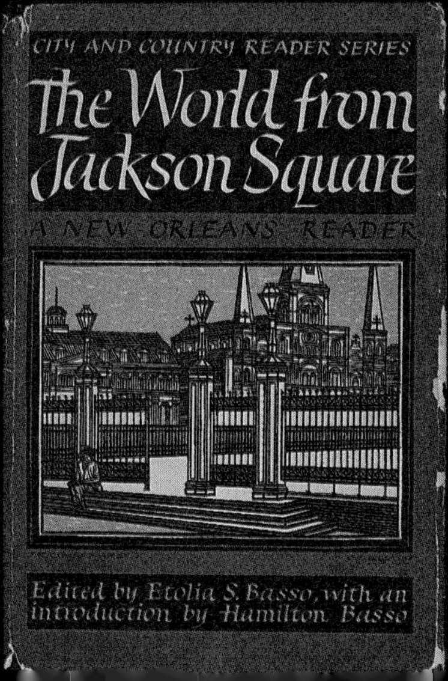

CITY AND COUNTRY READER SERIES
The World from Jackson Square
A NEW ORLEANS READER
Edited by Etolia S. Basso, with an introduction by Hamilton Basso

WILLIAM FAULKNER
MOSQUITOES
AN AVON BOOK

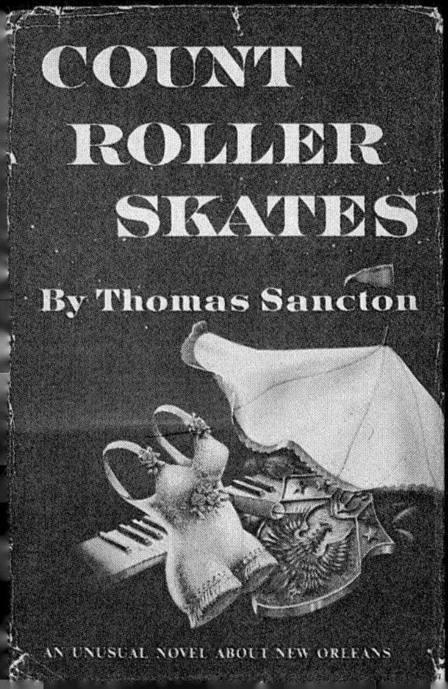

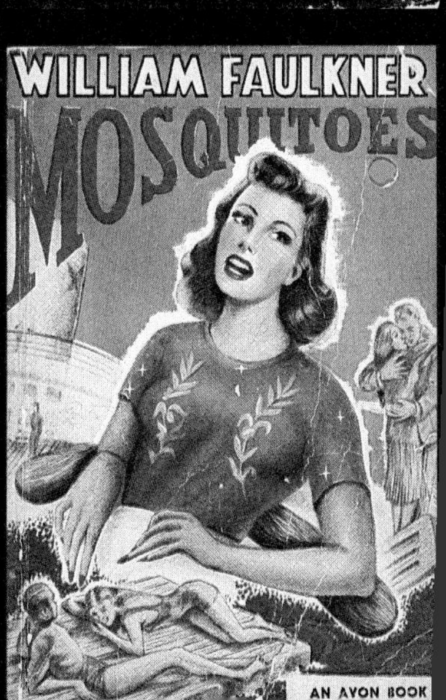

tary training site. These guys were training at Camp Shelby and may only have had one or two days left in the States before they were off to the Vietnam War. The place had a jukebox, and Buffett said, 'You want a tough crowd?' He had to unplug the jukebox each time he'd start playing. And some guy who's about to leave for Vietnam has just put his last quarter in the jukebox to hear his favorite song one time, and you have to go over and turn it off and start playing a guitar in front of him!"

Buffett lived to tell the tale, and continued to enjoy the fleshly pleasures of New Orleans while maintaining a semblance of academic respectability. His official bio has him graduating from USM in 1969 with a Bachelor of Arts Degree in History and Journalism. Unofficial accounts have him dropping out to gig fulltime at the Bayou Room, or being denied graduation for failure to pay $500 in campus parking tickets! Whatever the awful truth, two things evidently came of Buffett's college stint. In a 1976 *High Times* interview, Buffett told Bob Anderson that he studied poetry in college, "just for rhyme schemes and like that. I've always been interested in poetry. If I ever studied anything in college that I retained, it was that. Poetry." The other important connection he made at USM was with a fellow student who still plays with Buffett, harmonica ace Greg ("Fingers") Taylor. ("Fingers" comes from Taylor's less publicized talent as a boogie-woogie pianist.)

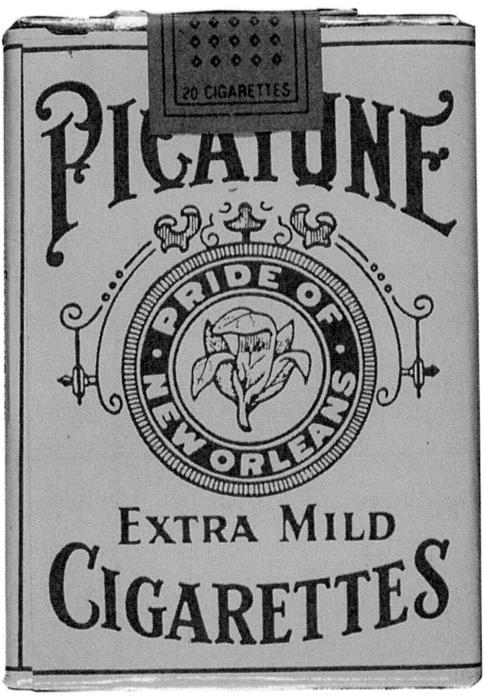

Harris Lewine Collection

Liggett & Myers' regional brand: savored by jazzman Lester Young and plentiful in Jimmy Buffett's French Quarter of the late sixties. (Opposite) The literature of New Orleans, 1927-80.

Buffettologist Curtis Rockwell collected this tale at a 1987 concert: "He was playing his guitar on the steps of the Hub, which is the student union at the University of Southern Mississippi. He's playing his guitar and thinking how great it would be to have a harmonica player. All of a sudden, some guy just walks up, sits down, and starts playing harmonica alongside of him. That's the roots of him and Fingers. Within a week, they were off to their first show in Jonesboro, Arkansas." The big time!

Latham remembers Buffett disappearing from the Quarter about the middle of 1969, which coincides with the end of his scholastic career. Like many postgraduates with uncertain futures, Buffett moved home for awhile and worked in the Mobile shipyards. He continued performing where he could, which was often the Admiral's Corner bar at the Admiral Semmes Hotel on Mobile's Government Street, where he played to "S.R.O. crowds at times," according to a 1970 piece in the *Mobile Press Register.* Choosing to ignore his long-standing, if low-paying, gig on Bourbon Street, which surely implied debauch to Mobilians, the *Register* reported: "Jimmy credits [Admiral Semmes] hotel manager Frank Taylor with giving him his first real break in the entertainment business."

We can only speculate as to what role "putting on a good front for the home folks" played in Buffett's first marriage. Margie Washichek, a onetime battleship queen (she had been Miss USS *Alabama*) became Mrs. Buffett in the summer of '69 following her graduation from Spring Hill College. As a sign of their times, Jimmy and Margie tied the knot in a Folk Mass at the Spring Hill College Chapel. As a sign of Buffett's taste in women, Margie, naturally, was a blonde.

"After college," Buffett told *Rolling Stone's* Chet Flippo in 1975, "I just went around, worked these joints, these Holiday Inn cocktail lounges. Things were ridiculous so I decided to get married and move to Nashville. I was gonna move to L.A.—I had an offer from Johnny Rivers' Soul City, but I didn't have enough money to buy gas to get there. So I went to Nashville and I couldn't even get a job at a cocktail lounge there. I was writin' songs but I couldn't plug songs, couldn't sell. I finally went to work for *Billboard* as a writer. That's where I learned about the politics and the workings of the music business."

Gris-Gris R&B: The New Orleans Tinge

Aside from Spike Jones, Mitch Miller, and the Mills Brothers, Buffett's early idols were the New Orleans Rhythm and Blues singers who came to him via radio. He cites WTIX as "the hot station" from New Orleans when he was growing up. For others in the South, it had been WJMR, home base to the legendary Poppa Stoppa, who urged listeners to his *Jam, Jive & Gumbo Show* to "get your jiver's license." Along with Jack the Cat and Doctor Daddy-O, Poppa Stoppa led the legion of Crescent City DJs who unleashed the second-line sass of New Orleans R&B on Southern radio. The segregationalist White Citizens Council of New Orleans was appalled, while the ears of pale young Southerners like Buffett were enthralled.

New Orleans R&B, no less than its jazz of an earlier generation, was rooted in the polyglot racial mixture that was the city's musical atmosphere. Jazz pioneer Ferdinand ("Jelly Roll") Morton spoke of the "Spanish tinge" in the music he played shortly after the turn of the century. It was still there a generation or more later in the rhumba-flavored music of Henry Roeland ("Roy") Byrd, better known as Professor Longhair, one of the most individualistic of New Orlean's long line of piano geniuses.

Shortly after World War II, trumpeter Dave Bartholomew began etching some new wrinkles in the old Crescent City sound with strong bass lines driven home by the likes of drummer Earl Palmer and tenor sax man Red Tyler. Cosimo Matassa had opened a recording studio on North Rampart and Dumaine in 1945, and by the year of Buffett's birth, the New Orleans R&B gumbo was boiling. An early entry was Roy Brown's 1947 hit, "Good Rockin' Tonight," a rave-up done blues

Frank Driggs Collection

Little Richard

Author's Collection

Dr. Demento

shouter style which would be covered seven years later by a young Elvis Presley.

Late in 1949, Bartholomew heard a rotund singer-pianist at the Hideaway Club belting "Junker Blues," a dope song first recorded by New Orleans' Champion Jack Dupree in 1941. Five months later, Fats Domino's first hit, "The Fat Man," was in the R&B Top 10. The Domino-Bartholomew team would enjoy even greater success in the era of rock 'n' roll, little changing their sound as their audience grew from black crowds at the Dew Drop Inn to auditoriums filled with white teenagers.

Befitting a city where funerals became raucous celebrations, New Orleans' R&B was infectiously fun and funky. The lyrics were often hip nonsense reflected in the titles of Crescent City hits: Art Neville's "Cha Dooky-Doo"; Lee Dorsey's "Ya Ya"; Jessie Hills's "Ooh Poo Pah Doo." Not everyone was amused, though. "It's not a music," Buffett's hero Mitch Miller grumbled when asked his opinion of Rhythm and Blues. "It's a disease." As if in response, the Crescent City's Huey "Piano" Smith cut "Rocking Pneumonia and the Boogie Woogie Flu" in 1957. The party rocked on, even if Mitch wouldn't sing along.

New Orleans tolerated, and in fact reveled in, the antics of characters who might have been run from other towns on the proverbial rail. Professor Longhair was as chrome-domed as Yul Brynner and sang of his admiration of a similarly hairless woman in "Bald Head." Guitar Slim wore cherry-red suits and brandished a mean guitar, piercing and distorted, which followed him (via a two-hundred-foot cord) into the streets from the club where he left his band grooving on stage, a sure crowd getter. ("He would create sensations within your body that really played tricks with your mind," marveled New Orleans songwriter Al Reed.) Clarence Henry sang like a girl and a frog ("I Ain't Got No Home"). Mac Rebennack, a white hipster with an innate feel for the local R&B, went from being a respected sideman to creating Dr. John the Night Tripper, a voodoo priest character who emerged at the height of psychedelia and shouted to Eastward-gazing hippies: "You want *weird?* Dig this!"

Little Richard was originally the Georgia

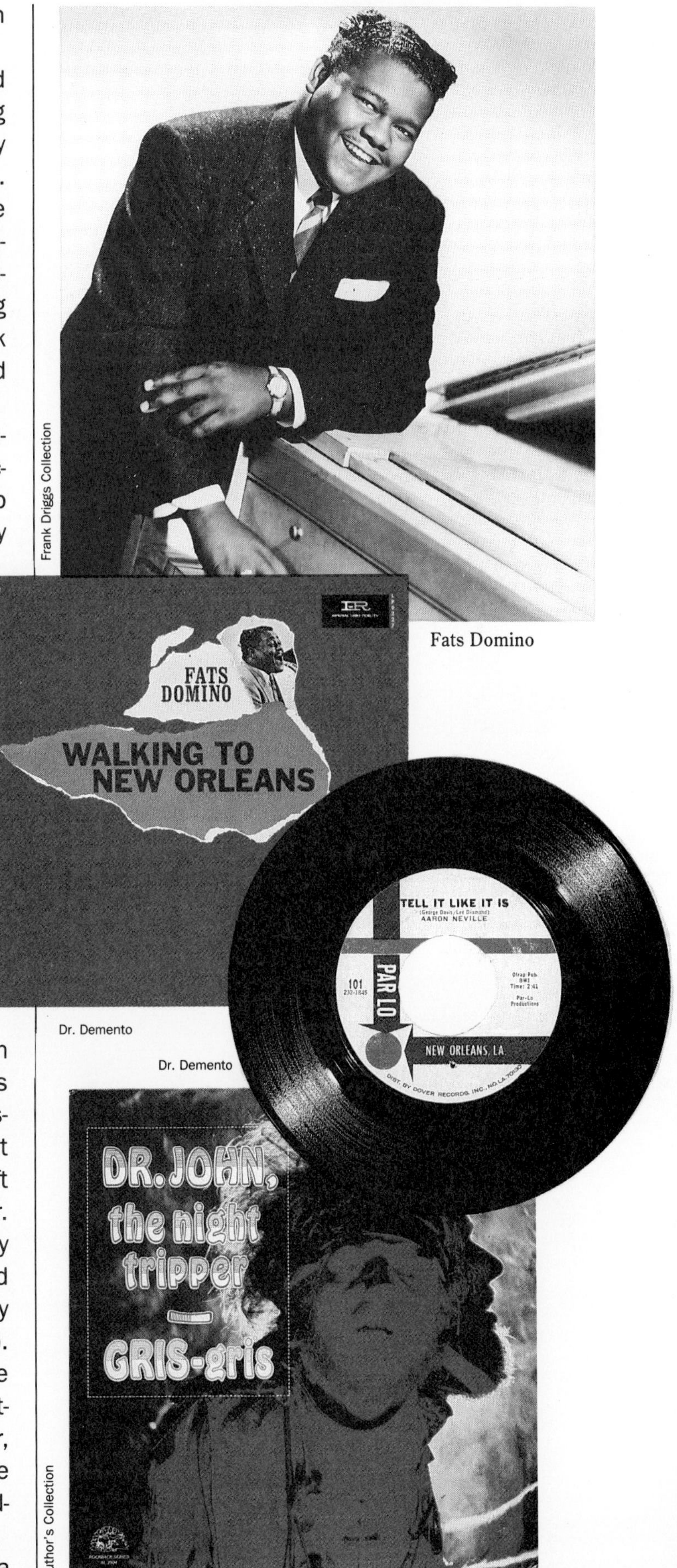

Frank Driggs Collection

Fats Domino

Dr. Demento

Dr. Demento

Author's Collection

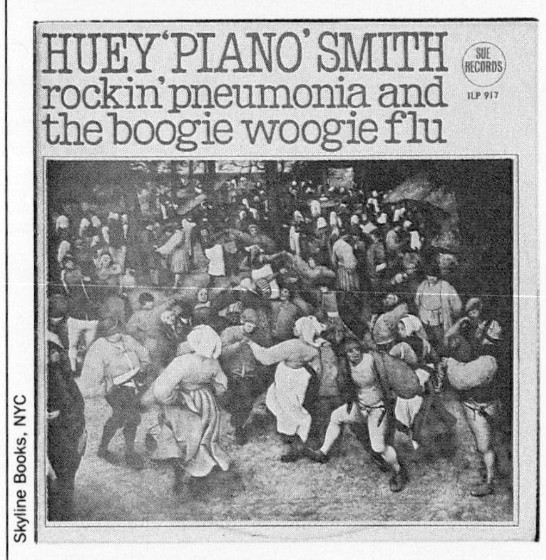

Skyline Books, NYC

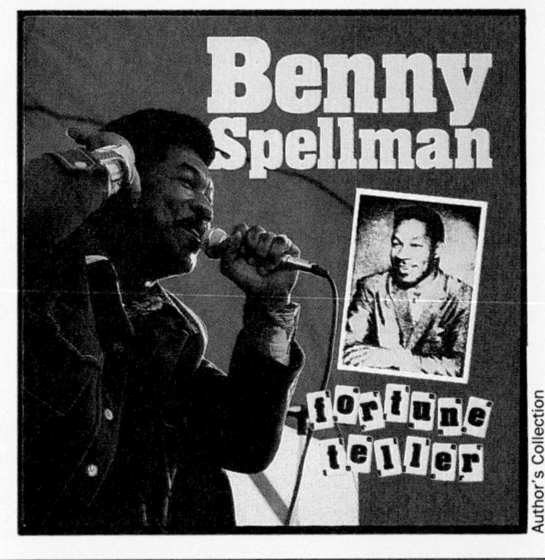

Author's Collection

Peach, but he honed his stage act—a bizarre gospel shouter/drag queen juxtaposition—and found the musicians to rocket his frenzy starward in New Orleans. Inspiration came via the example of a local drag queen named Esquerita, whose six-foot-six-inch frame was crowned by a towering bouffant which Richard emulated. Driven at a pace more possessed than even Richard's, Esquerita's records were way gone. Pat Boone might have blandly covered "Tutti Frutti," but "Esquerita and the Voola"? Not a chance. (Esquerita, AKA Fabulash, died of AIDS in 1986.)

The New Orleans R&B Buffett enjoyed as a kid wasn't quite so unhinged as that. "I cut my teeth on gumbo rock," he tells us in "Saxophones" (*Living and Dying in 3/4 Time*), and names Dr. John, Frogman Henry, Benny Spellman, and "Sweet Irma Thomas" as inspirations. Spellman was the unforgettable bass voice on Ernie K-Doe's "Mother-in-Law," and his own hits include "Fortune Teller" (covered by the Rolling Stones) and "Lipstick Traces" (covered by Ringo Starr). Buffett probably saw Spellman many times, since he constantly toured Gulf Coast clubs and

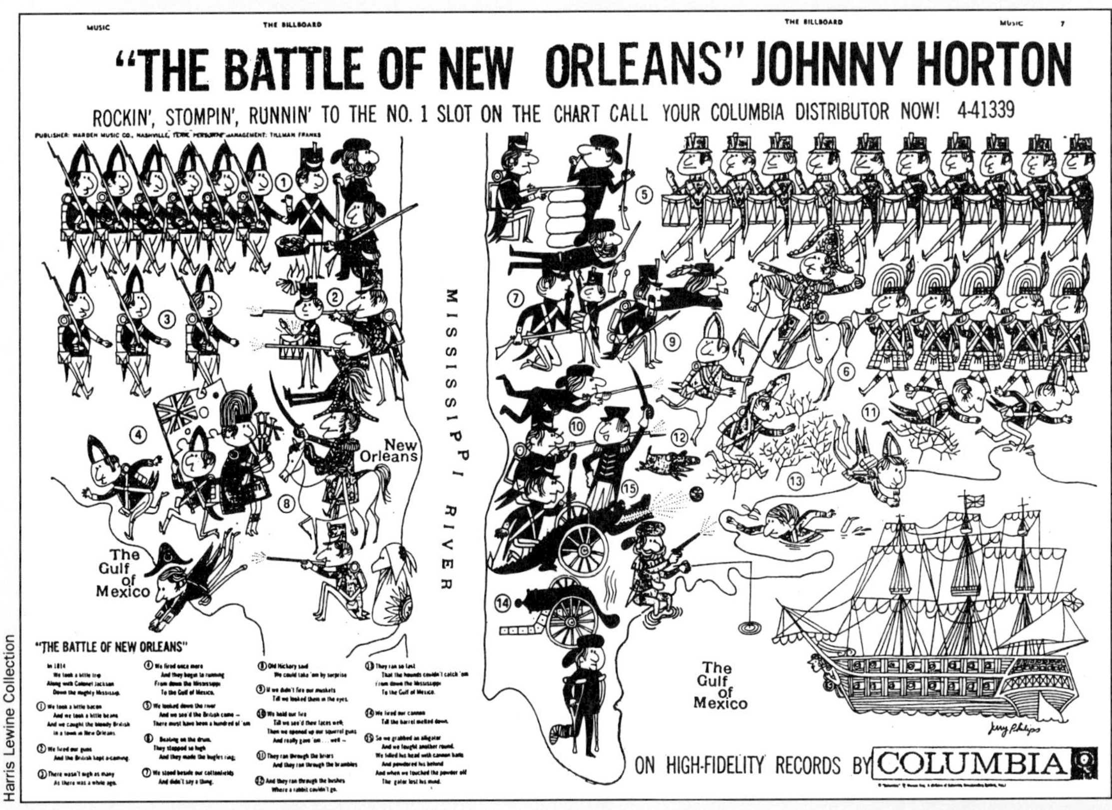

Harris Lewine Collection

colleges in the sixties. (He even once played a gig for the Ku Klux Klan in Jackson, Mississippi.)

Irma Thomas was a no-nonsense gal who urged her sisters, "(You Can Have My Husband But Please) Don't Mess With My Man," in 1960. She was back in the charts four years later with "Anyone Who Knows What Love Is," but is best known for the B side of that hit, "Time Is on My Side," a great testifyin' "you'll-get-yours" song covered by the Rolling Stones. Thomas enjoys a revitalized career today, and has recorded extensively in recent years for the rootsy Rounder label.

New Orleans R&B was populated by great characters, brilliant musicians whose tragicomic lives erupted in death-defying music (here comes that second line again). James Brooker was a child prodigy who became one of the greatest keyboard artists that this thick pianist's gene pool produced. He was as complex and idiosyncratic as Professor Longhair, and better schooled. He was also a junkie. His sole hit was a 1960 organ instrumental called "Gonzo." It was inspired, Booker told Bunny Matthews, by a movie called *The Pusher* which had a lead character nicknamed Gonzo. "That was one of the few pictures I ever saw about dope that came close to being like it *really* was," said Booker. Either the movie, or Booker's record, or both, made an impression on Buffett's 1970s Key West running mate, Hunter Thompson. Thompson, as every *Doonesbury* reader knows, proudly calls himself Dr. Gonzo.

As Buffett's "Saxophones" suggests, New Orleans R&B was a fat sax sound and a groove that would not behave. It perked up ears as far away as London, so there was no way you wouldn't notice it in nearby Mobile. Times have changed but the beat goes on, especially at the annual New Orleans Jazz and Heritage Festival, where Buffett is often a "surprise" guest with the likes of the Neville Brothers, who he used to enjoy at the Ivanhoe Piano Bar in his scuffling days and who he has worked with (co-writing and producing) in richer recent times. The free spirit of the Crescent's City's R&B pioneers was summed up nicely by Art Neville: "All we wanted to do was play," he told John Broven (*Rhythm & Blues in New Orleans,* Pelican Publishing Co., 1988). "We wanted a chick and $100 to play!"

Photo: Syndey Byrd

"Sweet Irma Thomas" is how Buffett described this great Crescent City soul chanteuse in his "Saxophones." Thomas was a churchy belter in the sixties and still moves body and spirit with her singing.

Photo: Syndey Byrd

Clarence "Frogman" Henry was one of the great eccentrics of New Orleans rhythm and blues. Singing falsetto ("like a girl") and basso ("like a frog"), Henry made a hit of "Ain't Got No Home" in 1956 and continued to chart in the sixties with such ballads as "But I Do."

Author's Collection

Author's Collection

The Ryman Auditorium in Nashville, 1946. "The mother church of country music"—where Roy Acuff, Eddy Arnold, and Ernest Tubb held services.

It was a valuable lesson. Years later, Buffett would dedicate 1981's *Somewhere Over China* to "Bill Williams, my old boss, who told me a long time ago that he knew that I knew that I could. Love, J.B." Williams, who died in the late 1970s, oversaw Buffett's work at *Billboard.* Taking the long view, Buffett was later able to see the good in his Nashville sojourn better than he had been in 1975 when he told *Rolling Stone's* Judith Sims: "I *hated* Nashville. It's too closed, too incompetent, and there's lots of nepotism." To *Stereo Review* in 1974 he recalled: "I spent two years in Nashville, working for *Billboard* and bummin' around. Couldn't get nothing recorded. Got depressed, got pissed off, got divorced, and left. Best move I ever made."

While her hubby wrote filler for *Billboard* and tried to plug his songs, Margie worked as a receptionist at the offices of ASCAP. Her proximity to the song publishing hub, however, didn't much help Buffett. "The Glasers (Tompall, Chuck, and Jim, whose studio was a hangout for Nashville's outlaws) were the most helpful," Buffett told England's *Country Music People* in 1976, "but with their own careers and various business activities they didn't really have the time to look after another hopeful songwriter." Buffett claims he was turned down by twenty-three record companies, and always ruefully recalled one rejection he took especially personally: "I remember going in one time to a guy at a record label," he told the *Nashville Tennessean's* Robert K. Oermann, "and playing a couple of my songs for him. One of them was 'The Captain and the Kid,' which I had just written because my grandfather had died. He turned off the tape machine after it was over and said, 'It's got potential, but the old man can't die in the end.'"

Despite the rounds of rejection, Buffett's persistence was rewarded, as reported in an uncredited feature in the *Mobile Press Register* from July 5, 1970. The earliest feature on Buffett's career appeared under the headline, BUFFETT SINGING, WRITING WAY TO TOP IN NASHVILLE.

"When Jimmy Buffett, former Mobile singer, married Margie Washichek, former Mobile beauty, and went off to Nashville to seek fame and fortune, it was just a matter of time before the big break came.

"Undoubtedly it is at hand!

"Jimmy, who has quite a following among the young in Mobile for the past few years, has a new record out, 'The Christian?'

"Co-written by Jimmy and Mobilian Milton Brown, 'The Christian?' has provoked some controversy since its release on the Barnaby label by Columbia Records a few weeks back. ... Special merit Spotlight in *Billboard* said, 'Strong debut out of the Nashville scene is a potent piece of material with a biting lyric line and a top vocal workout. Could make it big!'" (Later, the article points out that Buffett had to forfeit his *Billboard* job "in

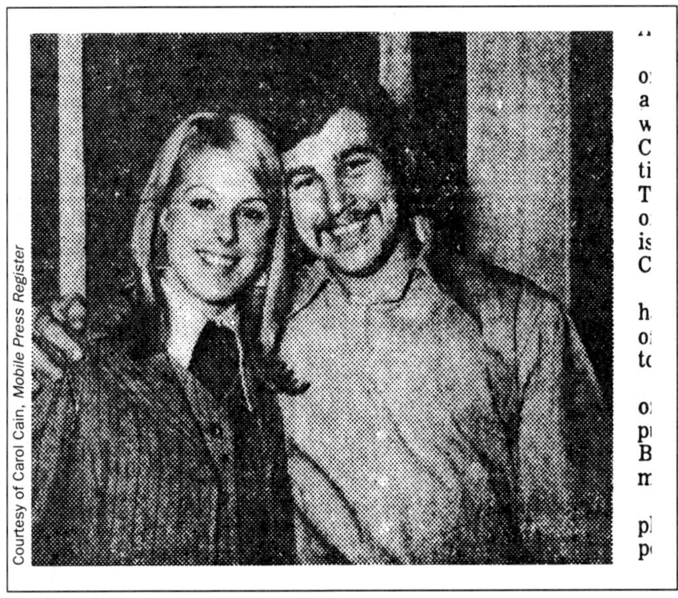

Courtesy of Carol Cain, *Mobile Press Register*

Jimmy Buffett and his first wife, the former Margie Washichek, in Nashville, 1969. Jimmy wrote filler for *Billboard* and hustled his songs for two years with little success.

Music City '69: Fear and Loathing in the Corn Field

Nineteen sixty-nine was the year Buffett's long-running love-hate thing with Nashville began. As bittersweet romances go, this one got off to a particularly rocky start. Long-haired folksingers were little more welcome that year in Nashville than were testimonials to the fighting pluck of Ho Chi Minh at a VFW dance. Yet that was when Buffett first moved there, confident fortune would wink and nod his way in Music City. Was he ahead of his time, or just sadly misinformed?

Polarization was the major media buzzword of 1969. It meant that, depending on the length of your hair, eligibility for the draft, and choice of leisure activities (cf., a future decade's buzzword, *lifestyle*), you likely felt superior to—and very different from—Americans with whom you did not share these elements. If you punched a clock and drove a pickup and your longest hair was your sideburns, for instance, there was a fair probability that you did not cheer with lusty abandon when privileged adolescents occupied university administration offices in protest, especially if your son had just been drafted to serve in Vietnam.

The film *Easy Rider,* directed by (and starring) Dennis Hopper, played up polarization paranoia that summer. Two motorcycle-riding freaks, Hopper and Peter Fonda, are blasted off their Harleys in the South by shotgun-wielding, pickup-driving rednecks. That was the price you paid for letting your freak flag fly in George Wallace country!

There was polarization within the counterculture, too. The year 1969 brought the summer of Woodstock (good hippies) and the winter of Altamont (bad hippies). For every American who cheered the idyllic mud wallow at Yasker's farm, there were others who thought the Woodstock Nation was riding a greased pole to perdition. In Nixon's America in 1969, no one dared call this

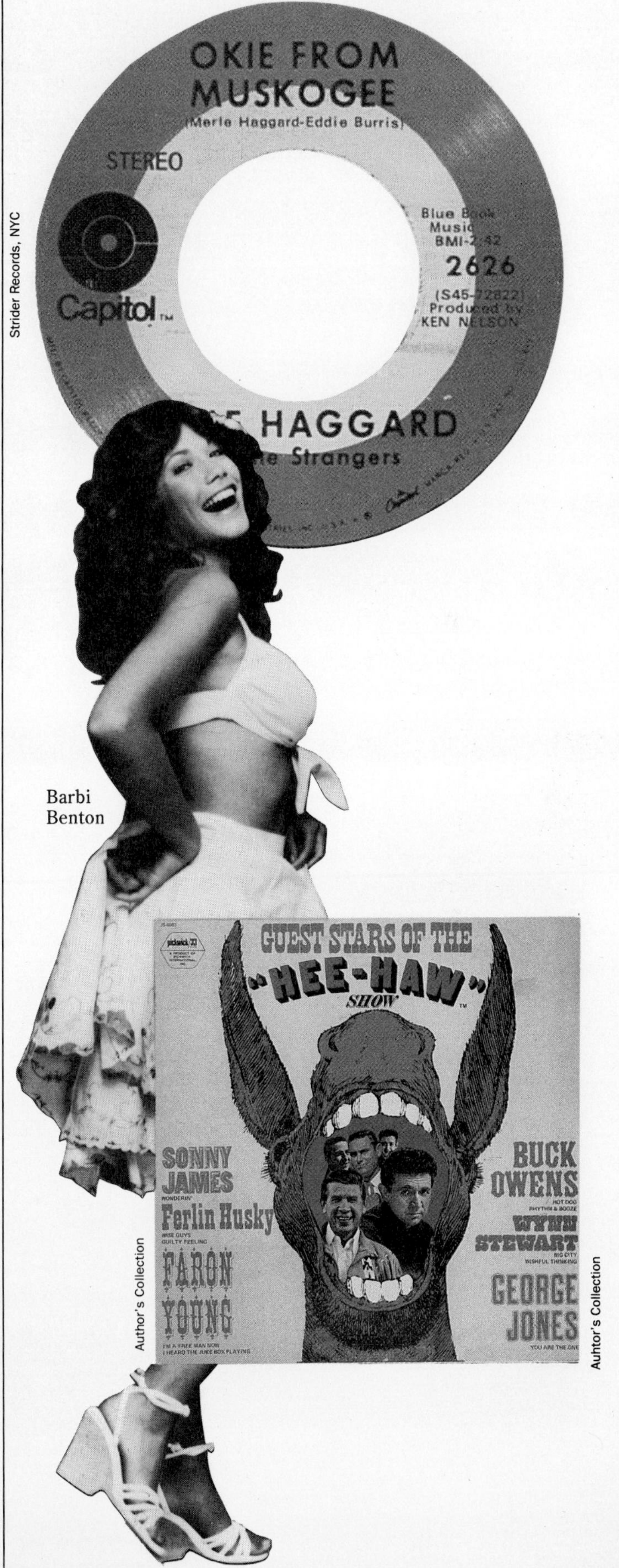

Strider Records, NYC

Barbi Benton

Author's Collection

Auhtor's Collection

class conflict. No one, that is, except Merle Haggard.

Haggard was the son of Steinbeck-style California Okies who ran away from home and into trouble at an early age. In and out of juvenile detention and San Quentin (he was there to cheer a Johnny Cash performance), Haggard finally straightened out in his twenties and became a vital part of the burgeoning Bakersfield, California, country scene. He already had four years of hits under his belt when, in 1969, a throwaway song about the simple pleasures of small-town America penned on a bus ride through Oklahoma became a blue-collar anthem.

"Okie From Muskogee" waved Old Glory and praised "holdin' hands and pitchin' woo" in a season of flag burning and Day-Glo daisy chains. Muskogee was a place where "beads and Roman sandals won't be seen," which sounded like heaven to many. Haggard's "Muskogee" spent four weeks at the top of the country charts, sounding a righteous vindication in some ears and, in others, an alarm that Dennis Hopper was right about those Neanderthals out there.

If further proof were needed, the other major blast in Nashville that year was the taping of a new CBS comedy-variety show called *Hee Haw.* It was a redneck *Laugh-In* starring country guitarist-comedian Roy Clark and veteran happy hitmaker Buck Owens, along with a supporting cast of the buck-toothed and cross-eyed. Owens played an acoustic guitar, instrument of choice of most folksingers. To assure *Hee Haw's* audience that he must not be mistaken for a folksinger and probable Communist, Owens painted patriotic bold red-white-and-blue stripes across his instrument.

Along with the jackass, the scarecrow, and the fat man (Junior Samples) who always flubbed his lines, buxom farmer's daughters would pop out of the cornfield to exchange witticisms with Buck and Roy to canned laughter. One of them was Barbie Benton, who pursued both Hugh Hefner and country stardom at the time. (Benton has since shunned both country singing and stripping in *Playboy* and now enjoys a career as New Age keyboardist.) These wholesome and ample young women were not the least of *Hee Haw's* attractions, and in 1978 they got their own syndicated sitcom, Hee Haw Honeys. One of the *Honeys,* Misty Rowe, did Barbie one better when she became an "adult" film starlet. *Hee Haw,* little changed from its original format, is still going strong in syndication.

What, then, in the year of Haggard and *Hee Haw* and a clenching of Nashville's jaw against strum-along pinkos and the whole filthy hippie mess, was Jimmy Buffett doing in Nashville? "The only reason I went to Nashville," he ruefully told *High Times* reporter Bob Anderson in 1976, "was because I didn't have the money to buy enough gas to get to L.A."

Author's Collection

Author's Collection

Merle Haggard (above) and "easy riders" Hopper, Fonda, and Nicholson.

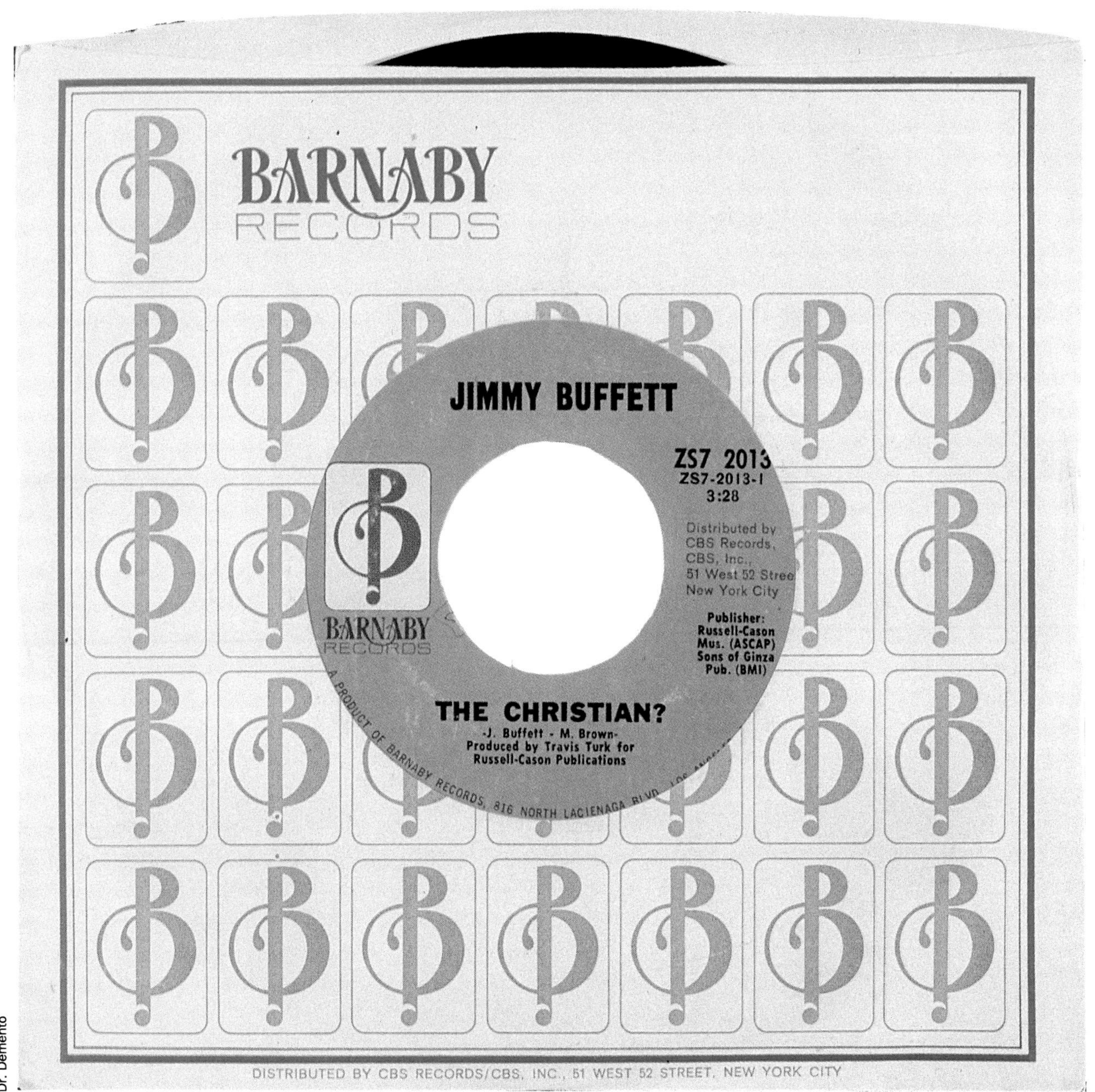

Dr. Demento

Buffett's 1970 debut single on Andy Williams's Barnaby label was hailed as the harbinger of fame and fortune, but made little splash and has yet to be reissued.

order to avoid conflicting interests.")

A Nashville publication was quoted as saying: "One of the heavy writers by the end of 1970 will be a guy named Jimmy Buffett. He's one of *Billboard's* editorial guys here and moonlights at tunesmithing ... and Buzz Cason and Travis Turk are producing a single and album by the guy using mostly (if not ALL) his own stuff for Barnaby Records, that's the Andy Williams label chiefed here by Mike Shepherd. Single by Buffett will probably be the left-fieldist thing you'll hear for a moon or two called 'The Christian?'—co-written by Milton Brown.'

"... A new label was established by Columbia Records early in 1970 and the first artist to record on the Barnaby label was Ray Stevens, whose 'Everything Is Beautiful' is making record history.

"The second single release by Barnaby was Buffett's 'The Christian?' This will be followed by another original composition entitled 'Captain America.'

"He has also cut an album of original songs which will be among presentations the last week of July at the annual Columbia Recording Convention in Freeport, Bahamas....

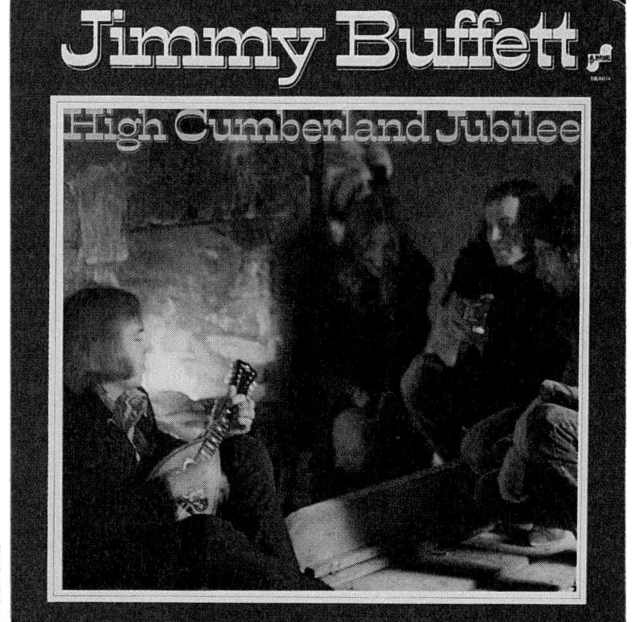

Dr. Demento

"Buffett is now devoting all of his time to songwriting and publishing in partnership with Buzz Cason and in the promotion of his records.

"Also in the making are plans for personal appearances at colleges as well as a possible television spot.

"'The Christian?' is available locally, though it hasn't been heard much here, if at all.

"'A prophet is not without honour, save in his own country, and in his own house.'"

Actually, Buffett's prophecies were widely ignored at the time his first album appeared. Legend has it *Down to Earth* sold a grand total of 374 copies. Not surprisingly, Barnaby "misplaced" the master tapes for the second Buffett album they were contract-bound to record. Though recorded in 1971, *High Cumberland Jubilee* wasn't released by Barnaby until 1977, in the wake of Buffett's success with *Changes in Latitudes, Changes in Attitudes.* He was selling far better in the late seventies than he was at the decade's onset, so Barnaby also released a double album of their Buffett sessions in 1979, *Before the Salt: Early Jimmy Buffett.* Margaritaville Records reprised this material, some of it twenty-three years old, on 1993's *Before the Beach.* But conspicuously absent on the Margaritaville reissue is "The Christian?" Buffett's fans will mostly be intrigued by early versions waxed for Barnaby of songs he would re-record between 1973 and 1976, "Livingston's Gone to Texas," "In the Shelter," and "The Captain and the Kid."

In 1977, Buffett told *Rolling Stone's* Chet Flippo, "I did a record, hired a complete band, went on the road and was broke in two months. Went back to Nashville, and my wife and I split up."

A has-been at twenty-four, broke and divorced, Buffett's fortuitous run-in with another free spirit steered him out of Music City and south to Florida. Jerry Jeff Walker would lead the Austin, Texas, "outlaws" a few short years later, but in 1971, Florida was his home base—Summerland Key, to be exact, about twenty-five miles from Key West. He invited Buffett to come check it out. "We'd both come to Nashville, and neither one of us liked it," Walker told the Winston-Salem, NC, Journal's Ed Bumgardner. "And I suppose it didn't like either one of us. So Buffett and I pulled out and hung out in Key West. Yes, I am the man who introduced Jimmy Buffett to Key West. I am responsible for all that island junk that he does so well—that golf-Gulf-and-Western music. Buffett thought Key West was heaven, man—the boats, the Caribbean. Me, I didn't like that whole steel drum thing. But I'd say it worked out nicely for Buffett."

Scamp Walker, Bojangles, and Redneck Motherhood

Buffett roared into Key West in the company of the man who wrote Richard Nixon's favorite song, "Mr. Bojangles." Jerry Jeff Walker wrote it after a night in a New Orleans drunk tank from which Vic Latham sprang him. "I remember him reading the lyrics to me in a little sub shop down on Dauphine Street," recalls the Key West bartender. Walker used a different name then, and wore an array of aliases between the birth of Ronald Crosby in Oneonta, New York, in 1942 and that of Jerry Jeff Walker a couple of decades later, somewhere on the road.

Walker took the Kerouac trip to heart and became a beat-folk wandering minstrel during the early 1960s "folk scare." The West Coast and New Orleans were frequent ports of call, and it was there Vic Latham befriended Walker. "Jerry and I go way back to the early sixties when I first got to the Quarter," recalls Latham, "and he could play maybe three songs on the guitar. The one that comes to mind immediately, because he played it twenty times a day, every day of the week, is [Woody Guthrie's] 'Hard Travelin'.' He would just play it and play it—I still kinda cringe when I hear it. I think of him sitting on the floor, about half a case of beer later, playing that same song!"

Walker credits New Orleans bluesman Babe Stovall with showing him "how to play with a little flair," which served him well in his days as street singer. Walker was off the streets long enough to form a psychedelic band, Circus Maximus, in 1967, which recorded for the eclectic Vanguard label, followed by solo albums for Atlantic's Atco subsidiary. Though commercial duds, these yielded the plum song ("Mr. Bojangles") which

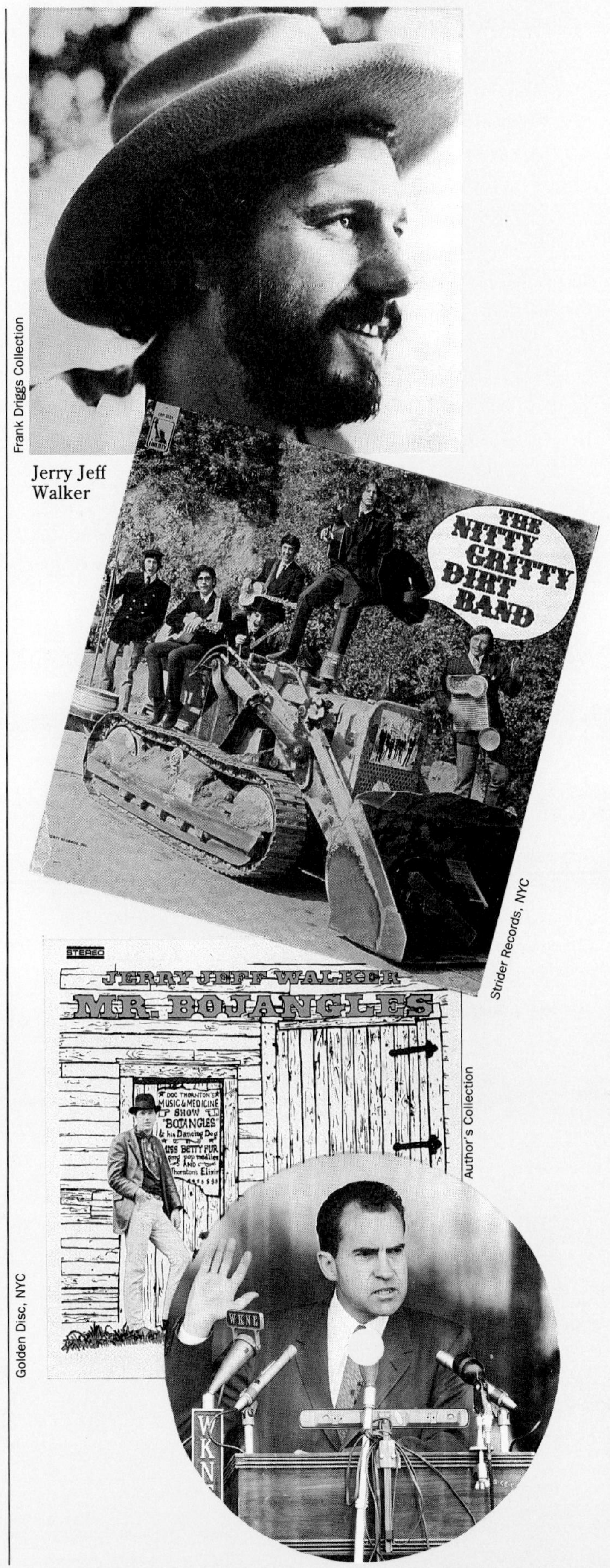

Frank Driggs Collection

Jerry Jeff Walker

Strider Records, NYC

Author's Collection

Golden Disc, NYC

reduced Nixon to tears and was covered by everyone from Neil Diamond to Nina Simone (the Nitty Gritty Dirt Band had the major hit version). Royalties from "Bojangles" supported Walker in high wastrel style through the swingin' seventies.

Watching him play avuncular host nowadays on *The Texas Connection,* an Austin-based music show aired on the Nashville Network, Walker's legendary past as the reddest-eyed rowdy on the Austin "outlaw" country scene could not be guessed at. But in the days when he served as role model for Buffett and on through much of the seventies, Walker wore his insobriety as a red badge of courage and, according to Larry L. King's account of him in *Of Outlaws, Con Men, Whores, Politicians, and Other Artists* (Viking Press, 1980), might answer to several descriptive monikers: Scamp Walker, Dr. Snowflake, and Jacky Jack Doubletrouble.

"Once I was hosting this sedate cocktail party at Princeton," writes King, "when Jerry Jeff Walker—who'd been playing a club in New York—appeared very much unannounced, dressed like a buffalo hunter, and looking like three months on field bivouac complicated by the blind staggers. Jacky Jack Doubletrouble proved that he was a natural showman by immediately imitating the walks and lisps of sherry-sipping academicians; he crashed about, stepping on long gowns, and howling for Lone Star Beer...."

Rolling Stone reporter Jan Reid caught up with Walker at an Austin club in 1973: "He was propped against the wall by the restrooms, tall and stoop-shouldered, hat pulled low over a stubble of beard, an oft-broken nose, a sleepy look, a cockeyed grin," Reif wrote in *The Improbable Rise of Redneck Rock* (Heidelburg Publishers, 1974). Walker and his Lost Gonzo Band were hellbent on keeping his legend alive and rarely performed unless they were severely stoned and stupefied. "My God," said a club manager over a handful of pills and half-smoked joints cleaned out of Walker's dressing room the morning after the night before. "They were so far gone they couldn't even get these things to their mouths." Walker waxed philosophical: "It's damned hard to sing," he said, "when you're throwing up."

When he *could* sing, one he loved to do was "Up Against the Wall, Redneck," an anti-"Okie from Muskogee" anthem penned by Austin's Ray Wylie Hubbard which laid Freudian blame on a "redneck mother" for her son's "kickin' hippies' asses 'n' raisin' hell." It was the sort of provocative lyric which, in 1973, could well incite the sort of mayhem it described. And Walker loved that.

"Everybody wanted Jerry Jeff to play his classic 'Mr. Bojangles,'" Willie Nelson wrote in his autobiography, *Willie* (Simon & Schuster, 1988), "but he never did like to be told what to play or when to play it. If some host asked Jerry Jeff to play 'Mr. Bojangles' or anything else at the wrong moment in the wrong tone of voice, he was liable to whip out his dick and piss in the potted ficus plant, and the fight would start." Nothing so pleased this gonzo cowboy who reduced Nixon to tears as an old-fashioned brawl, even if he got the worst of it. "After these rodeo cowboys beat Jacky Jack up," wrote Larry L. King,"—I mean stomped a *mudhole* in his ass—he lay in a buncha broken furniture and looked up through the blood and said, 'Y'all ain't so fuckin' tough. I been beat up worse than this by motorcycle gangs.'"

CHAPTER FOUR

Nautical Wheelers

I reckon I got to light out for the territory...because Aunt Sally she's going to adopt me and sivilize me...I been there before.
—Mark Twain, *The Adventures of Huckleberry Finn*

It was the seventies, and Key West was cooking. A strange collection of shrimpers, gays, dope dealers, crooked politicians, hippies, and tourists roamed the quaint streets of the little town at the end of the world.
—Jimmy Buffett, *Where Is Joe Merchant?*

When Buffett arrived in Key West in 1971, "it was November, eighty-five degrees, and everybody was swimming," he told *USA Today* in 1987. "I said, 'This looks like the kind of place I ought to consider living in.' It had a very good feeling about it."

The feeling of Key West is central to Buffett's best songs and to his success as what MCA marketing vice president Geoff Bywater calls "a lifestyle artist." While Buffett will philosophically say that his "Margaritaville" is less a place than a state of mind (not to mention blood alcohol content), many of his fans believe that it is on the map, and that its name is Key West. "The perception of Key West and 'Margaritaville' are pretty interchangeable," says Carol Shaughnessy, who edited Buffett's *Coconut Telegraph* in the mid-1980s and fielded fan calls and letters. "The perception was that people cared about stuff that people in the real world didn't have time to care about, and you lived closer to nature, the sun was always shining, and you could party and you never got stressed out. I think you never had a hangover. If you *did,* it was a very *picturesque* hangover.

"One fan came to our attention because he had painted 'Margaritaville' symbols all over a Barracuda, and he'd send us photographs of his car in various stages of its creation. He came down to visit Key West on his fortieth birthday, because he was 'A Pirate Looking at Forty,' and after he and his wife had enough money, they

Scotty Hillman Collection

Scotty Hillman Collection

bought a house and live here now." Key West is truly Parrot Head Mecca.

To the Spanish, it was *Cayo Hueso*—"Island of Bones." Cayos meant "little islands," hence, keys (*cayos*). Key West was an anglicization of Cayo Hueso. The bones the Spaniards found bleached on the beach may once have supported the frames of Caloosa Indians, a fierce but long-extinct tribe (they apparently weren't laid-back enough to last in Key West).

Ponce de Leon went looking for the Fountain of Youth and found the Florida Keys in 1513. Jimmy Buffett arrived at the same destination 458 years later, announced that he and his conquistadores would "Grow Older But Not Up," and proceeded to pump out a lucrative Fountain of Youth strongly laced with tequila.

Buffett wasn't the first Mobilian to leave a mark on Key West. That distinction goes to John Simonton, a Mobile businessman who, in 1822, made a dubious investment when he bought Key West for $2,000 from Juan Salas. Matthew Perry raised the American flag over Key West that year, and our Navy launched a protracted campaign against the pirates who sported in Key West's warm waters. The Navy eventually drove off the pirates, but there was no securing ships from hurricanes or treacherous reefs. The predictable frequency of shipwrecks became the lifeblood of Key West's economy.

The locals were expert at the lucrative business of "wreck and salvage." Principally of New England or English Bahamian stock, they were (and their descendants are still) called *Conchs* after the large sea snail they ate, and whose shell they blew as a signal trumpet to announce, "Wreck ashore."

"It was an educated and colorful group on this tiny island far from mainland America," writes Joy Williams in *The Florida Keys: A History and Guide* (Random House, 1987). "The men wore silk hats, the ladies served suppers on fine china, on occa-

Scotty Hillman Collection

Scotty Hillman Collection

Souvenir Folder of
QUAINT
KEY WEST FLA.
PLACE STAMP HERE
New Highway Built Over the Old Florida East Coast Railway Viaducts

Scotty Hillman Collection

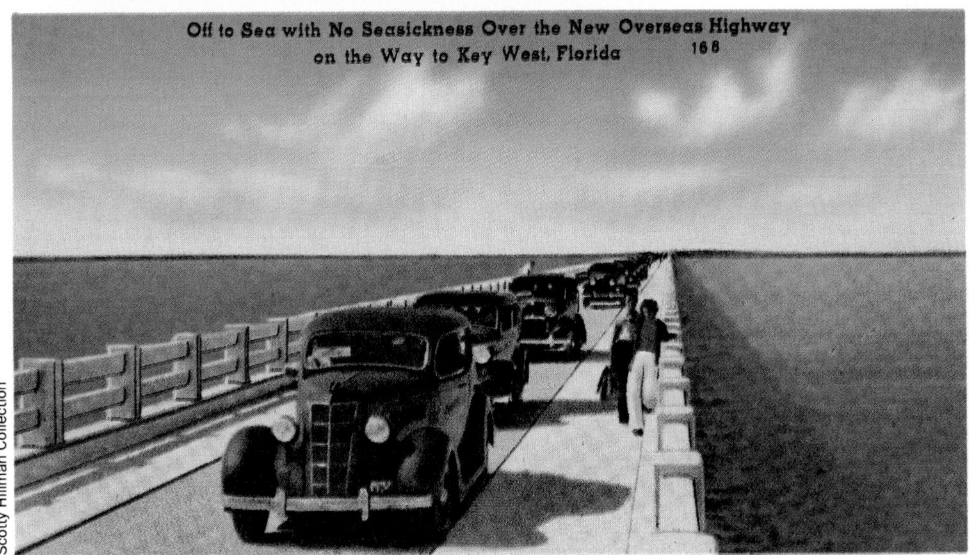

Off to Sea with No Seasickness Over the New Overseas Highway on the Way to Key West, Florida 168

Oil magnate Henry Flagler's Florida East Coast Railroad linked Key West with the mainland in 1912, but little changed at the remote outpost. Later, Flagler's tracks were replaced by the highway that brought Buffett to Key West, A1A.

Scotty Hillman Collection

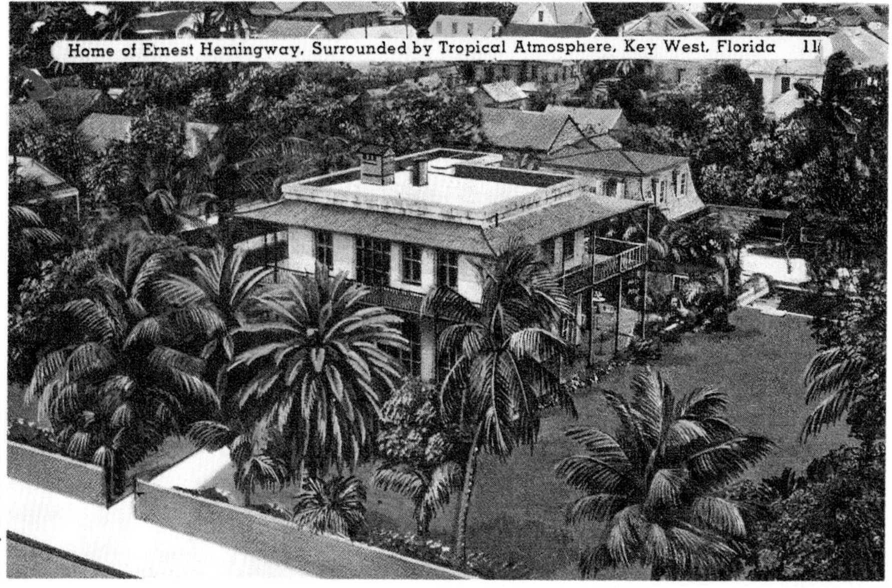

Scotty Hillman Collection

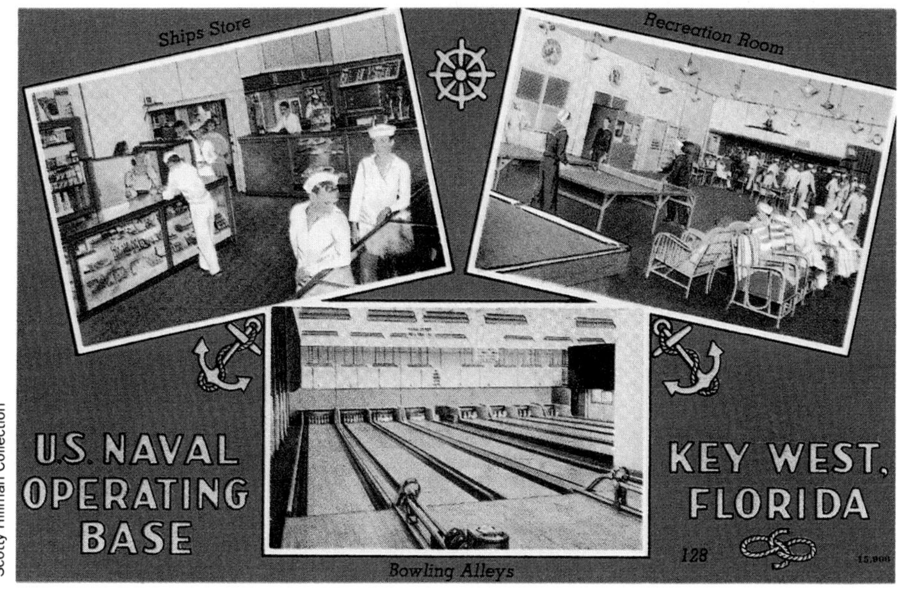

Scotty Hillman Collection

Scotty Hillman Collection

Wright Langley Collection

Nineteenth-century Key West was home to the Conchs, whose "wreck and salvage" talents were legendary. Lighthouses drove the Conchs to more conventional maritime pursuits like sponging, but their remoteness from the American mainland—and nearness to Cuba—gave Key West a character unlike any other town in America. (Top) Bird's-eye view of 1884 Key West. (Bottom) Key West waterfront, 1904.

sion, gold plates. All the wealth was wrecking wealth. Indeed, much of the exotic furnishings that filled the houses, and the formal clothes the people wore, came directly from the foundered ships."

That party ended when lighthouses began appearing on the Keys in the 1850s. By then, Key West had 2,700 citizens, and continued to grow in the latter nineteenth century as sponging and cigar making replaced wrecking as the heart of the local economy. The naval presence also played a role in the town's growth and character. Then as now, it was an eccentric outpost, as noted by one visitor in the 1880s, who called Key West "about as un-American as possible, bearing a strong resemblance to a West Indian town."

The mainland finally reached out to it in the early years of this century when Henry Flagler, Standard Oil magnate and President of the Florida East Coast Railroad, began laying track which would end in Key West. (Let it be noted that Flagler's general manager was a man named Joseph Parott.) Construction on the Seven-Mile Bridge brought Key West boomtown prosperity and vices, such as floating whorehouses. When Flagler's Overseas Railroad was completed in January of 1912 and the old robber baron christened it with a triumphant ride in his private car, one Marathon Key man celebrated the journey by going on a week-long drunk, ending with his death by alcohol poisoning. He had the seventies party spirit, but was really sixty years ahead of schedule.

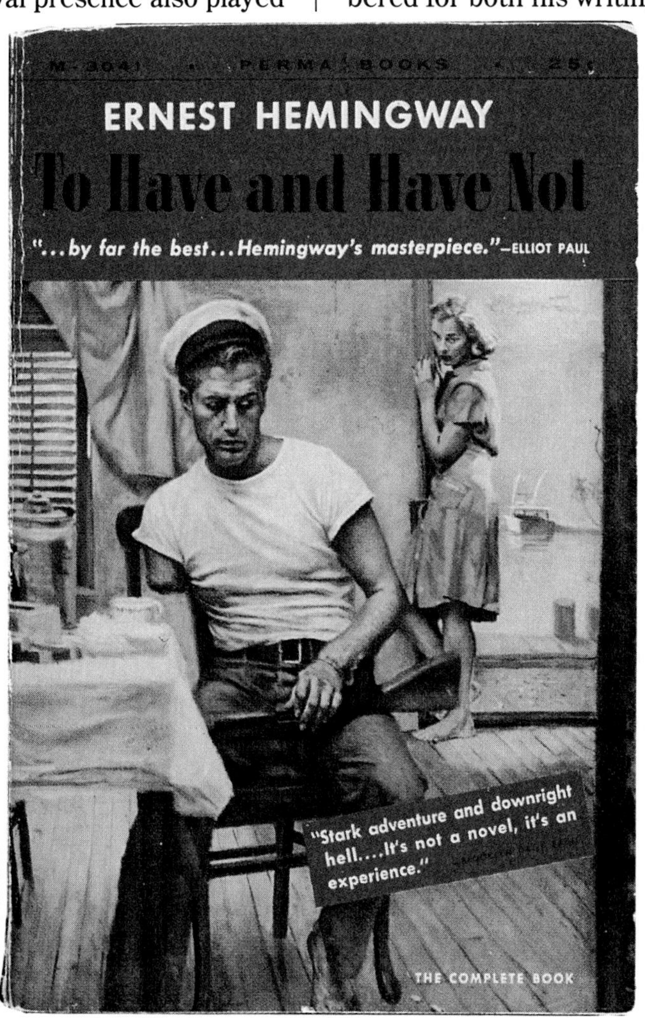

Harris Lewine Collection

A prophetic Hemingway, 1937: "No matter how a man alone ain't got no bloody f—ing chance."

Along with pirates, Conchs, and the Navy, Key West has long been famous for the literary lights who have shone on its sleepy shores. Western writer Zane Grey must be mentioned as the first famous novelist to "discover" the Keys, though he actually sojourned at Flagler's Long Key Fishing Club, considerably north of Key West. Grey alternately worked on such books as *Code of the West* and went sailfishing, a sport he is credited with popularizing.

Ernest Hemingway is certainly better remembered for both his writing and fishing in Key West, where he and his second wife, Pauline, bought an 1850s-vintage house in 1931. After much restoration (it would boast Key West's first swimming pool), it became Hemingway's primary residence for the next nine years.

To Hemingway's door at 907 Whitehead a young would-be writer from Minneapolis named Arnold Samuelson traveled by freight in 1934, ignoring the warning of the bum who told him, "Hey, Bub, you're headed the wrong way.... That train's headed for Key West. There ain't nothing there. When you get there all you can do is turn around and come back. If you can get back. If they find you panhandling in Key West, the cops don't fool with you. They throw your ass in jail." (From *With Hemingway: A Year in Key West and Cuba,* by Arnold Samuelson, Random House, 1984.)

Given its Depression-blighted economy, panhandlers would have found slim pickings in Key West, where 80 percent of the citizenry was on welfare. Things were so bad it was suggested the 12,000 isolated Key Westers simply ask the government to relocate them somewhere—perhaps

Wright Langley Collection

Hemingway, with sailfish catch, Key West waterfront, 1934: "Harry . . . went back to running liquor when the depression had put charter-boat fishing on the bum. . . . 'It's a strange place,' said Professor MacWalsey. 'Fascinating, really. They call it the Gibraltar of America and it's three hundred and seventy-five miles south of Cairo, Egypt.'" —Ernest Hemingway, *To Have and Have Not.*

anywhere—else. Instead, Florida's Federal Relief Administrator, Julius Stone, set about finding ways to make Key West an attractive vacation spot for those few Americans who could afford them.

Hemingway had predicted as much in his 1934 Key West novel, *To Have and Have Not:* "What they're trying to do is starve you Conchs out of here so they can burn down the shacks and put up apartments and make this a tourist town. That's what I hear. I hear they're buying up lots, and then after the poor people are starved out and gone somewhere else to starve some more they're going to come in and make it into a beauty spot for tourists."

Arnold Samuelson, Hemingway's 1934 houseguest/writing student, offered a telling portrait of Mrs. Hemingway's reaction to Key West improvement: "Pauline worried about the WPA program turning Key West into a tourist town, on account of what it would do to the cost of keeping servants. Tourists would be competing for servants and raising wages. She liked Key West the way it was, a town everybody was leaving who could leave; those who stayed were the cheapest labor in America."

Hemingway's *To Have and Have Not* protagonist, Harry Morgan, was not unlike many desperate Conchs who "went back to running liquor when the depression had put charter boat fishing on the bum." Rum-running was both an easy way to make money in a strapped economy and an act of defiance against an unpopular prohibition, exactly what dope smuggling would become in Buffett's day.

Key West was only beginning its transformation into a "beauty spot for tourists" when a hellacious hurricane ripped through the Middle Keys on Labor Day, 1935. Its two-hundred-mph winds destroyed the railway and, on Upper Matecumbe Key, a tidal wave demolished a train intended to rescue hundreds of road crew workers, who perished in the hurricane. The devastation effectively ended Key West's recovery, though the town would boom again during World War II, thanks to the Navy and the local eagerness to live up to a lascivious reputation as "the Singapore of the West."

There was a lull after the War, though the town Hemingway had abandoned would soon be embraced by other writers. The poet Elizabeth Bishop had lived and worked in Key West between 1938 and 1942, writing many of her *Poems: North and South,* which won the Pulitzer Prize for Poetry in 1946. But a far more influential presence settled on the local scene after World War II, when playwright Tennessee Williams decided to check out Hemingway's Depression-era port, liked it, and stayed.

Tennessee Williams's *A Streetcar Named Desire* electrified the New York theater world when it had its debut in 1947 with Marlon Brando playing the loutish Stanley Kowalski. *Streetcar* and *The Glass Menagerie* were the first of an extraordinary string of plays Williams wrote about people at society's fringe, characters he etched with the poetry and violence of Greek tragedy. Many of

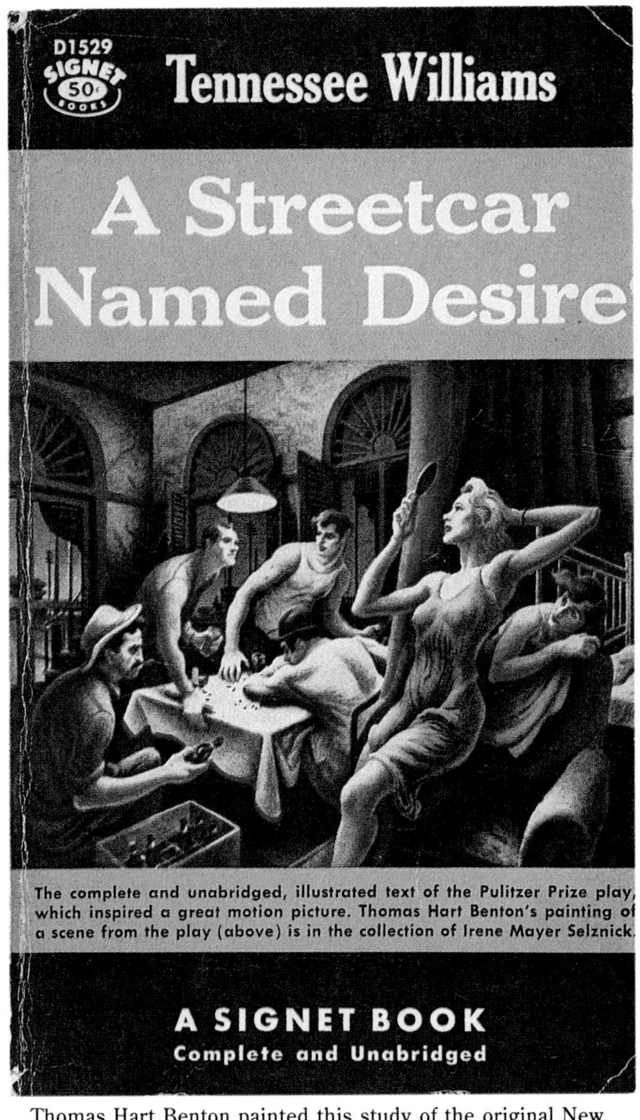

Phil Ahrens, Gotham Book Mart

Thomas Hart Benton painted this study of the original New York cast of Tennessee Williams's *A Streetcar Named Desire,* which brought stardom to Marlon Brando.

Photo: Wright Langley

Tennessee Williams (here at home, at 1431 Duval Street) loved bulldogs and loved Key West, even though it never served as setting for the many plays he wrote there.

Celluloid Keys

Hollywood came to Key West—and vice versa—en route from Hemingway's Key Wet-inspired fiction. Typical of Hollywood, the route from novel to screen tended to obscure all traces of the point of embarkation, but some fine journeys were made anyway.

The first and finest was *To Have and Have Not* (1944), directed by Howard Hawks from a script co-written by William Faulkner and Jules Furthman, lending this film, as critic Pauline Kael points out, the distinction of having the hands of two Nobel Prize-winning authors in it. "Don't be misled," Kael cautioned, "it's the Warners' mixture as before—sex and politics—but better this time."

Sexual politics were essayed here by Humphrey Bogart and a sultry ingenue, Lauren Bacall, whose role was surely one of the most memorable screen debuts of its time (and, for pure heat, perhaps of all time). Bacall was not yet twenty, but appeared deliciously and dangerously worldly-wise as she volleyed slinky come-ons to Bogie: "You know how to whistle, dontcha, Harry? Just put your lips together and *blow!*" Warner Bros' resident anarchist animator, Tex Avery, parodied this in a cartoon with an audience of eye-popping, tongue-wagging wolves, blowing enthusiastic wolf whistles at Bacall.

Readers of Hemingway's novel may have wondered, as they watched the film, just where it went. Apparently director Howard Hawks and his screenwriters opted to scrap Hemingway's Depression-era novel in favor of what its characters may have been up to prior to its beginning, only World War II was on, so there had to be Nazis a-lurk, and ... we assume Papa was well paid for the use of his novel's name, at least.

Legendary songwriter Hoagy Carmichael ("Stardust") accompanied Bacall's langorous songs in the film. (Perhaps as tribute to that role, Hoagy became the name of Frank Bama's dog in Buffett's novel, *Where Is Joe Merchant?*). The

Frank Driggs Collection

Author's Collection

singer's voice on the soundtrack belonged not to Bacall but to a young man named Andy Williams. A quarter of a century later, Williams would start a short-lived record label, Barnaby, for which Jimmy Buffett made his first album.

Hemingway's *To Have and Have Not* continued to be recycled by Hollywood long after 1944. Michael Curtiz, who had directed *Casablanca,* used its plot for his 1950 film, *The Breaking Point.* Tough-guy director Don Siegel and tough-guy actor Audie Murphy teamed in 1958 to make *The Gun Runners,* based on Hemingway's short story "One Trip Across," the kernel of *To Have and Have Not.*

Perhaps the most ironic recycling of *To Have and Have Not* was the tacking of its ending on to the 1948 film version of Maxwell Anderson's play *Key Largo*. John Huston directed Bogie and Bacall in this one, along with a malevolent Edward G. Robinson as a racketeer holding a hotel full of hostages in the Florida Keys. Though shot primarily in Hollywood (a few interior shots were done "on location" at the Caribbean Club), the movie was surefire tourist bait, which the town of Rock Harbor cast out when it changed its name to Key Largo in 1952. Party poopers point not only to the West Coast filming of most of *Key Largo* but to such anomalies as fog and kelp (not in the Keys there aren't) in Huston's melodrama. This hasn't abashed the local Holiday Inn's bogus Bogie boast that "Key Largo is laden with memories of the great actor." Anyone anxious to relive them can float there aboard a riverboat used in *The African Queen,* though there is no connection whatsoever between that film and the Florida Keys.

If some films set in the Keys were made elsewhere, at least one shot in the Keys wasn't set there at all. *The Rose Tattoo* (1955) was written by Tennessee Williams at his home in Key West, and Hollywood's bowdlerization of his 1951 play (set somewhere on the Gulf Coast) at least starred the woman for whom he created the passionate role of Serafina Delle Rose, the fiery Anna Magnani. Much of the film was shot where *The Rose Tattoo* was hatched, at Williams's house at 1431 Duncan Street. In a casino scene, Williams and producer Hal Wallis can be seen among the extras.

Finally, a bit of Key West history made it onto film in 1953's *Beneath the Twelve Mile Reef.* The "sponge wars" between Greeks and Conchs, spiced by an intra-ethnic love between Greek Robert Wagner (you read it right) and Conch Terry Moore, was the film's topic. Leonard Bernstein didn't turn it into a musical.

Harris Lewine Collection

Edward G. Robinson

Harris Lewine Collection

Photos: Chris Robinson

Buffett's friend Chris Robinson took these snapshots of the Tequila Regatta the singer celebrated in the song "Nautical Wheelers." At the top are Buffett, Sonia (who later became Mrs. Chris Robinson), Phil Clark, and Mason on the Pier House beach, 1971.

Williams's plays were written in Key West, and while Hemingway, who vacated in 1940 and never looked back, became the literary tourist attraction in town, Williams has the distinction of being the major American writer who lived longest and wrote most in Key West, even though it never served as a setting for his plays.

Like Buffett and many of his contemporaries, Williams was a Southern misfit with an appetite for life who had honed a few of his appetites in the French Quarter. He was openly gay, and probably his presence (and celebrity status) had significant impact on the early development of Key West's sizable and influential gay community.

In 1958 the Conch Train, a kind of kiddie-park tram with tour guide, began running the streets of Key West, and was symptomatic of the town's gradual attempts to realize Hemingway's 1934 prediction that it would become a "beauty spot for tourists." Aside from tourists, there were shrimpers and sailors on sprees in the town's plentiful Duvall Street bars, writers (famous and unknown), and a smattering of gays. Key West changed at its own languid pace and still managed to retain much of the neo-Caribbean flavor noted nearly a century before by the author who saw it as "about as un-American as possible, bearing a strong resemblance to a West Indian town."

By 1971, lifelong locals could lament the destruction in the 1960s of such landmarks as the coral-rock Convent of Mary Immaculate, a beautiful structure doomed to the wreckers' ball in 1966, but the new kids in town—like Buffett—weren't in a mood to mourn for a past they never knew. Vic Latham came to Key West in 1970, and wasted little time in getting the party going at the Chart Room, "an infamous bar where a lot of writers and musicians and smugglers and politicians, every *imaginable* type of heavy drinker, hung out," recalls Latham. It was there that Buffett and Jerry Jeff Walker renewed their friendship with this old New Orleans crony. "There was a group of maybe ten or fifteen of us who *were* the Fast Lane down here for a good while," says Latham. "Several of us had French Quarter backgrounds. I'm not talking about just musicians. Along with Jerry Jeff, Jimmy, and myself, there was [writer] Tom McGuane, who later married Jimmy's sister, Laurie; Jim Harrison, who is, to my mind, perhaps the finest writer in America today; Dan Gerber, the heir apparent to Gerber Baby Foods; a French count by the name of Guy de la Valdene; and a lot of smugglers, including Phil Clark, about whom 'A Pirate Looks at Forty' was written. All of us had a thing for having a good time, and were a little more creative at it than most. Jimmy managed to chronicle a lot of that in his songs."

"Whenever there was a gathering," recalls Phil Tenney, current owner of the landmark Key West restaurant, Louie's Backyard, "he was there.

Courtesy of Chris Robinson

Chris Robinson, Baby Cory, and wife Sonia, at the height of the Key West Boogie, 1974.

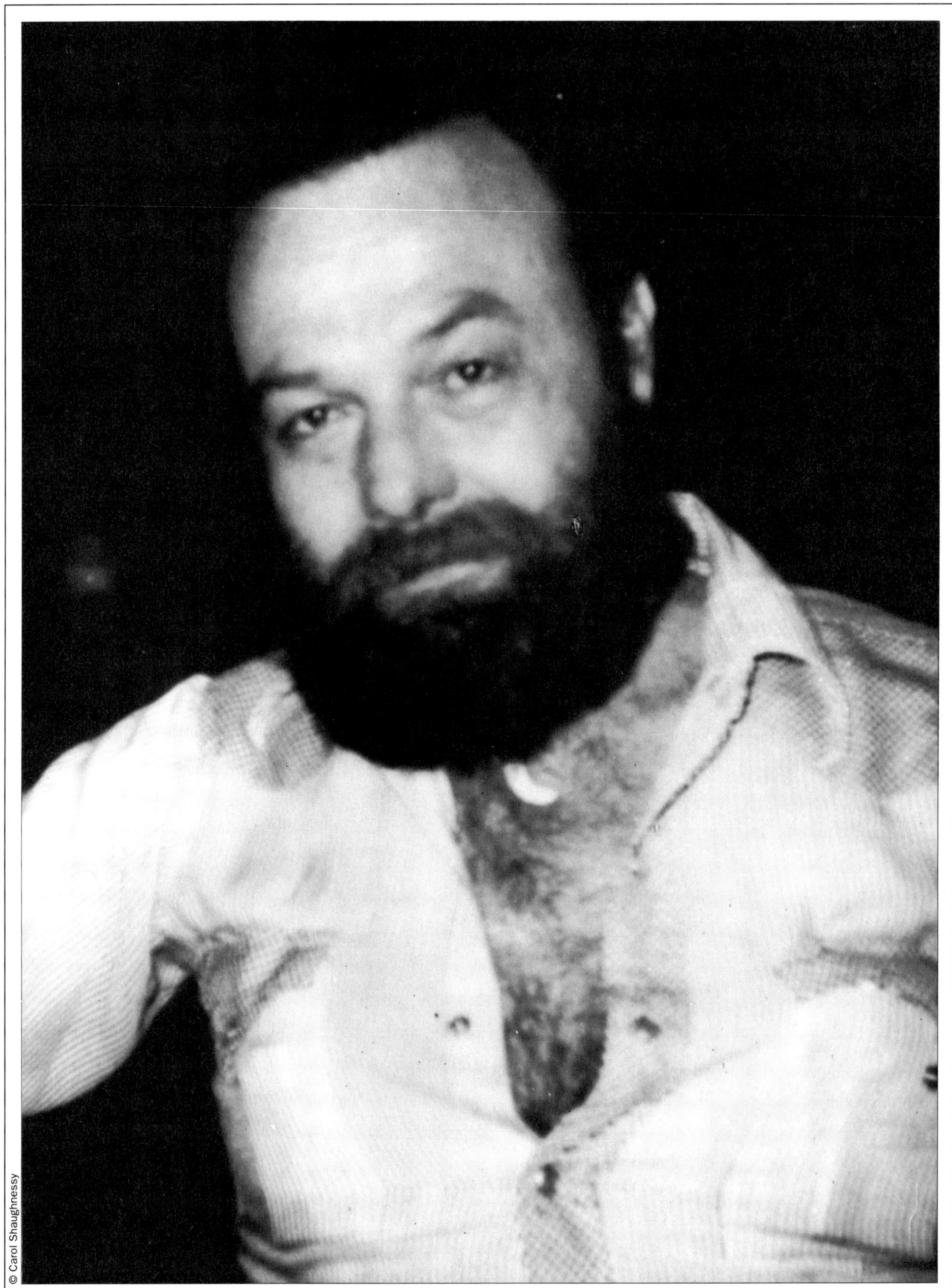

© Carol Shaughnessy

"Jimmy literally made Phil a legend with that one song ["A Pirate Looks at Forty"]. It was one of the high points of Phil's life, I would say."—Vic Latham

We'd all sing, or he'd sing, or they'd jam. I first heard him at Howie's Lounge on lower Duvall. It was really seedy! Then he played at Crazy Ophelia's. I met him at the Chart Room. The city was run from the Chart Room. The mayor, chief of police, *everyone* was there.

"We had things like the Ballast Key weekend, where we'd take seven or eight boats and go out to this little key west of Key West. We used to go out there and have parties, fix great big fifty-five gallon drums full of punches, and just be bad."

"Back in the seventies," says Chris Robinson, a bartender at Louie's who once lived downstairs from Buffett, "we were all young and had nothing to worry about. No families at that point. Just the *boogie!*" John Helen, who tends bar at Vic Latham's Full Moon Saloon, fondly recalls the Key West boogie: "It was a bicycle society," he says. "Flip-flops and cut-offs. Beards and long hair. Bars. Beaches. As little work as possible. Rents were very affordable: $60 a month for apartments that are now $400 and $500 a month.... Wages were real low, but the price of alcohol was real low too."

It was to this Southern/borderline Caribbean bohemia at the beach that Buffett came in late 1971, eager to participate in—and chronicle—what Robinson calls its "decade of decadence." "I don't know why I didn't fit into Nashville," Buffett told the British fanzine *Country Music People* in 1976. "Maybe it was the continuous battle for success. The place seemed a little weird to me. I wanted space and time to evaluate people and places. This is what I found in Key West."

The songs Buffett started writing there reflected the quirky local counterculture, or what Vic Latham calls "just a bunch of fools having fun." "Nautical Wheelers" is a good example: "'Sonia's just grinnin' and Phil is ecstatic, and Mason just jumped in the sea,'" says Chris Robinson, quoting the lyric. "They were on what was called the first Tequila Regatta. Swindle Wendel's Trimarans used to rent these little trimarans at the Pier House. You would do a shot of tequila at the Chart Room; you'd run out to the pool. You'd dive in the pool. You'd do your second shot of tequila. Run down to the beach, jump in the water, swim out to the raft in front of the Pier House. Do your third shot, sail a sailboat out to a little designated area. Come back and do your fourth shot. Dive in the water, run up the beach, hit the pool. Do your fifth shot. Dive in the pool, hit the Chart Room, and do your sixth shot of tequila.

Courtesy Illustration House, Inc.

"Fifteen men on the Dead Man's Chest—Yo-ho-ho, and a bottle of rum!" N. C. Wyeth's cover illustration for Robert Louis Stevenson's *Treasure Island.*

"They were out in the middle of the harbor and the wind kind of died and there's a good current out there—they were being swept out to sea. So Mason—she was one of Jimmy's girlfriends, I think—took off her clothes and flagged down this shrimp boat. So when this shrimper came over to tow 'em in, she had to jump in the water 'cause she was naked. So that was where 'Sonia's just grinnin' and Phil is ecstatic, and Mason just jumped in the sea' came from. That was Phil Clark, that he wrote 'A Pirate Looks at Forty' about. Sonia was Phil's girlfriend, who ended up being my ex-wife." A small world.

Clark's cameo in "Nautical Wheelers" was overshadowed by the full-blown portrait, "A Pirate Looks at Forty," both on the A1A album. Many consider it Buffett's finest song, and its wistful celebration of a drug smuggler made it an underground favorite in the mid-seventies. "He was proud as he could be," Latham says of Clark's reaction to Buffett's portrait of him in song. "It was one of the high points of Phil's life, I would say."

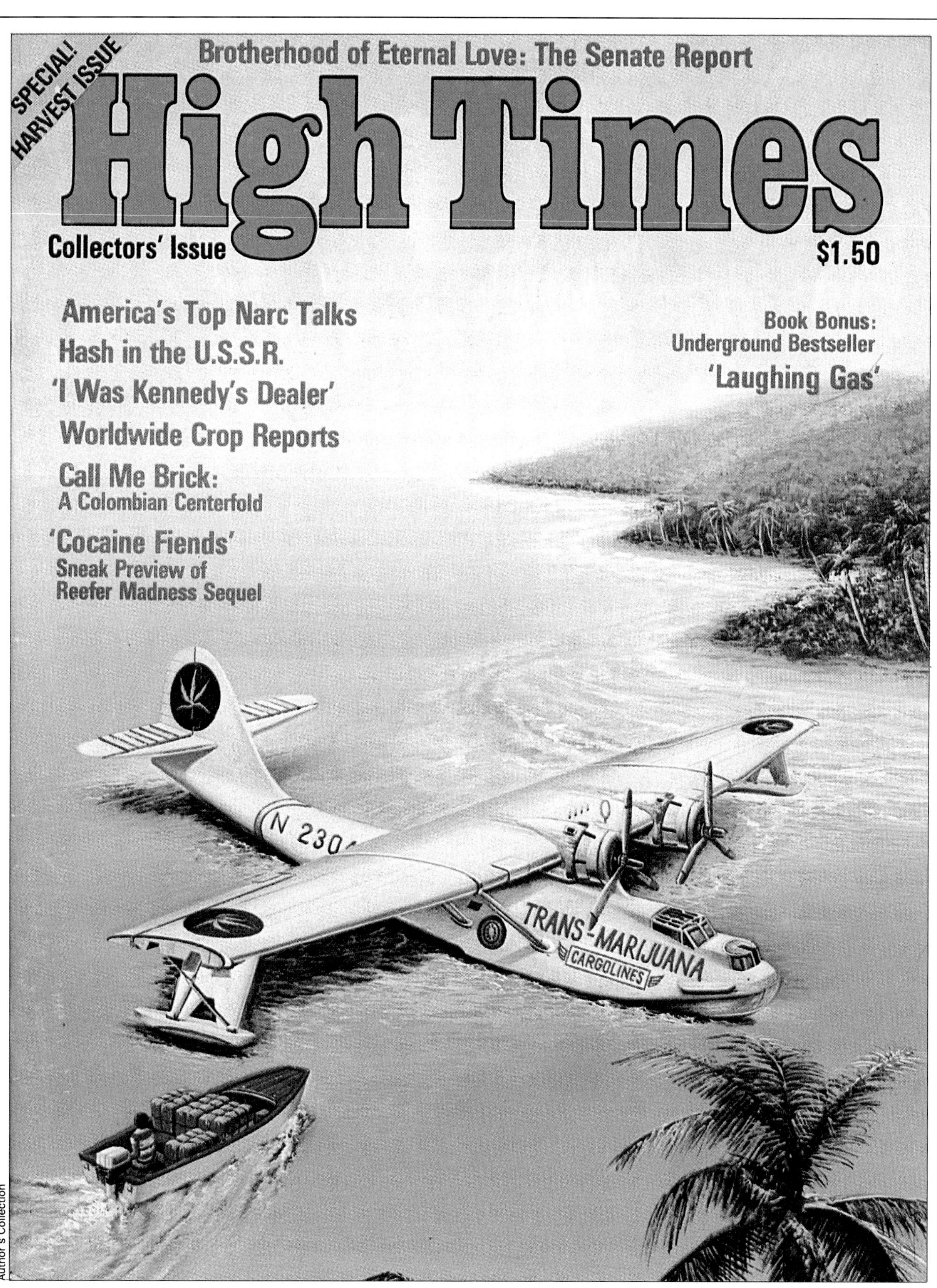

SPECIAL! HARVEST ISSUE
Brotherhood of Eternal Love: The Senate Report
High Times
Collectors' Issue
$1.50
America's Top Narc Talks
Hash in the U.S.S.R.
'I Was Kennedy's Dealer'
Worldwide Crop Reports
Call Me Brick:
A Colombian Centerfold
'Cocaine Fiends'
Sneak Preview of
Reefer Madness Sequel
Book Bonus:
Underground Bestseller
'Laughing Gas'
TRANS-MARIJUANA
CARGOLINES
Author's Collection

High Times celebrated the seventies dope culture and the allure of smuggling. Key West thrived on smuggling money, and local officials looked the other way. Marijuana was a major cash crop, and Buffett's tapes were among the standard accessories on most smuggling voyages or flights.

Clark was in his late thirties when he and Latham were running the Chart Room, the sort of larger-than-life character who could well inspire a young songwriter like Buffett. "Phil was good-looking," recalls Latham. "*Big*—probably stood six-feet-two, maybe 215 pounds. Phil had as beautiful a basso speaking voice as I've ever heard. I know a hundred disc jockeys throughout the country who would give their left ball to have Phil's voice. He had run a couple of bars in New York City. He had spent a lot of time in St. Thomas, both on sailboats and probably doing some smuggling or some kind of nefarious ways of making money. He worked as a fisherman a good bit. Didn't seem to handle being ashore as well as he did being on the water, which is not unusual. You'll find a lot of committed seamen just kind of lose their shit when they get onshore. I frequently called the shrimpers the true modern-day cowboys, because when they came in from a two-week shrimping trip, it was just like coming in off a trail drive. They'd come to town and just go crazy. Fortunately, they didn't carry guns. They had knives instead."

It wasn't for shrimping, though, that Phil Clark is remembered. "In the early seventies" recalls Chris Robinson, "there were shrimp boats bringing in 30,000 pounds [of marijuana], and it was piled everywhere. No one looked down on you for smuggling then. It was a romance adventure!" Buffett told *Rolling Stone's* Chet Flippo in 1977: "If I hadn't gotten into rock and roll seriously, I'd still be out there smuggling my ass off, because I was *good* at it, the few times I did it. I thought, yeah, I am livin' my life as a song."

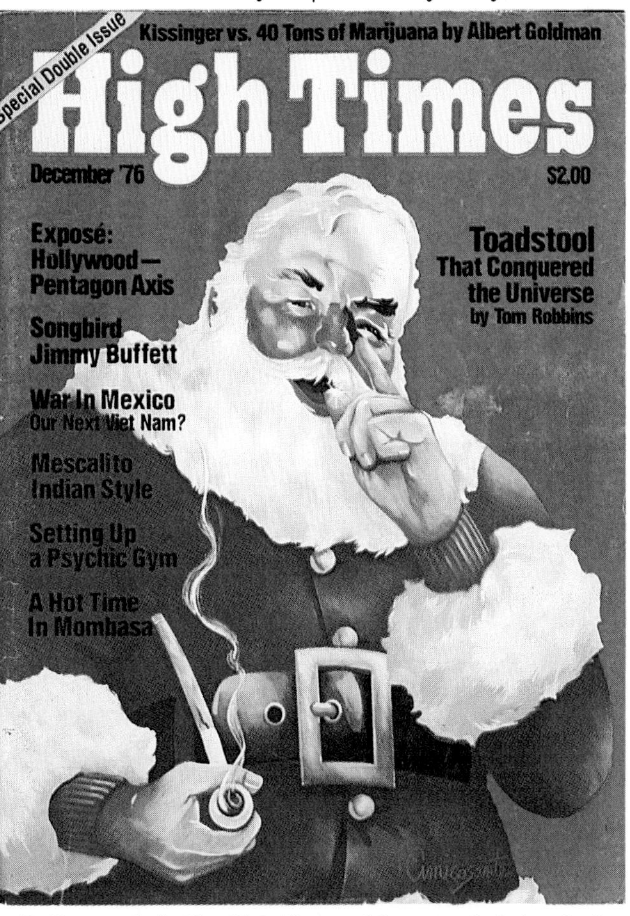

Buffett was hailed by *High Times* as "the smuggler's favorite," and he granted a candid interview to the magazine for its Christmas 1976 issue.

Discussing "A Pirate Looks at Forty" in a 1976 *High Times* interview, Buffett told Bob Anderson: "Smuggling and piracy have always been associated with coastal areas. The shrimpers on the Gulf used to run cigarettes to South America in the holds of their ships, 'cause they could get a ton of money. That's how it started. Then they decided to pick up a load of weed on the way back.... I guess everybody would like to be a smuggler. I mean, it's a fascinating thing, right? It's adventurous, romantic, swashbuckling. There's something about going to sea—there's this mystery and romance that I think is carried over in literature and music.... Everybody would love to be a rock star or a smuggler."

"Everybody in town was involved in it in one way or another," says Vic Latham of drug smuggling's impact on Key West's economy. "It was a cottage industry, a mom-and-pop type situation. Business was done on a handshake down here. There weren't guns." Chris Robinson confirms Latham's picture of Key West's smugglers: "The only time you carried guns," he says, "you carried guns to go down for the Colombians hijacking your boat. They'd shoot you and steal your load. Your guns weren't for backup here. It was just local people, the Smiths and the Joneses. And it put money back into the economy. There were lots of hundred dollar bills and no credit cards floating around. You'd go out to eat for dinner in some of the nicer restaurants and there's six or seven people going through six or seven bottles of Dom, you know they've just had a successful run! People had money, and money went a whole lot farther back then than it does now." The local

Bambú
PAPEL
DE
FUMAR
BAMBÚ
For a poster size, full color reproduction, send $2.00 to:
Bambú Sales, Inc., Dept. P, 338 Westbury Ave., Carle Place, N.Y. 11514.

Author's Collection

Ad for a popular brand of "rolling paper" expresses the open commerce in dope accessories during the 1970s.

Author's Collection

Buffett bragged of dope smuggling in the seventies and cultivated the image of the affable rogue whose "water sports" might include importation of Colombian weed.

Cadillac dealership enjoyed the nation's biggest cash Cadillac trade for a few years in the seventies.

Phil Clark held court in Key West when smuggling was "a gentlemanly sport," recalls Robinson. "Mostly it was marijuana, not cocaine, and it fit in with the Key West pirate atmosphere, 'cause everyone in Key West was noted for their shipwrecking abilities." Writing in *Crawdaddy* in 1977, Buffett's photographer friend Tom Corcoran noted of smugglers trying to outrun the Coast Guard: "If capture is unavoidable, there occurs an instant and practical definition of the price of freedom: sink the boat and get rescued. The purchase price of the boat plus cargo rarely exceeds lawyers' fees. Better luck next time."

Smuggling was risky and macho and high-profit countercultural derring-do. In *Grass Roots: Marijuana in America Today* (Harper & Row, 1979), Albert Goldman wrote: "... nothing is more characteristic of the fantasy life of America in the mid-seventies than the dream of standing stripped to the waist behind a wonderfully knurled and spoked yacht wheel with your old lady at your side as you cast a keen eye to windward and bring on home that big load of gold that is gonna put you on Easy Street!... The smuggler's public image is a fusion of the outlaw bravado of the Wild West with the sex-drugs-and-money glamour of the rock star.... In a world where the power of illusion and the illusion of power are so hard to distinguish, the dope smuggler is an exemplary contemporary character."

Given that, it would have been easy for Buffett to make a kind of cartoon song about the 1970s pirate-smuggler, which he did not do. "A Pirate Looks at Forty" opens with a sort of prayer to "Mother Ocean," and develops into a well-crafted and sensitive character study. Few singer-songwriters of the seventies were as poetically inventive as Buffett in the song's "invocation," which paraphrases a stanza of Lord Byron's *Childe Harold's Pilgrimage,* Canto I:

And I have loved thee, Ocean! and my joy
Of youthful sports was on thy breast to be
Borne, like thy bubbles, onward; from a boy
I wantoned with thy breakers,...
And I trusted to thy billows far and near,
And laid my hand upon thy mane,—as I do here.

"Jimmy captured him pretty well," Chris Robinson recalls of Phil Clark. "'I passed out and I rallied,' that's in the song. Phil would stand at the bar and get so drunk he would almost pass out. But he'd wake up and kick his little boot down on the ground and toss back another beer. He always had his shoulders back and had this great grin."

"He was a born romantic," says Vic Latham, "but he was also born restless," which may account for the five successive wives Robinson recalls Clark had. In his last years, he was engaged to Carol Shaughnessy. Asked to describe Clark, she says, "God, it's hard to put somebody that you lived with for five years into about three sentences! Phil was a gentleman of the old school. He had a sense of honor that you rarely find today. Combine that with an absolute lunacy! I would catch him playing like a kid with our dog. I wish I had been old enough at the time we were together to understand him better. It was the time when there were legends in Key West, and he was one. Sometimes he abused it. And yet, if a friend of his was in trouble, he would do literally everything in his power to help that friend with money or a place to stay or anything that was needed."

The magnanimous pirate's luck ran out in the mid-eighties as both the local scene and the tolerance for smugglers deteriorated. He had been too visibly active for too long, and a lengthy prison term looked like the inevitable outcome of a bust. "He got caught that last time and he didn't want to go to jail," explains Robinson. "The pirate was like fifty then, and I don't think he wanted to go to jail, so he split and I think went to Michigan and up through Canada and down back to California, where he ended up."

"When he left," says Shaughnessy, "I had a very strong feeling that in about two years somebody's going to come to me and tell me that he's dead. It was about a year and a half."

"He had gone pretty well downhill," recalls Latham. "Phil was drinking far more than he should have." The circumstances of his death in 1986 are unknown, but this much is certain: "He fell off a boat in Sausalito Bay and drowned," says Robinson. "Probably got drunk or something."

"Vic [Latham] and [partner] Sid [Snelgrove] put out a bucket for contributions at the Full Moon Saloon," recalls Shaughnessy. "It said,

'Bring the pirate home.'" The ashes of Clark, who died broke under an assumed name, were eventually returned to Shaughnessy. "I kept 'em around for awhile," she says. "That sounds so morbid, but I did. Then I got a little pirate's chest for the ashes, and people carried the treasure chest around to all of his favorite bars and I guess drank Johnny Walker Black [a Clark favorite] in his memory."

"We all had a drink with Phil," says Robinson. "We all had a drink and poured a little of the drink over the pirate's chest." Latham recalls a further wrinkle to the pirate's sendoff: "We all got together for our rather bizarre memorial service," he says, "and to scatter his ashes out on the Gulf of Mexico. Somebody, I don't remember who now, had the brilliant idea that it would be a lasting tribute if we snorted a line of his ashes. So where Jimmy came up with this business of the ashes being in the spittoon, which he describes as an urn, on the bar at the Full Moon is beyond me. It's our tip cup he's talking about. [Buffett refers to this in his *Parrot Head Handbook.*] What ashes that aren't in the Gulf of Mexico are walking around up several people's noses."

"Some friends of ours eventually took him out on a boat," Shaughnessy says of Clark's ashes. "I had given them a little pirate flag that we sold in the Margaritaville store. I gave them a little pirate flag, and they took the ashes out to the Gulf Stream and flew the pirate flag and scattered the ashes. And that was Phil. And I still have the pirate flag."

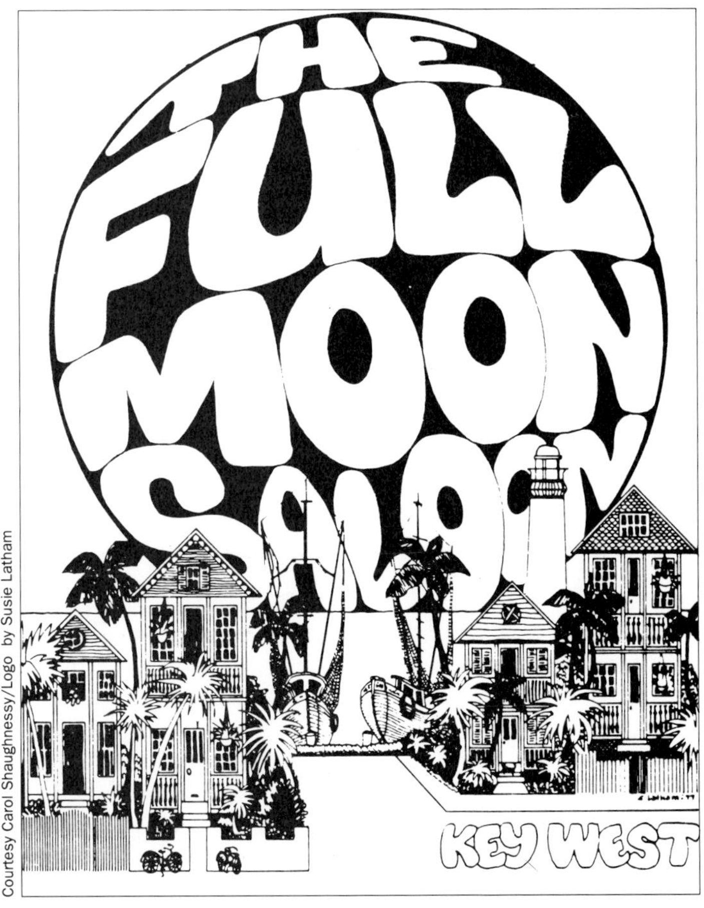

Courtesy Carol Shaughnessy/Logo by Susie Latham

Sundown, Clouds, and the Great Folk Gestalt: Singer-Songwriters of the Seventies

When Buffett was eleven, the nation was singing along with the Kingston Trio's pin-striped purling of an old murder ballad, "Tom Dooley." Buffett loved it, and ordered all the Kingston Trio's albums (he had them sent to a fake address so he wouldn't have to pay). Buffett and his collegiate elders gazed thoughtfully to the Trio for the aged-in-wood story songs that were a thinking kid's alternative in the late 1950s to rock 'n' roll, then deep in Bobby Vees and other dreamy guys marketed to the libidos of thirteen-year-old girls.

The Kingston Trio begat the Limelighters, the Brothers Four, and other bands of clean-cut, guitar-and-banjo strumming guys who stood somewhere between the earthen shanty and the frat house den. They were the Disney version of folk music, and matched the *Davy Crockett* sensibility of the time. They were *not* closet Communists or hopheads, and inspired many a future MBA to take up the banjo.

Meanwhile, in Greenwich Village, scruffier sorts were poised to wreak havoc with wholesome folk fever. Inspired by the topical songs and Okie bohoe antics of Woody Guthrie, whose wanderlust and inattention to personal hygiene caused one admirer to dub him "the original hippie," these unkempt lads lampooned the John Birch Society, championed civil rights, went to art films and read Ginsberg's *Howl.* These "sons of Woody" included Bob Dylan, Phil Ochs, and Tom Paxton. Commercially, they were co-opted by Peter, Paul and Mary, who were the Kingston Trio with goatees and sex appeal.

Phil Ahrens, Gotham Book Mart

The Kingston Trio

Frank Driggs Collection

Strider Records, NYC

Time passed. Surf music, psychedelia, and Soul all came and went. The Beatles disbanded, and the great pop party hit a deep lull. That's when the folksingers returned, this time more inward-looking than the sing-along frat folk or the confrontational protesters of the previous decade. Buffett was again listening: "I wanted to write clever, good songs like those people," he tells us in *The Parrot Head Handbook.*

Gordon Lightfoot was one of those people, the singer-songwriters of the seventies. Lightfoot was older than most, a Canadian who worked for a while writing commercial jingles in Los Angeles. In the mid-sixties, his songs came to the attention of Canadian folk stars Ian and Sylvia, whose recordings of Lightfoot's "For Loving Me" and "Early Morning Rain" inspired Peter, Paul and Mary to cover them. His songs made it to Nashville, too, where Marty Robbins turned Lightfoot's "Ribbon of Darkness" into a number-one country hit in 1965. Lightfoot's own recordings began to yield hits in the early seventies: "If You Could Read My Mind" is one which evidently influenced Buffett's ballad writing. Lightfoot survived a three-year relationship with Cathy Smith, the woman who gave John Belushi his fatal dose and provided probable inspiration for Lightfoot's 1974 hit, "Sundown," in which a "hard-lovin' woman" has got him feelin' mean.

Another Canadian Buffett admired was Roberta Joan Anderson, who dropped the name (and a husband) after moving south in the sixties to become Joni Mitchell. Like Lightfoot, her star rose with other artists' recordings of her work: Judy Collins changed the title of "Clouds" to "Both Sides Now," a major hit in 1968 which threw a spotlight on Mitchell's writing talent. "As a songwriter," gushed a Detroit reviewer, "she plays Yang to Dylan's Yin...." (Huh?) It didn't hurt that she was a lithesome, angelic blonde with a voice to match, either. Mitchell's penchant for romantic entanglements with equally pretty-guy singer-songwriters (Jackson Browne) lent gossipy spice to concept albums like 1971's Blue. Later, she would dabble in jazz, and was working with composer-bassist Charles Mingus on what became the *Mingus* album at the time of his death in 1979.

Frank Driggs Collection

Gordon Lightfoot

Strider Records, NYC

Photo: Norman Seef

Joni Mitchell

Van Morrison sang spirited grunge ("Gloria") with Them before going solo and becoming one of the singer-songwriters who inspired Buffett. The beefy Belfast native had a hit in 1967 with "Brown-Eyed Girl," which Buffett fondly recalls from his New Orleans days (and which he later covered). Other hits, "Tupelo Honey" among them, followed. Morrison's distinctive Celtic Soul sound, as the PR flack on one of his early albums put it, "expresses the real *now!*"

James Taylor, according to Buffett's old pal, Chris Robinson, was "Jimmy's idol," so it must have been especially satisfying when Taylor joined Buffett for the *Volcano* sessions. More than anyone else, Taylor typified the sensitive singer-songwriter in the early 1970s. He was a rich kid with scars: A heroin habit which he kicked, followed by depression and institutionalization. "Fire and Rain," a major hit in 1970, was supposedly inspired by the suicide of a young woman Taylor had grown attached to at a Massachusetts mental hospital.

A cheerier sort of misfit was Willis Alan Ramsey, whose atypically brooding "Ballad of Spider John" Buffett covered on *Living and Dying in 3/4 Time.* Ramsey made one great album and then walked away from recording, thereby assuming legendary status. It took nearly twenty years to break his silence. Asked when he would make his next record, the laconic Texan would reply, "What was wrong with the first one?"

Strider records, NYC

Frank Driggs Collection

James Taylor

CHAPTER FIVE

TRYING TO REASON WITH HURRICANE SEASON

Key West was a town where you had to pick and choose.
It was always a favorite of pirates.
—Thomas McGuane, *Ninety-Two in the Shade*

You are a fine player, and I'm not much of a player.
But I'm a poet and a businessman, and one day I'll be rich
and famous. And you'll always be a bellboy.
—Jimmy Buffett explains the hierarchy of the universe
to a guitar-playing bellboy, circa 1973

The 1970s were high times in Key West. Rent was cheap; living was easy. "He lived right over the top of me for seven and a half years," recalls Chris Robinson, who was downstairs from Buffett at 704 Waddell Street in Key West between 1972 and 1979. "The house had two apartments, but we had the same nice, wonderful backyard we used to boogie in. It's right on the water there, right on the Atlantic. We had parties in the backyard: We'd have *killer* parties! You'd walk in the front door, and somebody would hand you a joint. Some electric stuff [i.e., acid] and 151 rum-filled watermelons. At a good party, you were blitzed by the time you hit the back door."

This was the era of full-tilt boogie: "My boogie span reaches about three days," Buffett informed *Stereo Review* in 1974. He boogied frequently in the company of novelist Tom McGuane. "He was really straight and just startin' to come out and boogie," Buffett told *Rolling Stone,* "and I was just comin' off my divorce so it was just sort of this intenseness together. So we just tore at it." McGuane's fiercesome tearing at booze and dope in the seventies was typified in a recent Hunter

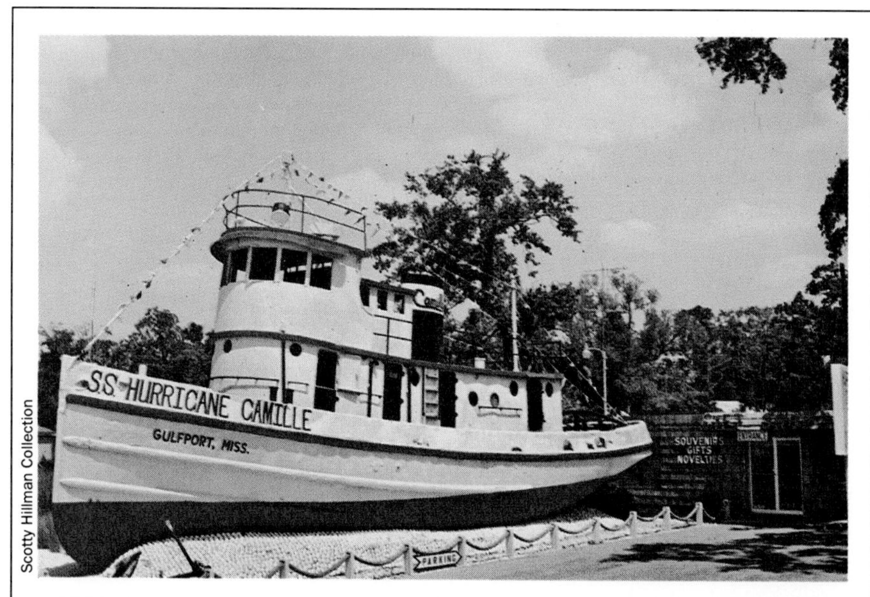

Scotty Hillman Collection

There was no reasoning with Camille, whose fury devastated the Gulf Coast in 1969. Buffett's early songs suggested the "live for the moment" fatalism of hurricane-coast culture.

Photo: Chris Robinson

Jane Slagsvol ran away from South Carolina privilege and headlong into Key West's "boogie." She knocked Buffett for a loop, and he dedicated albums to "Miss Jane." In "My Lovely Lady," on the shellfish-fixated *A White Sport Coat and a Pink Crustacean* album, he praised her appetite for crabmeat.

Thompson biography which depicts McGuane and Dr. Gonzo squaring off in a contest of who could snort the most dope and live.

"Jimmy had an apartment right next to a restaurant I built in 1972, Louie's Backyard," recalls Vic Latham. "The outside bar at Louie's was his neighborhood bar. In fact, there was even a gate in the fence where he just came and went at will." When he made his first ABC albums, Buffett told Nashville session guitarist Reggie Young that "... he was living over a bar in Key West, and he would go down and play for his dinner." Louie's current owner, Phil Tenney, says, "It could well be true. When I took over this restaurant, there were a lot of old books, and we found all his bills that were signed but never paid for. It was a hell of a stack!"

Latham fondly recalls the laid-back Louie's days of the early seventies. "That was when he and I hung out together so much," he says. "We used to sit and talk for hour after hour about writing and our reaction to people and books and music and so forth. It would start in the early afternoon, or maybe sometimes in the morning with a Bloody Mary and next thing you'd know, it would be six o'clock the next morning and we were still drinking and discussing the eternal verities." Along with hangovers, inspiration sometimes came of all this. "He and I had been sitting in the backyard at my house," recalls Latham, "and we had been at it all day until about six o'clock in the morning. It was champagne and aqua vitae and scotch and nose candy and everything else. I brought him home and left him lying face down in his hammock. He was just a mess! Later, I was laughing at him about how drunk he was, and he said, 'Well, one good thing came out of it,' and that morning he woke up and wrote 'Trying to Reason With Hurricane Season.'"

Photo: Chris Robinson

Playback time. Christmas in Key West, 1976. Buffett's "big ears" (and "big eyes" for Jane) hastened the singer-songwriter's success.

Hurricanes and hangovers were acts of nature common in Key West's landscape, and Buffett was writing songs which captured the town's "sleaze with honor," as Robinson characterizes it, as well as some of its notable characters. *Stereo Review's* Peter Reilly described Buffett's "Woman Going Crazy on Caroline Street" as being "about one of those Blanche DuBois types one can find in almost any bar, the ghostlike aura of once-splendid good looks still hovering about her, drinking too much and talking too much and flirting with a desperate, lonely urgency."

The song's inspiration is rumored both to have "had a fling" with Buffett and, more recently, to have been active in Ross Perot's 1992 presidential campaign.

Aside from his picturesque hangovers and the local characters with whom he shared them, Buffett also wrote about their haunts. None was more infamous than the one he called "the snakepit," the Old Anchor Inn. "It was dark, cavelike," recalls John Hellen, who tended bar there. "Right on the main street. It was where the so-called hip people hung out in those days." The hip people included Buffett and McGuane, who started the Club Mandible McGuane cryptically alluded to in his notes to Buffett's *A White Sport Coat and a Pink Crustacean*. "Club Mandible meant everybody talked about each other," says Hellen. "The jawbone is what it referred to." Dink Bruce, another veteran of the Key West Boogie, remembers: "In the midst of a drunken, drugged stupor, McGuane came up with this concept of the Club Mandible. The only requirement to be a member of the Club was that you buy a purple shirt without a collar and put some stupid name on it that you dreamed up. That made you a member of the Club Mandible, and you just sat in the bar with these purple shirts on at the Old Anchor Inn."

Greetings
FROM

Scotty Hillman Collection

UAINT

WEST

TY

FLORIDA

"I don't know how I can explain the Club Mandible," says Robinson, "but there were about twenty or thirty members and they had shirts and they had their different club names. They had Lieutenant Barko, and there was General Chaos, and Private Parts. We'd always go out en masse and boogie. It was like a big party when we'd go out on weekends. Then we'd take a few days to recover, go down to Fausto's, get some chocolate milk. That's one of the classic grocery stores on Fleming Street down here. We've all done it. We've all gone out and boogied so hard that 'If I don't die by Thursday, I'll be roaring Friday night,'" a line from Buffett's "My Head Hurts, My Feet Stink, and I Don't Love Jesus."

"'Margaritaville' basically was about a place where we all used to drink called the Old Anchor Inn," says Latham. "It was just as bizarre as it could be. It was the kind of place that, one bartender would open the beer cooler to get a beer out and find the other bartender curled up asleep on top of the beer, because it wasn't air-conditioned in there and the beer coolers were cool. It was just total insanity. They finally closed it down, I think, in '73 because it was so insane."

"I don't care how high you were when you went in the Anchor Inn," recalls Robinson, "somebody else was worse off in there! The bouncer was about a three-hundred-pound woman named Tiny who sat out in front on this little stool by the picket fence. You walked in the Anchor Inn, and some people were passed out on the bar. They had a little jukebox over in the corner." (Along with Jimi Hendrix, it also spun that perennial drunk's favorite of the thirties, Bunny Berigan's "I Can't Get Started.") "Most of the time you didn't even go in the bathroom because there was so much urine on the floor. You went out back in the wrecked, junked cars in the vacant lot and took a pee out there. That was like 1972. There's a friend of ours who had a little bottle of liquid amyl nitrate, and he'd go around the dance floor and hit up everybody. Everybody would just be going crazy!"

Such was the scene that inspired Buffett's early Key West songs, believed by many to be his best. "It was a different era then," says Robinson. "That was the era of free love. No herpes. No AIDS. People were having affairs with everybody's girlfriend, and nobody kinda cared." The living was easy, and Buffett had dibs on the role of town troubadour. A 1974 *Miami Herald* piece by Candice Russell portrays Buffett "... holding court at the Chart House Bar, a sandy-haired prodigal son to a legion of admirers. He is in his metier, sharing a laugh with the guys at the bar, girls coming up to rub his back, and the phone ringing for him. On an impromptu basis, this is where he plays and sings for his friends."

Years later, Buffett would write of "The tourist girls who came to ride the Conch Train and fall in love for the weekend" in *Where Is Joe Merchant?* One of those girls would stay more than a weekend and consequently change Buffett's life. Jane

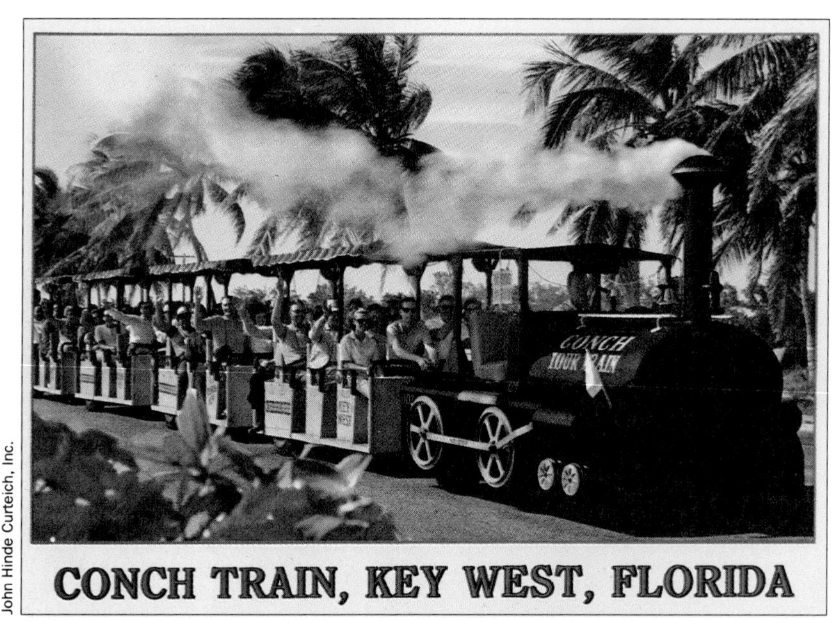

CONCH TRAIN, KEY WEST, FLORIDA

John Hinde Curteich, Inc.

Slagsvol came from "a pretty wealthy, influential family in Columbia, South Carolina," says Latham, who claims he introduced her to Buffett. Latham characterizes Buffett's reaction to Jane as "lust at first sight. She's a beautiful woman. Maybe the name that she's known by describes her as well as anything. We all call her Lady Jane. She and two or three other South Carolina runaways came down here, so she had a wild streak in her."

One observer recalls that Jane "sort of squared him away about paying his bills" and generally was a good influence on Buffett. Robinson fondly recalls going mutton snapper fishing with his wife, Sonia, Jane, and Buffett in his first Key West boat, "a little thirteen-foot Boston whaler." The man who would vehemently decry the evils of jet skis ("... dangerous torpedoes in the hands of the incompetent people who rented them") in *Where Is Joe Merchant?* was, in his hell-raising twenties, often seen blasting over the waves in powerboats. The romantic—and *expensive*—sailing ships came later. "In the days when he was doing so much creative work," recalls Latham of the boating Buffett, "it was predominantly power craft."

On land, Buffett might tool around on the red bike he mentioned in his *Parrot Head Handbook,* or, for longer junkets, cruise in the cab of the '53 Chevy pickup he called God's Own Truck. "I love my truck," Buffett told the *Miami Herald's* Candice Russell in 1974. "I bought it for one hundred dollars. It had the Monroe County Glass and Mirror Company stenciled on the driver's door." Russell described Buffett's vehicle as green and rusted out. God's Own Truck became an eccentric calling card for Buffett, but the pickup was destined for scrap long before he bought it. "He had thought at one time to have it mashed into a cube and made into a coffee table," recalls Dink Bruce. "The only problem was figuring out how to get it up to the second story in this tiny little staircase." God's Own Coffeetable was a stoned fantasy which never came to life.

Into Buffett's idyllic life of sex, drugs, and rusted pickups came an awful spoiler: success. He had never really given up wanting it, despite his "kicked back" Key Westerly attitude. Vic Latham told Miami's *New Times* reporter Tom Finkel the following illustrative tale, heard from the lips of "the guy who ... was working as the night clerk at the La Concha Hotel on Duvall Street, when it was old, seedy, beat-up, back before it was the Holiday

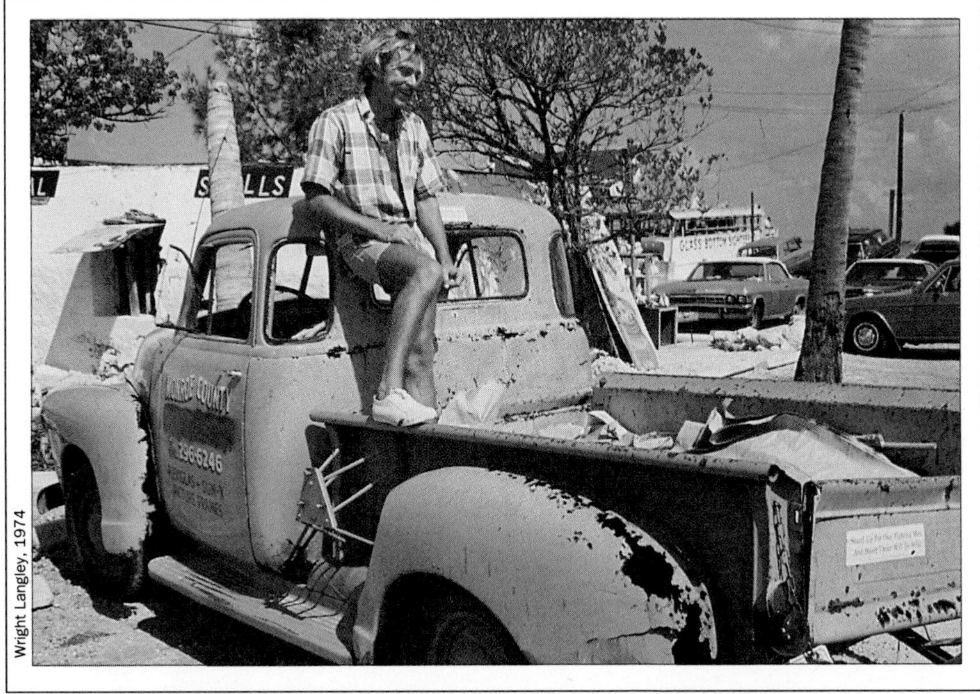

Wright Langley, 1974

"God's Own Truck" was the name Buffett gave the rusted heap he bought for $100 from the Monroe County Glass & Mirror Co. The '53 Chevy pickup was the perfect antistatus vehicle for him in his "professional misfit" days. The truck's name punned on the Lord Buckley monologue Buffett loved, "God's Own Drunk." (Following spread) Jimmy closeup.

Wright Langley, 1974

UNTY

Author's Collection

Marty Robbins's 1957 recording of "A White Sport Coat (and a Pink Carnation)," produced by Buffett's boyhood idol, Mitch Miller, made it to number 2 on the pop charts and number 1 on the country charts. Robbins was thirty-two when he wrote and recorded his ode to teen prom angst, still an "oldies" radio favorite.

Inn. The place was semi-closed down, and this other kid who worked there as a bellboy spent a lot of time outside, sitting on the front steps playing guitar. One time the clerk was outside talking with the kid while he was picking, when Jimmy walked by. This was in the days when Jimmy had put out some records but he hadn't become famous. Jimmy listens to the kid awhile, and the kid is a pretty good picker. So he says, 'Well, you play pretty good. You mind if I use your guitar for a few minutes?' The kid hands it to him, and Buffett starts playing. He plays probably half a song, just picking around, when the kid, all smartass and uppity, says, 'Gimme that guitar back. You can't play a *lick!'* So Jimmy, without being at all upset, hands the guitar back and says, 'You know, boy, you're absolutely right. You are a fine player, and I'm not much of a player. But I'm a poet and a businessman, and one day I'll be rich and famous. And you'll always be a bellboy.'"

The bell rang for Buffett in 1973, and the call came from Nashville. "When I got my deal with ABC," Buffett told the *New York Times's* John Rockwell in 1978, "it was my last chance—I'd done the rounds." Two years after his break, Buffett told Judith Sims of *Rolling Stone:* "There was a lot of spontaneity on that first [ABC] album; it'd been three years since I'd been in the studio, and like it or not, you write your best songs in hard times."

Session guitarist Reggie Young, who played on Buffett's first three ABC albums, remembers ABC Nashville producer Don Gant as "a songwriter person. He had great ideas. I think he was sort of a sounding board [for Buffett]." Young had just moved from Memphis to Nashville, and notes that many of the players on what became A *White Sport Coat and a Pink Crustacean* had similar backgrounds. It wasn't a typical country session of the time, Young recalls, and was "kicked back" in a Key Westerly way. "We weren't in any hurry to do anything," he says. "Mostly Buffett would just sing songs, we'd run it down a few times and cut it."

The result appeared in June 1973 on the ABC/Dunhill label as A *White Sport Coat and a Pink Crustacean.* With its title pun on a 1957 Marty Robbins hit, "A White Sport Coat (and a Pink Carnation)," it was a tough album not to notice. On the cover, Buffett appeared with a sheepish stoned grin slumped over crates of shrimp. On the back sleeve, he thanked "Bob Hall and the Thompson O'Neal Shrimp Co. for supplying the pink crustaceans which made a great cover and a fine dinner." McGuane penned a

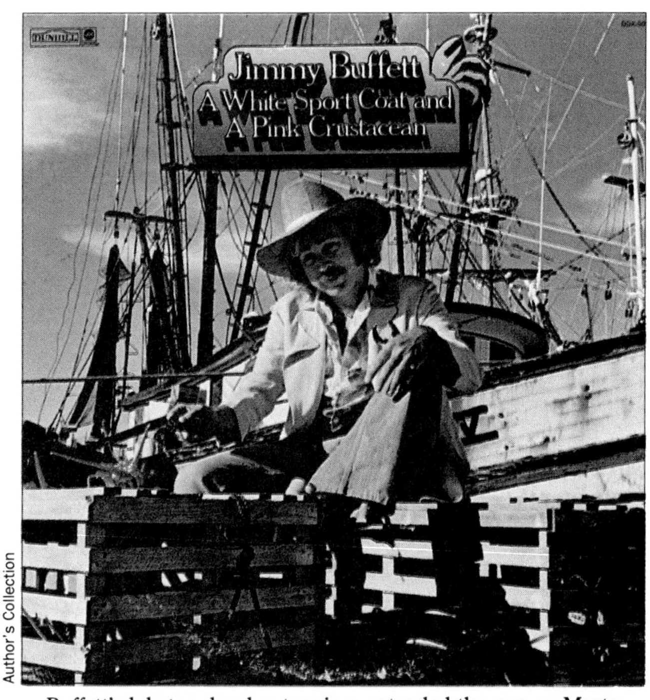

Author's Collection

Buffett's lobster-claw boutonniere extended the pun on Marty Robbins's "coat/carnation" in the title of Buffett's cheeky "they-can't-miss-this-one" ABC/Dunhill debut album in 1973.

Author's Collection

One of the most imitated voices in country music, Lefty Frizzell's soft Texas drawl, took Buffett and Jerry Jeff Walker's "Railroad Lady" saga to country jukeboxes in 1974.

"meet-the-new-artist" squib which described his friend as "... this throwback altarboy of Mobile, Alabama," whose album offers "spacey up-country tunes strewn with forgotten crabtraps...." Recalling McGuane's notes to *Rolling Stone's* Chet Flippo in 1977, Buffett said, "I still have no idea what he meant by 'sucking chest-wound singer.' But, 'the first to sleep on the yellow line' was fact, the fact that we did get so loaded one night that we were crawlin' down the street."

Sport Coat opened with the song ABC released as a single in May in advance of the album, "The Great Filling Station Holdup." Buffett spread his Gulf Coast drawl thick and played the part of a dim good ol' boy who learned the hard way that crime won't pay. "There was a Rebel Oil station near where I grew up," Buffett told Candice Russell. "Every week or so, I'd see a filler item in the paper about how the station was robbed of $20 and three cases of soft drinks." "The Great Filling Station Holdup" (a pun on the creaky 1903 silent Western, *The Great Train Robbery*) peaked at number 58 on Billboard's country charts, not bad for a song which plainly parodied country music.

Sport Coat's second offering was closer to country's heart, which may be because "Railroad Lady" was co-written with Jerry Jeff Walker. Like his "Mr. Bojangles," "Railroad Lady" told a hard-luck story with a balance of humor and sentimentality. "It matches Steve Goodman's 'City of New Orleans' as one of the finest train songs of recent years," enthused Alan Cackett in *Country Music People*. "There are echoes of the legendary Jimmie Rodgers running through the song...."

A man who idolized Rodgers and covered many of his songs, Lefty Frizzell, then had the same producer at ABC as Buffett, Don Gant. "Railroad Lady" came to Frizzell via Gant, and it would become one of a half dozen songs from his two ABC albums which made a showing on the country charts during a Frizzell "comeback" which ended with his death at age forty-seven in 1975. Twenty-some years earlier, the onetime boxer with a distinctive Texas drawl had given Hank Williams a hard run for the country money with such honky-tonk ballads as "I Love You a Thousand Ways" and "Always Late (With Your Kisses)." Drink and age had taken their toll, though such admirers as Merle Haggard still praised Frizzell as an important influence, one which grew more evident in country music in the 1980s when such "new traditionalists" as John

Author's Collection

Hank Williams was Lefty's chief rival in early 1950s Nashville, and "the hillbilly Shakespeare" exerted a magnetic pull on a later decade's folksinger-songwriters.

Anderson and Randy Travis sounded uncannily like Frizzell.

Curiously, both Frizzell's recording of "Railroad Lady" and Buffett's first real hit, "Come Monday," debuted on *Billboard's* country charts on the same day, June 15, 1974. Both enjoyed similar modest success. Buffett's "Come Monday" peaked at number 58, the same position "The Great Filling Station Holdup" attained the year before. Frizzell did slightly better with his recording of "Railroad Lady," getting up to number 52 before the song disappeared from the charts in late August.

Despite the presence of a steel guitar, the third song on *A White Sport Coat* was less "country" than its predecessors and more reflective of Buffett's folk circuit background. "'He Went to Paris' tells with economy and controlled sentiment of an old man's backward glance at the pains and forgotten questions of a lifetime," wrote Candice Russell in the *Miami Herald.* The old man who inspired the song was a one-armed pianist and janitor who befriended Buffett during his early stints as warm-up act at Chicago's The Quiet Knight.

"Jimmy was in here one night," Vic Latham told Tom Finkel of New Times, "sitting on the [Full Moon Saloon] bar and picking, singing one of my favorite songs of his, 'He Went to Paris.' There's a particular line that I like, and when he sang it, he leaned back to get my attention. Well, he leaned too far and fell in the beer box. Two weeks later we read about it in *Rolling Stone.* We still don't know how it got in there."

Another side of Buffett emerged via the playful "Grapefruit—Juicy Fruit," which winked and nudged at the conventions of the cocktail pop song as it offered lapsed Catholic advice: "Commit a little mortal sin / It's good for the soul." The song's "mortal sin" was committed at the Islander Drive-In Theater, Buffett recalled in his *Parrot Head Handbook,* where "the movie was *Payday,* starring Rip Torn." Torn's over-the-top portrayal of a stoned country star was just the thing, along with willing female company and cold beer, to inspire Buffett.

Buffett trivia experts will note the earliest recorded reference (a spoken aside, "Ah, take it, Reefers") in "Grapefruit—Juicy Fruit" to Buffett's then-mythical (except in the studio) band, the Coral Reefers. Like much else on *Sport Coat,* the band's name was a pun sure to evoke knowing smiles. An old-time Hawaiian combo or even a surf band might once have been named the Coral Reefers, but Buffett knew that "reefer," in 1973, would be taken to mean a marijuana cigarette. By then, of course, "reefer" was camp slang, since "joint" was the term of the day. Reefer evoked hidden vices of the Prohibition era and the marijuana melodrama of the kitsch film favorite of American campuses, *Reefer Madness.*

Buffett's first musical trip to the tropics, "Cuban Crime of Passion," sprang next from *Sport Coat's* grooves. Inspired by a love triangle turned homicidal and co-written with his photographer pal Tom Corcoran, it was, Buffett told *High Times* reporter Bob Anderson, a rare example of pure fiction in his songs. "They're about 90 percent based on fact," he said, "things that I've done or seen other people do. The only one that is really more fiction than fact would be 'Cuban Crime of Passion.'"

Dr. Demento

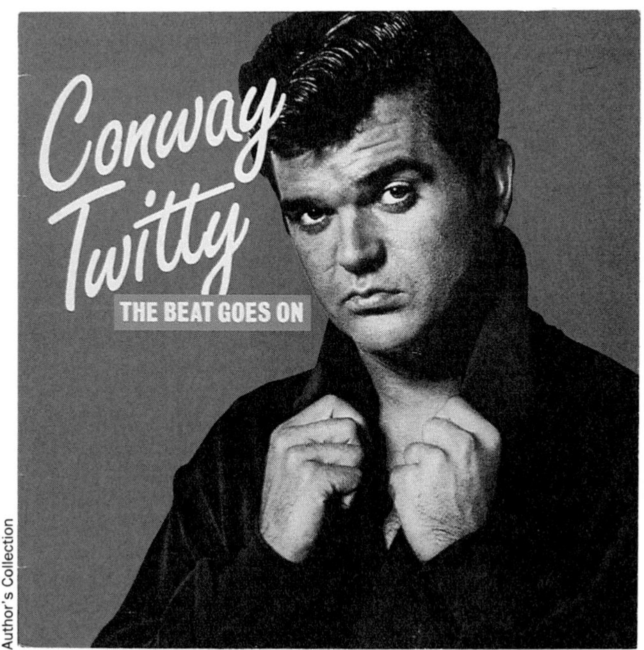

Author's Collection

Country superstar Conway Twitty (né Harold Llyod Jenkins) took his snazzy stage name from Conway, Arkansas, and Twitty, Texas, and along the way has had sixty three Top 10 hits on the *Billboard* country charts. In 1958 Twitty scored his biggest hit with the Elvis Presley-inspired weeper, "It's Only Make Believe," which soared to number 1 on the pop charts.

The first side of Buffett's major label debut album closed with a song which shall live in infamy, "Why Don't We Get Drunk (and Screw)." "We all loved that song," recalls Chris Robinson, "because we used to go down and do that exact thing." Barry Hansen has played novelty records on his syndicated *Dr. Demento Show* since 1970, and remembers when he used to field requests for Buffett's song in Los Angeles radio station KMET in the days of "underground" FM radio. "It's a great song for people who were getting drunk and screwing," says Hansen, "or wished they were. I still have a 45 of that that gets a turn on the jukebox now and then."

Buffett told *Los Angeles Times* pop critic Robert Hilburn that the song was written as a country parody. "There was a controversial song by Conway Twitty at the time called 'Let's Go All the Way,'" said Buffett. "So I thought, okay, I'll really take a song all the way." Buffett's memory of the inspiration for "Drunk and Screw" is, perhaps for good reason, a mite blurry. "Let's Go All the Way" was the title of a 1964 country hit by Norma Jean, the perky blonde Porter Wagoner replaced on his TV show with Dolly Parton in 1967. Conway Twitty *did* have a controversial song in 1973, but its title was "You've Never Been This Far Before," in which he sang, "My trembling fingers touch forbidden places ..." It was the sweatiest, sexiest thing in country music history thus far, and was number one on *Billboard's* country charts for three weeks that summer. But by the time Twitty's trembling fingers were wreaking moral havoc, Buffett's blunter approach to the matter was already out. "Why Don't We Get Drunk (and Screw)" was the B-side of his first ABC single, "The Great Filling Station Holdup."

More inspiring than the trembling Twitty was "this businessman drunk trying to pick up these hookers," Buffett told Hilburn, recalling a scenario witnessed at an Atlanta hotel. "I just wrote the whole thing down. I never even though it'd actually end up on a record, but everybody loved it because it really does touch on human nature, I guess. It's something everyone can laugh at."

Laugh we did, and do still in concert as

Frank Driggs Collection

"Only jazz musicians smoke marijuana" was Buffett's take on 1930s dope culture in "Pencil Thin Mustache." The "grass" of the 1970s had formerly been tea, boo, gage, pot, reefer, and Mary Jane. United States Commissioner of Narcotics H. J. Anslinger reported in 1946 (the year of Buffett's birth): "Marihuana arrested and seizures increased . . . seizures aggregated 12,445 ounces against 12,325 ounces in 1945." A slow week in 1970s Key West.

Rednecks and Reefers, Rockers and Weepers: The Country-Rock Thang

Hearing Buffett talk about country can be a bit like hearing someone admit to being related (but *distantly,* they insist) to a dimwit closeted in a back room, the family shame. "I heard plenty of country music," Buffett confessed to England's *Country Music People* in 1976, "but didn't take too much notice of it. Much too busy enjoying myself."

Country, with its hungover guilt about back street affairs and losers imprisoned by bad marriages and grim jobs wasn't exactly the sound track of the Pleasure Principle. Yet it was impossible for Buffett to ignore (try as he might), for it was America's foremost pop music storytelling genre. And if you read Faulkner, Erskine Caldwell, and other chroniclers of Southern life, as did Buffett, how could you not notice the more Snopesian casting of Faulkner's themes in country song?

It was natural you would, especially if you played acoustic guitar and sang Bob Dylan's songs and aspired to be a famous folknik one day. Dylan, even at his coolest and most cryptic (circa 1965 and *Highway 61 Revisited*), professed an admiration for Hank Williams ("Like a Rolling Stone" took its title/tag line from a song Williams recorded, "Lost Highway"). And Dylan's original idol had been Woody Guthrie, the populist Okie who tacked his socialist realism lyrics onto tunes cribbed from the Carter Family, a group that was among the earliest and most influential in country music history. So even as country music made the South's better-educated sons and daughters queasy, they were never far from it, even in the psychodramatic songs of Greenwich Village bohoes.

Laments for lust-lorn truckers (Loretta Lynn's

Authro' Collection

Harris Lewine Collection

The Carter Family

Frank Driggs Collection

"What Kind of a Girl Do You Think I Am?") and Dylan's Guthrie-meets-Ginsberg hipsterism ("Subterranean Homesick Blues") played to audiences with wildly divergent attitudes, but they were bound, by some strange alchemy, for a harmonic convergence (with *twang*). The resultant sound came to be labeled country-rock, and would profoundly affect both country and pop music in the 1970s.

Author's Collection

The original standard-bearer for all this was a rich kid from the South named Gram Parsons, whose L.A.-based International Submarine Band surfaced briefly in 1966 and is widely cited as the first country-rock band. Parsons' Submarine soon sank, but by late 1967 he had joined the popular folk-rock band, the Byrds, best-known for their jangly cover of Dylan's "Mr. Tambourine Man" and the early psychedelia of "Eight Miles High." Parsons steered the Byrds toward twangier waters, and in 1968 the band released *Sweetheart of the Rodeo,* which brimmed with a down-home hippie back-to-earthiness and covered country chestnuts with gen-u-ine affection. The Byrds even appeared on Grand Ole Opry in 1968, which extended polite but cool applause to the long-haired California kids.

By 1969, Parsons and fellow country enthusiast Chris Hillman had splintered from the Byrds to form the Flying Burrito Brothers, a band whose legend far exceeds its modest success during its lifetime. Bedecked in sequined Nudie suits asparkle with rhinestone marijuana leaves and peyote buttons, the Burrito Brothers were both an outrageous parody of and a loving tribute to country traditionalism. At their ragged best, the Burritos sounded akin to a hillbilly brother duo zonked on acid, staggering and howling down Sunset Strip on a warm summer's night. Too good to last and too stoned to care, the Burritos scattered to various fates: Parsons to a desert drug overdose in 1973, and Hillman eventually to middle-aged sobriety and respectability fronting the Desert Rose Band, which sounds like a tamer, more polished version of the Burritos.

Strider Records, NYC

By the time Hillman disbanded the Burritos

Frank Driggs Collection

The Eagles

Strider Records, NYC

in 1971 (Parsons was already gone), that band, along with the twangier performances of the Byrds, had created a ripple, if not a wave, with the likes of Poco (on the mellower side) and Commander Cody's Last Planet Airmen (on the cheekier side) trailing in their wake. The Nitty Gritty Dirt Band, another group of California longhairs with country leanings, penetrated Nashville's pine curtain in 1971 and recorded *Will the Circle Be Unbroken,* an influential celebration of country roots with Roy Acuff, Mother Maybelle Carter, and a host of similarly sainted hillbillies.

The awkward courtship dance of hippies and hillbillies was picking up steam, turning into a well-lathered two-step as some of the Nashvillians reckoned these kids *meant* well, and the longhairs flashed that these gap-toothed moonshine cookers were realer elderfolk than Mom and Dad in the suburbs, what with their martinis, Valiums, and uptightness. It was "Take Me Home, Country Roads" (a John Denver hit in 1971) as the children of urban stockbrokers donned overalls and headed for the hills to explore herbs and horticulture and invent themselves some roots. The soundtrack to all this well-meant playacting was country-rock, not country as wailed through clenched teeth by George Jones or rock as throttled by Grand Funk Railroad but a gently kicking groove that was indebted as much to the coffeehouse folky background of its best performers, such as Emmylou Harris, as it was to either the honky-tonk or the rock arena. The Eagles' "Take It Easy" was, in 1972, a mellow anthem for this post-Woodstock counterculture, laid back and hardly confrontational. Five years later, Jimmy Buffett was being managed by the Eagles' business wizard, Irving Azoff, and opening shows for that band, one of the biggest of its day. It fit: Buffett may have been more gently irreverent, but he, too, was mellowed out, kicked back, feelin' peaceful 'n' easy.

Buffett alters lyrics to fit changed times: "I just bought a waterbed, it's filled up for me and you" has become "I guess I'll get a designated driver and buy a condom or two." Part of what made "Drunk and Screw" funny was that it sounded like a gen-u-ine Nashville twanger, even though no country star in his right mind would have cut such a thing. Buffett recorded it with some of Music City's ace session men: the tipsy fiddle that bobs and weaves through the record was bowed by Vassar Clements, once one of Bill Monroe's Blue Grass Boys and famed for both his bluegrass and Western Swing stylings. "We cut it honky and loose and it's on every jukebox wherever we go," Buffett bragged in 1974. In those days, a jukebox hit still meant something.

Unless you were part of the Nashville scene twenty-some years ago, the song's references to the object of its lust as a possible "snuff queen" may need explaining. John Grissim's *Country Music: White Man's Blues* (Coronet Communications, New York, 1970) has a chapter, *Snuff Queens and Cheap Thrills,* which defines the country groupie: "... in just about every town where an act may perform there's bound to be several gals who not only love singin' cowboys and anybody who has anything to do with them, but who also desire the anonymity of casual sexual encounters.... Country music people call them snuff queens.... The average snuff queen tends to be older (sometimes much older) than her counterpart of the rock world. She wears shorter hair, less exotic dress, and seldom employs the direct 'I'm-clean-I'm-over-eighteen-let's-fuck' approach...." An unidentified "popular artist" told Grissim: "The girls aren't pushy or forward.... They let you know they're available but they don't make any big show of it." Another "young performer well-known for his sex appeal" bragged: "Some of these gals will be so hot and bothered they'll be speechless. All you gotta do is touch 'em and they go BANG!"

Buffett's "Why Don't We Get Drunk (and Screw)" ushered in a spate of lewd parodies of country songs in the seventies. From Austin, Texas, came Rusty Wier with "I Heard You Been Layin' My Old Lady" and a frank rebuff of feminism in Kinky Friedman's "Get Your Biscuits in the Oven and Your Buns in the Bed." Someone known as Chinga Chavin even cut a whole album called *Country Porn* ("Asshole From El Paso" was a send-up of the endlessly spoofable "Okie From Muskogee.") Most of this stuff is forgotten today, though Buffett's summer tours have turned "Drunk and Screw" into a naughty sing-along favorite.

Side two of *Sport Coat* opened on a slightly less outrageous note with "Peanut Butter Conspiracy," the album's second hymn to petty larceny. This time the pleasures of shoplifting are recalled from a time when Buffett was "Workin' in a dive for twenty-six dollars, spendin' it all on grass." This was probably in the French Quarter in the late 1960s. Buffett's penchant for wordplay is at large in the title of the song about hungry hippies heisting canned goods. The Peanut Butter Conspiracy was a sixties psychedelic band which was likewise fond of puns, evidenced by such album titles as *The Conspiracy Is Spreading.*

"They Don't Dance Like Carmen No More" is a song Buffett attributes to his "Cuban period," "when I first got to Key West and came in contact

Dr. Demento

with the Latin passion for fun." It's a nostalgic tribute to Carmen Miranda (1909-1955), the "Brazilian Bombshell" whose comic tropical storm blew through a host of 1940s Hollywood musicals, among them *That Night in Rio* and *Copacabana,* in which she costarred with Groucho Marx. The irrepressible singer/dancer, famed for her towering fruit-filled headdresses, died of a sudden heart attack following a demanding number on a Jimmy Durante TV show. ("Good night, Mrs. Calabash, wherever you are.")

"I Have Found Me a Home" was Buffett's first recorded love letter to Key West, which also played a role in "My Lovely Lady," a song as much about the pleasures of "sailing in those warm December breezes" as about "Miss Jane," here credited with consuming her weight in crabmeat!

"Someone once asked me," Buffett told audiences in the late seventies, "'How can you write those real sensitive songs and then write those real trashy songs?' 'Well,' I told him, 'sometimes I feel real sensitive and sometimes I feel real trashy!'" Buffett's first important album swung wildly between his "real trashy and real sensitive" sides, but ended on a sensitive note. "Death of an Unpopular Poet" was "melodically the most sophisticated cut on his first album," wrote Candice Russell, "besides being lyrically subtle, ironic and sad." Buffett told Bob Anderson that his song was inspired by the 1972 death of poet Kenneth Patchen. "I was watching Walter Cronkite one night," Buffett recalled in his *High Times* interview, "and he had a little blurb on there that Kenneth Patchen had died. That surprised me, because hardly anybody ever heard of Patchen except in small circles. He was one of my favorite poets. So I was thinking about him, and then I thought about Richard Farina.... They starved their asses off and didn't get to stick around to reap their rewards."

Harris Lewine Collection

Groucho Marx played Carmen Miranda's agent in *Copacabana* (1947). "The Brazilian Bombshell," whose dancing Buffett admired, complained of Hollywood directors in *Modern Screen:* "Dey holler at me and tell me to seeng in Souse American, like I talk! Dey must be notts!"

Neither Patchen nor Farina bore much resemblance to the "Unpopular Poet" Buffett described in his song, but they're laudable inspirations. Patchen fought crippling back pain much of his life to produce several volumes of verse which led him to be variously labeled a proletarian poet, a surrealist, and a beat. Among his admirers were both Henry Miller and Allen Ginsberg. Patchen was one of the poets whose "word jazz" was performed and recorded with jazz ensembles in the 1950s. In his "Elegy on the Death of Kenneth Patchen," his friend Lawrence Ferlinghetti wrote:

> A poet is born
> A poet dies
> And all that lies between
> is us
> and the world.

Richard Farina was nearer Buffett's generation, a singer/songwriter and novelist whose *Been Down So Long It Looks Like Up to Me* became a campus favorite in the late 1960s. Part Cuban, part Irish, handsome and intense, Farina would claim to have moved among both the Irish Republican Army and Castro's forces in his late adolescence, and to have done bohemian service in Paris at "music, street-singing, scriptwriting, acting, a little smuggling...."

Farina's sister-in-law was Joan Baez, and with his wife, Mimi, he made memorable recordings for the Vanguard label: he played dulcimer, she guitar, and both sang. Peter, Paul and Mary recorded his "Pack Up Your Sorrows," and his literary work was bought by such magazines as *The Atlantic.* The day after the publication of Farina's novel, *Been Down So Long It Looks Like Up to Me,* he was killed in a high-speed motorcycle crash on the Carmel coast after a party celebrating the publication of his book. Farina was twenty-nine. "And everybody wonders did he really lose his mind, / No, he was just a poet who lived before his time."

Unlike his composite poet, Buffett was very much in tune with his time. During the strange Watergate-obsessed summer of '73, Buffett wasn't the only weirdo to mirror country music in a stoned looking glass. Another freshman member of the class of '73 was an Austin professor's son who wore both a Stetson and a Star of David and performed as Kinky Friedman and His Texas Jewboys. His *Sold American* album appeared about the same time as Buffett's *Sport Coat* and included such songs as "Ride 'Em Jewboy" and "We Reserve the Right to Refuse Service to You," in which a long-haired Jewish kid is offered this advice in a redneck bar:

Take your business back to Walgreen's,
Have you tried the local zoo?
You smell just like a Communist,
You come through just like a Jew.

Friedman would precede Buffett into the craft of fiction writing, and now has five successful mystery novels under his belt. The first, 1986's *Greenwich Killing Time,* had a "street-smart country singer named Kinky" as a central character and opened with this morning-after-the-margaritas sentence: "I held the mescal up to the light and watched the worm slide across the bottom of the bottle."

As for Buffett, his books were a distant glimmer at best in 1973, but he really didn't mind then. "ABC decided they liked me and they were gonna give me $25,000 to do a record," Buffett told *Rolling Stone*'s Chet Flippo in 1977. "I said, 'Shit man, I can do it for ten and have fifteen left over to buy a boat.'"

Along with the jukebox notoriety of "Drunk and Screw" and the modest country success of "The Great Filling Station Holdup," *Sport Coat* earned Buffett attention as a quirky new voice among folk-rooted country singer-songwriters. *Stereo Review* called his album "a disarming and delightful surprise." His appearances to support its release got reviewed in the right places: a set at Hollywood's Troubadour prompted *Daily Variety* to praise Buffett's "auspicious L.A. debut with low-key charm and humor and superb original tunes."

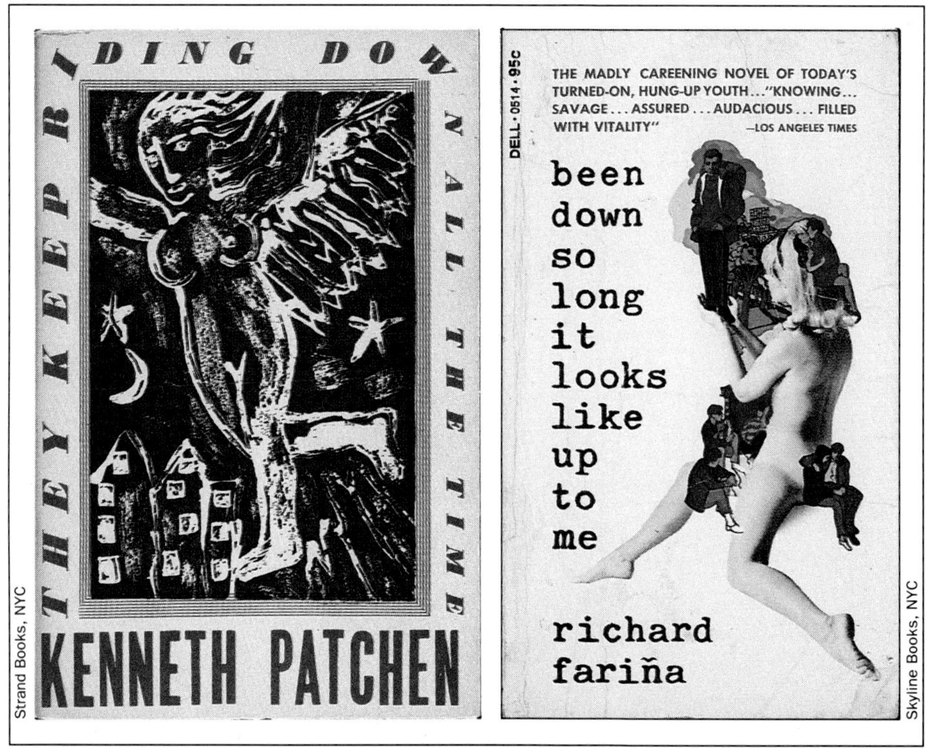

Poet (and sometime prose writer) Kenneth Patchen and novelist (and sometime songwriter) Richard Farina were the composite inspiration for Buffett's "Death of an Unpopular Poet," a fate he vowed not to suffer.

Across the country, Buffett was hailed by the *New York Times* for a gig at Max's Kansas City: "... the imagery of the country singer (and writer) Jimmy Buffett was clear and clean, rooted firmly in Buffett's own existence," raved Ian Dove. "Buffett looks outside and takes notes."

A White Sport Coat and a Pink Crustacean may not have sold a million copies, but it was sure a leg up on *Down to Earth.* It got Buffett's "trashy but sensitive songs" heard by the right ears and opened doors to key venues. "Since then," Buffett told Chet Flippo four years later, "it's been full-tilt boogie all the way."

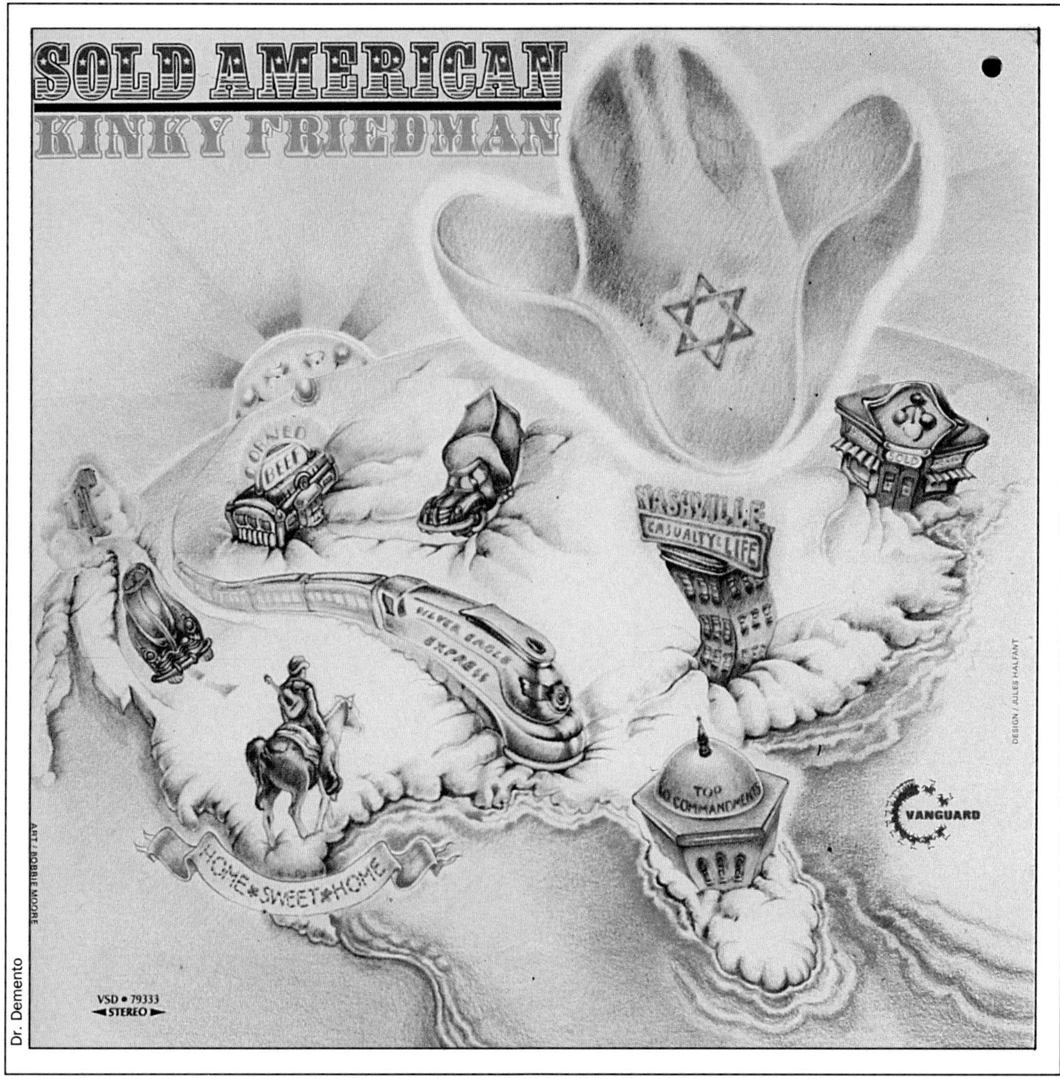

Tweaking country sanctimony was a popular pastime in 1973. The spectre of Hasidic honky-tonk loomed in the person of Kinky Friedman and His Texas Jewboys, welcomed to the Opry by the Rev. Jimmie Rodgers Snow as the "first full-blooded Jews" to play country's mother church. After the novelty of this act wore thin, Friedman pursued a successful career as a mystery writer.

Confessions of a Parrot Head III: Terry Brykczynski

I went to high school in Pensacola, Florida. This friend and I had worked as shrimpers, because his father was a shrimper. I had lost track of this guy for a couple of years—I was living in New York City then—and finally went down to see him. He was a forest ranger south of Gainesville, Florida. He had built his own house out of cement blocks in the woods, and we were driving around in the truck and stopping the truck to gather road kills and throwing alligators in the back of the truck. He was living an *incredible* life, it seemed to me, coming from New York City. And he said, 'You gotta listen to this!' He turned on *A White Sport Coat and a Pink Crustacean.* This was the first time that I heard lyrics like this which seemed to really address specifically some of the things that I had gone through, living for a couple of years in the South. To talk about pink crustaceans just bowled me over, because it was so specific and such an in-joke, it seemed to me, at the time. I figured, 'How could anyone else think this is as funny as I think it is?'

"It was a key to a subculture. It was like finding a map. McGuane had written the liner notes. It was a little bombastic, but it was also one of my first inroads into McGuane. One name led to another, and every one of them had something to offer. There was the relationship of that whole group living down in Key West, which suddenly became a focal point. There was [the film of McGuane's novel] *92 in the Shade* with Margot Kidder, who I was in love with at the time from a distance. So it was this incredible bubbling pot of cultural excitement to me to find this group of people that really spoke to my generation. I remember sitting in the chair and listening in that old cement block house in Gainesville and thinking, 'Wow! What incredible music!'

"I think he's captured a regional element, sort of the forgotten South ... which is one step beyond a fantasy for most of the people in the South. They've always wanted to reach for something, and he propels 'em, he gives 'em the engine to do it in dreams.... And the pirate element, too. I think of the South, the element of getting something for nothing, and so many lines come to memory from his lyrics, the one about

Photos: Margaret Miller

'Made all the money in Miami and pissed it away on grass' or something. I guess the undercurrent of the South is to amass something and then to piss it all away in one night. That's the fatalistic, dark side of the South, too....

"He's a real survivor. I remember we were in Australia one time, and he was coming over there, maybe it was for the yacht races or something. You'd always see his picture in the paper at these parties. Maybe he's looking for material or something. It seems like he's a magnet for where the action is.

"We just came back from Grand Cayman. We go there often, and there's a guy who's a local celebrity called the Barefoot Man. He has regular shows at the Holiday Inn, and he just hates it because people will ask him to sing Jimmy Buffett songs instead of his own. You can see the hurt on his face as he has to go through one more Jimmy Buffett number. He's ruined so many lounge performer's lives!"

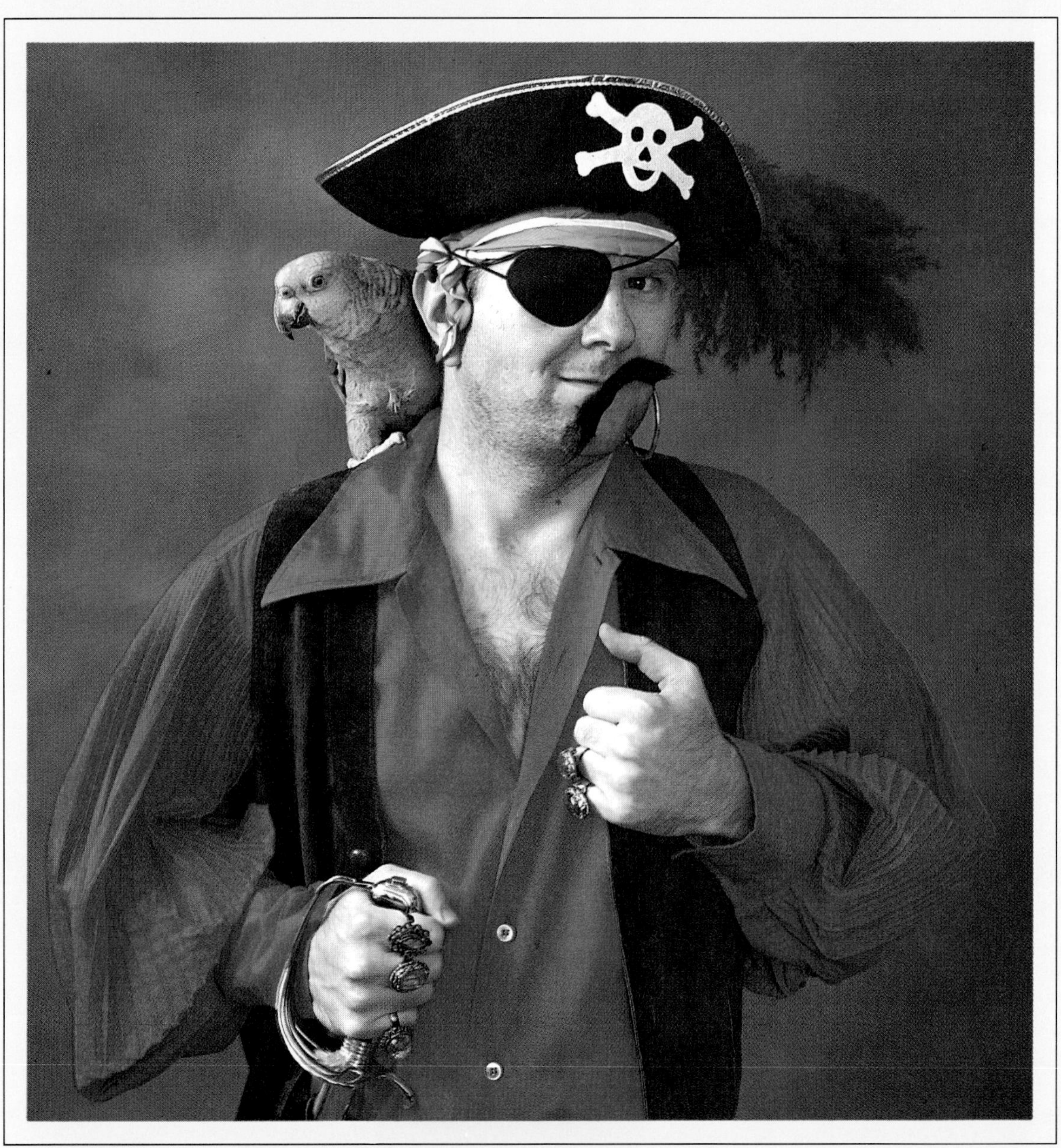

CHAPTER SIX

MARGARITAVILLE

There are enough people out there writing moan music.
—Jimmy Buffett, 1978

This is the first time I've worked without a net. I want to tell the truth.
At the same time, I don't want to start a feeding frenzy.
—Thomas McGuane, *Panama,* 1978

"I remember some friends meeting him at the airport with a banner, 'Welcome Home, Mr. Entertainment,'" says Chris Robinson of Buffett's return to Key West from promoting *A White Sport Coat and a Pink Crustacean.* Mr. Entertainment had taken harmonica ace "Fingers" Taylor and a Key West crony, Vaughn Cochran, with him to New York. (Cochran played washboard then; *New York Times* reviewer Ian Dove called him a "low-phosphate washboard scrubber." Today Cochran is president of Sportfishing World Headquarters and his paintings of fish adorn T-shirts sold through Buffett's *Coconut Telegraph*). Taylor and Cochran were a big band for Buffett, who soloed a lot in those days, though his "schtick" included introducing an invisible Coral Reefer Band by name, among them Miss Que Pasa, Miss Kitty Litter, and Mr. Marvin Gardens, accredited songwriter of "Drunk and Screw."

Just four months after *Sport Coat* appeared in June of 1973, Buffett was back in a Nashville studio with producer Don Gant to record his second ABC/Dunhill album, *Living and Dying in 3/4 Time.* The first album was doing well, but not so well that a record label would normally start work on a new artist's second album so quickly. Fate played a hand in ABC's accelerated interest in Buffett. "At the time he was working for ABC Records," recalls Chris Robinson, "so was Jim Croce. When Croce died, they [ABC] pushed Jimmy. I think they put their energy into Jimmy more after Jim Croce died."

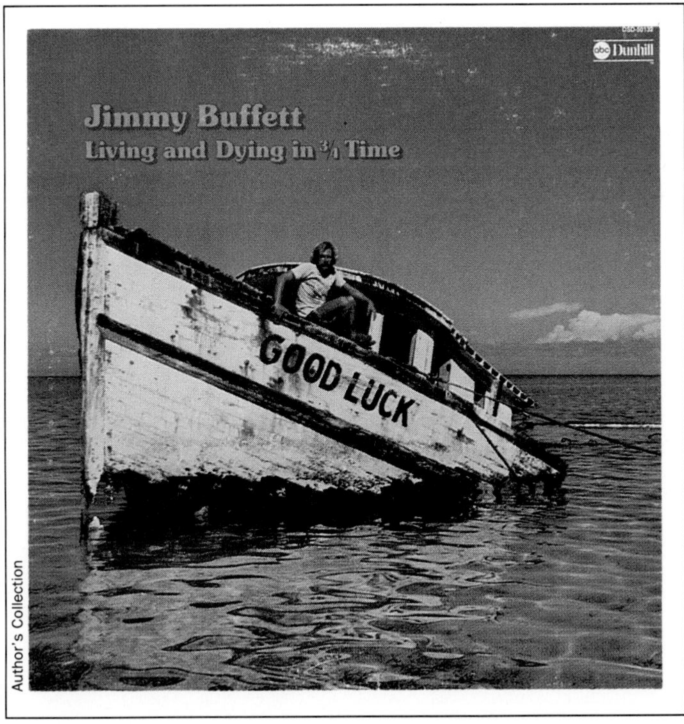

Author's Collection

Author's Collection

After years of scuffling, likable Jim Croce hit paydirt with the comic urban fable of "Bad Bad Leroy Brown" in 1973. The previous year's "You Don't Mess Around With Jim" paved the way, and Croce enjoyed phenomenal success (many TV appearances, including guest-hosting the popular *Midnight Special*) all too briefly. His death in a 1973 plane crash left fans mourning a down-to-earth star. His label, ABC, gazing at a deep sink in future revenues, picked newcomer Jimmy Buffett as the nearest thing to Croce on its artist roster and pushed Buffett with a pre–music video promotional film.

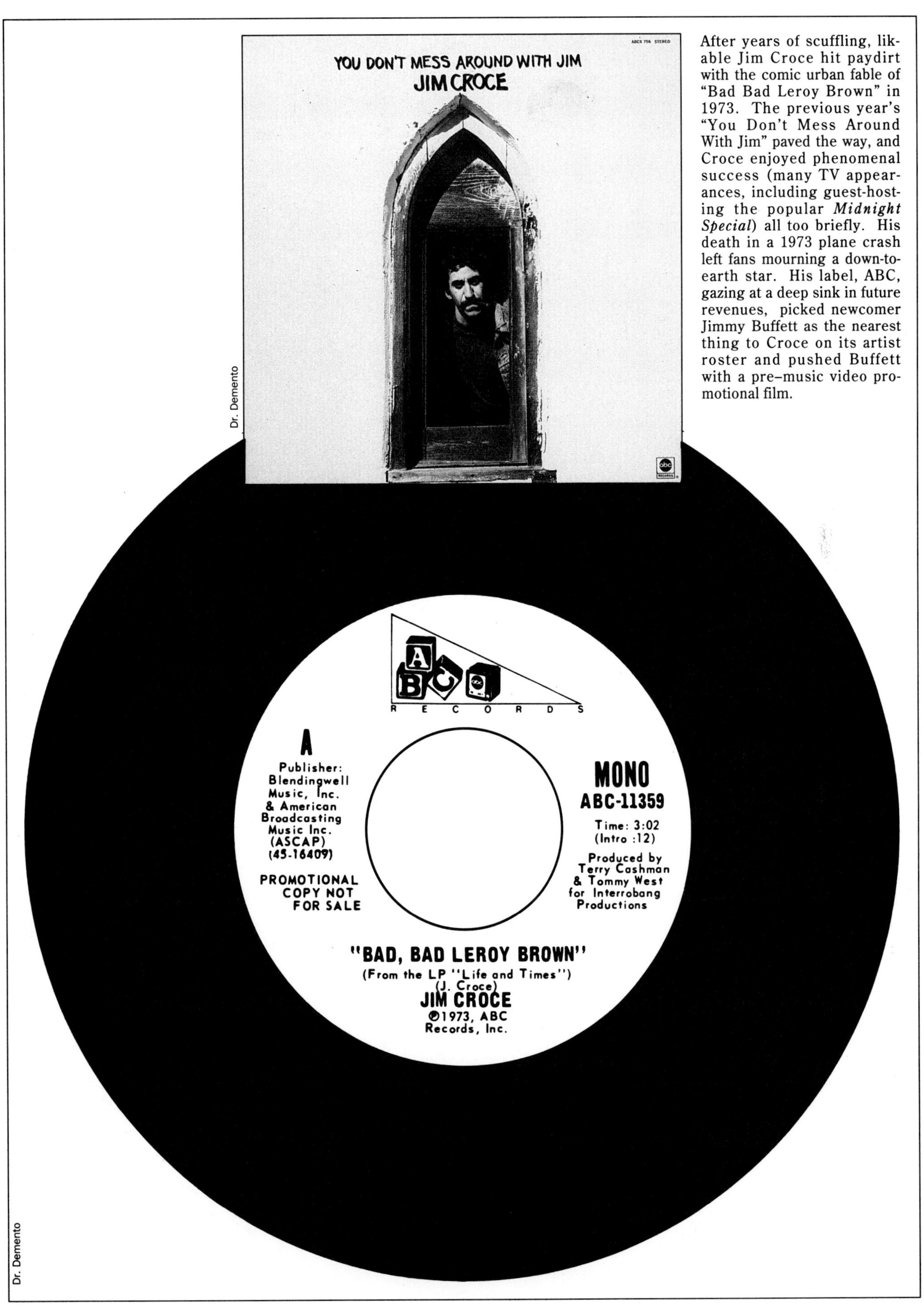

Dr. Demento

Dr. Demento

Strider records, NYC

The beautiful crossover hit "Come Monday" established Buffett on the pop charts, hitting number 30 in 1974.

Croce and Buffett shared more than the same label. Both told stories with their songs, some satiric, others sentimental. Both wore mustaches. "I get a lot of comparisons with Jim Croce," Buffett told *Stereo Review* a year after Croce's death. "I guess that's because we were on the same label and we were good friends. He used to visit me down in Key West."

At twenty years' remove, it's easy to forget just how popular Jim Croce was for a brief while. A Philadelphian, Croce knocked around New York coffeehouses in the late 1960s (one album for Capitol, *Approaching Day,* bombed) and supported himself driving trucks. An old buddy from Croce's Villanova College days, Tommy West, took a shine to Croce's songs and coproduced the sessions which became the *You Don't Mess Around With Jim* album. The title song was an updated "Stagolee" variant, nicely balanced by the James Taylor-style sensitivity of "Operator," a song which made Croce a heartthrob of Ma Bell's daughters.

Croce's talent as singer-songwriter was abetted by an appealing personality. His lived-in face was simultaneously ugly-handsome and comic. He chewed cigars and had a low-key likability. Sure, he could write a sensitive ballad ("Time in a Bottle"), but he seemed free of pretense and self-absorption. After all, he was a former truck driver.

Croce hit the singer-songwriter's jackpot in 1973 with "Bad, Bad Leroy Brown," a song which effectively recycled "Don't Mess Around With Jim" to greater commercial effect. It was number one on the pop charts, and even Frank Sinatra covered it! (Are you listening, Mitch?) At age thirty, Croce was one of pop's hottest properties the summer Buffett's *Sport Coat* appeared, and it couldn't have happened to a nicer guy. It was with genuine grief that the world responded to news that Croce and five band members were killed on September 20, 1973: his chartered plane crashed into a tree shortly after takeoff in Nachitoches, Louisiana.

With pragmatic promptness, ABC looked at its artist roster for the Next Best Thing and decided Buffett was it. "It has now become apparent what ABC/Dunhill had in mind during their lengthy and admirable support of Jimmy Buffett," *Billboard* wrote in 1974. "ABC saw the next Jim Croce." The comparison to Croce shows up in several reviews that year of *Living and Dying in 3/4 Time.* Two years later, an ABC press release on Buffett would say: "He was compared to writers like Kris Kristofferson and he was expected to fill the space left by Jim Croce."

His label was so committed to promoting Buffett that it produced a fifteen-minute promotional film shot in "his natural Key West habitat" for showing in ABC-owned theaters to hype *Living and Dying in 3/4 Time.* Improbably enough, Buffett showed some of this twenty-year-old pre-MTV promo among the video clips screened during his 1993 Chameleon Caravan Tour.

Auhtor's Collection

Photo: Michael Abramson

Author's Collection

Jeff Bridges (left) and Sam Waterston played self-proclaimed chainsaw rustlers in *Rancho Deluxe,* Frank Perry's 1975 production of Tom McGuane's absurdist western. Buffett wrote the score and made a cameo appearance singing "Livingston Saturday Night." (Top) McGuane's Paradise Valley, Montana, retreat inspired the country-flavored songs of Buffett's *Living and Dying in 3/4 Time* album.

Buffett's Etiquette Lesson From a Legend in Law Enforcement

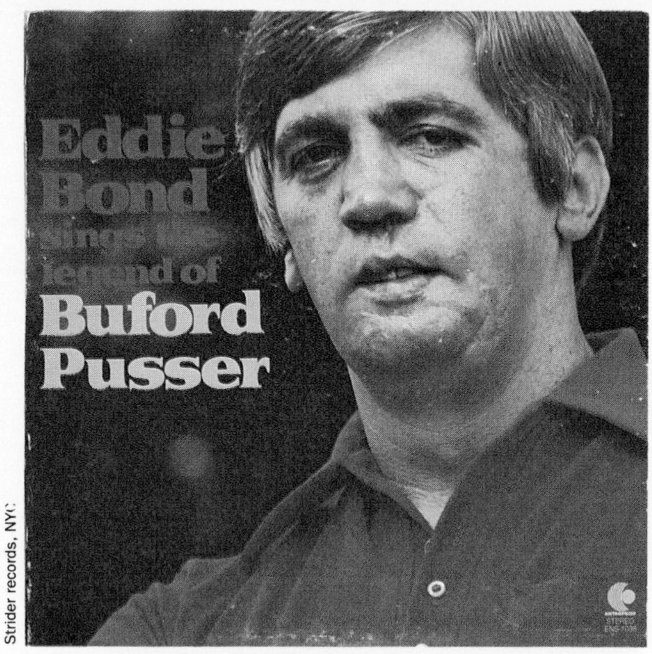

Strider records, NYC

Great men surely touched Buffett's life. One nearly beat him within an inch of it. The occasion was the recording of his second ABC album, *Living and Dying in 3/4 Time.* It was October 1973 (a month after Jim Croce's death). According to the version of the tale Buffett told Noel Coppage in a 1974 *Stereo Review* feature, "We had just recorded 'God's Own Drunk,' and we were shit-faced drunk ourselves." Buffett had revised a Lord Buckley monologue concerning a usually sober man who agrees to guard his brother-in-law's moonshine still. He yields to liquor's temptation and then blithely fends off a nine-foot bear, for "I was God's own drunk and a fearless man." Buffett had a crowd egging him on in the recording studio, and felt the need (like any good method actor) to get into character.

This helped his performance but hindered his ability to recall where he'd left his car, a rented Gremlin. Drummer Sammy Creason accompanied Buffett on his search. "So we got up on the hood of a parked car," Buffett told *Stereo Review,* "and we were standing there looking around, and it turns out to be Buford Pusser's car." Pusser's legend as head-cracking lawman was the topic of the Bubba film classic, *Walking Tall* ("Audiences are standing up and cheering ..."). Walking tall came naturally to Pusser, who stood six-feet-six. "We didn't know it was him," said Buffett. "We'd drunk a whole bottle of tequila, so we gave him a whole ration of shit, and he beat the hell out of both of us. Yanked my hair out, punched Sammy in the nose...."

Buffett claimed he kept an eight-inch lock of his hair in his bedroom dresser drawer as a souvenir of the encounter. He recounted the incident to *Rolling Stone's* Judith Sims in 1975. "There was a bald spot in the back of my head," he told her. "I looked like a monk." By the time of this retelling, the incident had sprouted additional details: "He followed us and jumped on the hood of *our* car," said Buffett. "He came over to the window and Sammy tried to apologize, but the guy grabbed me by the hair and started yanking it out and hitting me. Finally I got the window rolled up and and we tore out. I said, 'Oh my god, we've been threatened by that killer maniac; when we get back we've got to protect ourselves.' I got a tire tool out of the car . . . and went back to the hotel. There he was in the lobby. He grabbed the tool out of my pocket. People then started pulling us into the elevator and one of them said, 'We'll just take you to your room, that was Buford Pusser.' 'Oh my God,' I said. "Lock me in.'"

Buffett knew he had not been scalped by your garden-variety mean redneck. Pusser had cleaned up wretchedly corrupt McNairy County, Tennessee, in the 1960s, though its criminal element did not appreciate Sheriff Pusser's efforts. He was knifed, beaten, and thrown from a window. He and his wife, Pauline, were ambushed on a country road in 1967. The spray of .30-caliber bullets killed her and blew away half the sheriff's face. Undeterred but righteously angry, Pusser came back swinging the pickax he used to smash gambling equipment and carved a niche for himself in the folklore of the South. For a man like Pusser (pronounced like puss), ridding his car of a couple of unwanted hippie hood ornaments wasn't even sport. More like swatting gnats. For a longhair like Buffett, Pusser was his worst nightmare incarnate.

Walking Tall was Pusser's saga on film, courtesy of Bing Crosby productions, with its title song sung by Johnny Mathis! Joe Don Baker played Pusser, and the film was such a runaway success that it had grossed $10 million before it even opened in New York, where Vincent Canby called it "a relentlessly violent, small-town American melodrama" in the pages of the *New York Times.* "It generates a primitive, atavistic sort of power," marveled critic Gary Arnold. Gareth Jones called it "a terrifying image of Nixon's silent majority at work." But in "small-town America," as the movie's ad campaign proclaimed, "audiences are standing up and cheering!"

It's a wonder no country hits were inspired by Pusser's saga, though one artist at least tried. *The Legend of Buford Pusser* was a country concept album, ten songs about Pusser by Eddie Bond. After slim success with rockabilly songs ("Broke My Guitar") on Sun, the label that launched Elvis, Bond found himself employed in the late sixties as Pusser's chief deputy! His songs liken Pusser to Wyatt Earp and have such titles as "200 Lbs. o' Swingin' Hound" and "Buford Pusser Goes Bear Hunting With a Switch." This 1973 tribute album was issued by Stax, the Memphis-based Soul label whose biggest act at the time was the chain-bedecked Isaac Hayes (*Shaft*).

Photofest

Former football star Joe Don Baker became a working-class hero in *Walking Tall,* the saga of crusading real-life sheriff Buford Pusser. Not depicted in the popular film was Pusser's scalping of a tipsy Jimmy Buffett in a Nashville parking lot.

Bing Crosby Productions had a hot property in Pusser, and decided to star him in the sequel to *Walking Tall.* Hours after the agreement to launch Pusser's film career was struck, he was killed when his sports car careened off Highway 64 near Selmar, Tennessee, crashed into an embankment, and caught fire. Pusser's death on August 21, 1974, didn't slow the *Walking Tall* industry, however. Bo Svenson played Pusser in *Walking Tall, Part 2* and *Walking Tall—The Final Chapter.* His last portrayal of Pusser was in a short-lived NBC-TV *Walking Tall* series in 1981. Pusser's death car is now on view at Carbo's Police Museum in Pigeon Forge, Tennessee.

It wasn't every longhair who could claim to have been scalped by such a legend, and Buffett used to love retelling the incident, changing the details with his mood and the occasion. In one version, he was leaving a Nashville club, not the recording studio, when he encountered Pusser. In another, he left his hotel to look for his missing car. The constants in all accounts are Buffett's tequila intake, Creason's presence (he's credited as *bodyguard* on the sleeve of *Living and Dying in 3/4 Time*), and Pusser's rage. "He reached in and socked Sammy," Buffett told a Philadelphia crowd in 1974, "and Sammy tried to counterattack by jabbing at his fist with a Bic pen. And while this man was beating the hell out of us, we couldn't get the car started because we didn't have our seat belts fastened. The ignition switch was buzzing and I was saying, 'Oh, God! I don't want to die in Nashville in a rented Gremlin.'"

Fans saw a younger, hairier Buffett buss a golden-tressed and bell-bottomed Miss Jane and then take her for a ride in God's Own Truck. Buffett was also witnessed bouncing over the waves in a powerboat laden with female cargo.

Living and Dying in 3/4 Time was released in February of 1974. Later that year, The Jimmy Buffett Songbook, a collection of songs from his first two ABC/Dunhill albums, appeared. "Jimmy Buffett is a unique singer/songwriter with a knack for being able to completely defy categorization," says the songbook's introduction to the artist. "He's too musically soft-spoken to be a rocker and the madcap, elliptical point of view in his lyrics wouldn't really qualify him in the folk music camp. So where does that place the eclectic Mr. Buffett? Everywhere, evidently, and that seems to be a perfect pigeonholing for the sandy-haired, twenty-six-year-old Key Wester." ABC's publicist went on to say that Buffett was vying for a role in Robert Altman's film, *Nashville,* but that role never materialized. "Whether Jimmy Buffett is a film star, a pop star, or both in five years is anyone's conjecture," the songbook concludes. "What is not open to question is the fact that, given any artistic situation, Jimmy can be counted upon to brand his entire environment with his trademark wry/rustic sense of humor. Maybe the singer is 'Living in 3/4 Time' but from our vantage point here at ABC, his life looks more like a Whirlwind than a Waltz."

"Wrote practically all of that second album while I was lying around out in Montana," Buffett told *Stereo Review's* Noel Coppage. Perhaps that's why it is more country and less Caribbean than many Buffett albums. He returned to Montana during the summer of '74 to work on the soundtrack (and to make a cameo appearance) in Frank Perry's *Rancho Deluxe,* a New West parody film scripted by Buffett's pal Thomas McGuane. McGuane and some friends had "discovered" Paradise Valley on the edge of Yellowstone National Park, and by the mid-1970s it had acquired a national reputation as one of America's hippest retreats. "The interesting thing about Paradise Valley," recalls one observer of the scene, "is that it was basically a macho boy's writers' club," of which McGuane was the focal point. Buffett struck this same observer as "cold, surly, non-communicative" and spellbound by Jane, remembered as "one of the great ice princesses of western civilization. Jane called the shots. She had him in her pocket.... He couldn't move without her directing him."

Buffett would later recall *Rancho Deluxe* in the introduction to his novel, *Where Is Joe Merchant?* "I was exposed to the real world of filmmaking," he wrote. "I used to watch the setups, poke my head in an available window to watch interior shots, and was fascinated with the whole process." Given his attempts at scriptwriting and film production over the years, it evidently has been an enduring fascination.

Rancho Deluxe starred Jeff Bridges and Sam

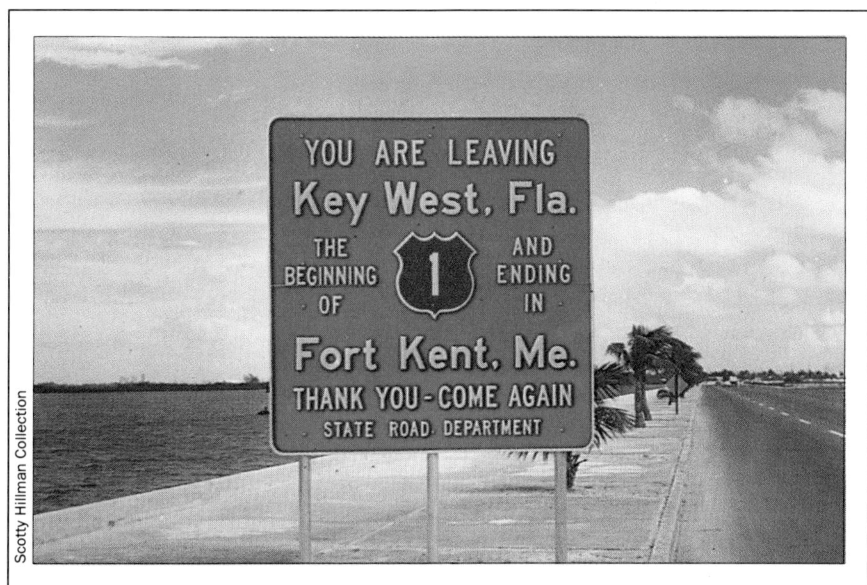

Highway 1 was both an end and a beginning in the 1940s. Buffett followed it to Key West in 1971, leaving Nashville and a failed marriage behind.

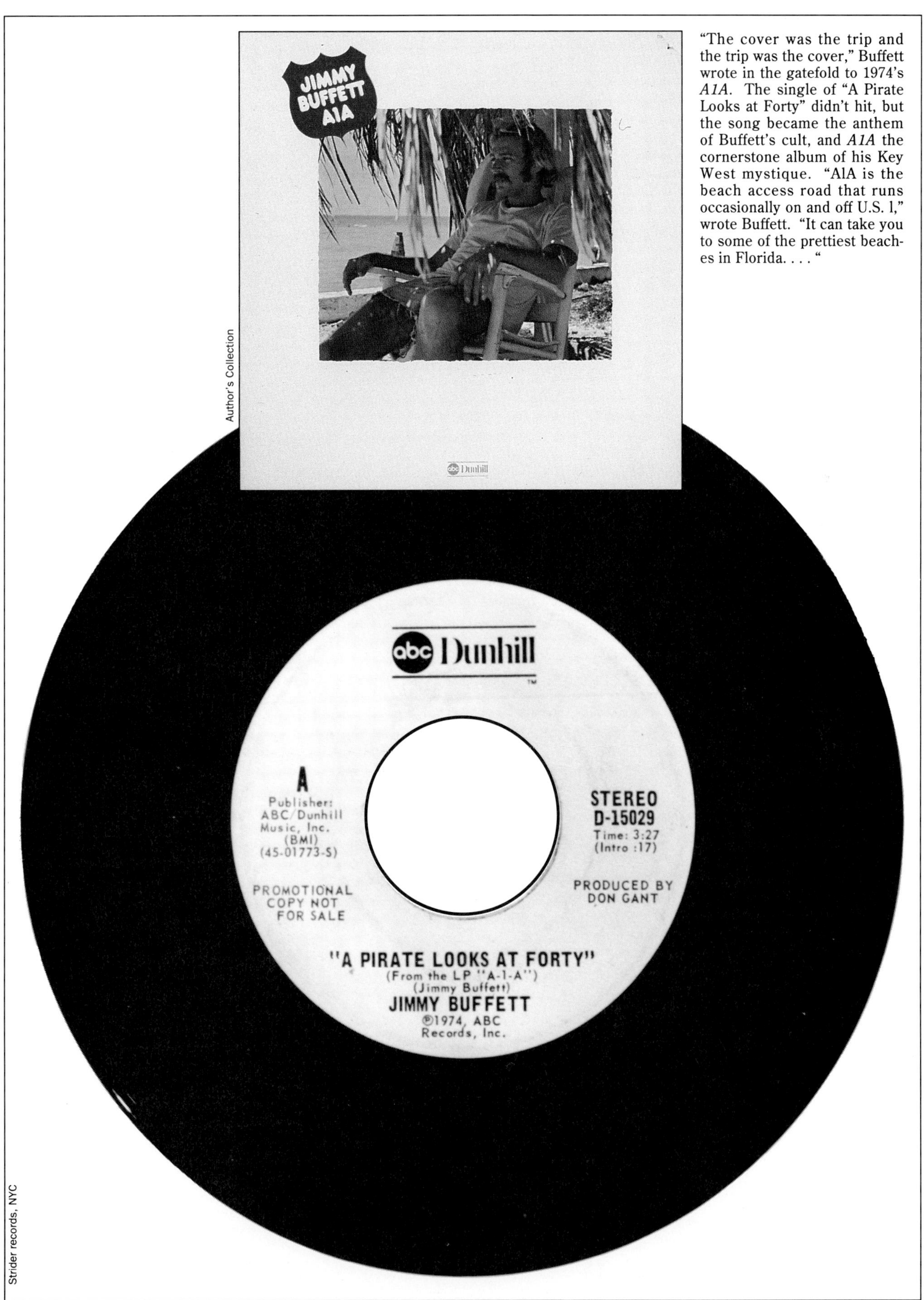

JIMMY BUFFETT A1A
abc Dunhill
A
Publisher: ABC/Dunhill Music, Inc. (BMI) (45-01773-S)
PROMOTIONAL COPY NOT FOR SALE
STEREO D-15029
Time: 3:27 (Intro :17)
PRODUCED BY DON GANT
"A PIRATE LOOKS AT FORTY"
(From the LP "A-1-A")
(Jimmy Buffett)
JIMMY BUFFETT
℗1974, ABC Records, Inc.

Author's Collection

Strider records, NYC

"The cover was the trip and the trip was the cover," Buffett wrote in the gatefold to 1974's *A1A*. The single of "A Pirate Looks at Forty" didn't hit, but the song became the anthem of Buffett's cult, and *A1A* the cornerstone album of his Key West mystique. "AlA is the beach access road that runs occasionally on and off U.S. l," wrote Buffett. "It can take you to some of the prettiest beaches in Florida. . . . "

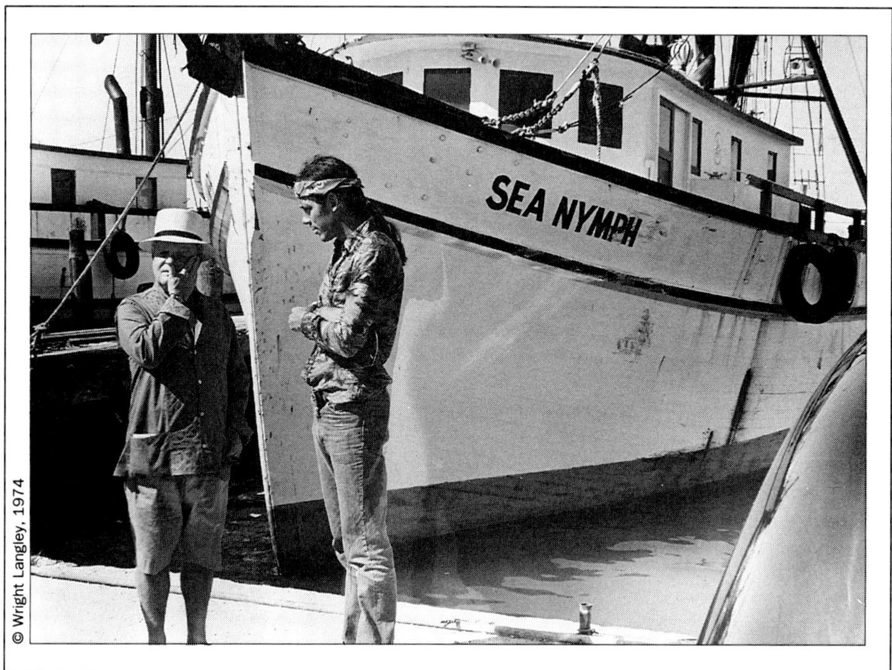

© Wright Langley, 1974

The author of *In Cold Blood,* Truman Capote, meets the author of *92 in the Shade,* Tom McGuane, in 1974, when McGuane directed the film version of his novel on location in Key West.

Waterston as two hip young "chainsaw rustlers" in the New West. Over the title credits, Buffett sang: "No, we're not outlaws or common thieves, just a few aces with cards up our sleeves." He was on screen less than a minute in a cowboy bar called the Wrangler performing "Livingston Saturday Night" with a band which included a long-haired McGuane on mandolin. The references to a whorehouse and the "shit" and "screw" in the R-rated movie song disappeared when Buffett recut "Livingston Saturday Night" for *Son of a Son of a Sailor* in 1978. Viewed today, *Rancho Deluxe* is less interesting as a film than it is as artifact of the seventies' country-rock lifestyle. When it appeared in 1975, *New York Times* critic Richard Eder called it "... a picture whose artfulness is marred by its own narcissistic excess."

The summer of '74 also saw Buffett penning songs for a French television documentary about tarpon fishing in the Keys, work offered via one of his Key West cronies, Count Guy de la Valdene, a French aristocrat who was a filmmaker. "I did that because it was a free trip to France," Buffett told *Rolling Stone.* Whilc singing about tarpons in

Phil Ahrens, Gotham Book Mart

Phil Ahrens, Gotham Book Mart

Phil Ahrens, Gotham Book Mart

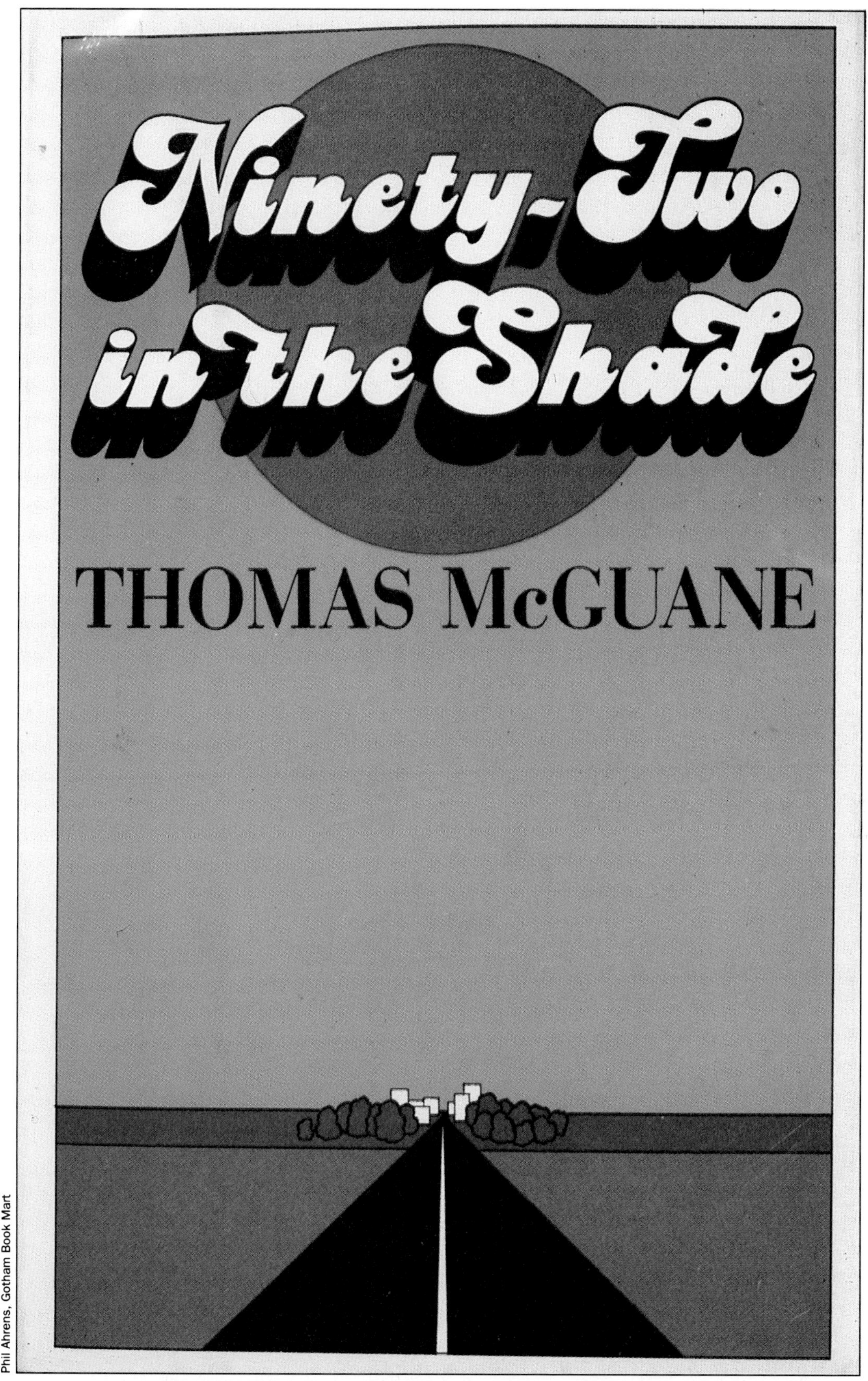

Phil Ahrens, Gotham Book Mart

One of the half-dozen major novelists of the 1970s, Tom McGuane sought out the rogue sanctuaries of the continental U.S. from Key West to the New West. "Like Mailer and Pynchon, Thomas McGuane makes the page, the paragraph, the sentence itself a record of continuous imaginative activity."—*New York Times Book Review*

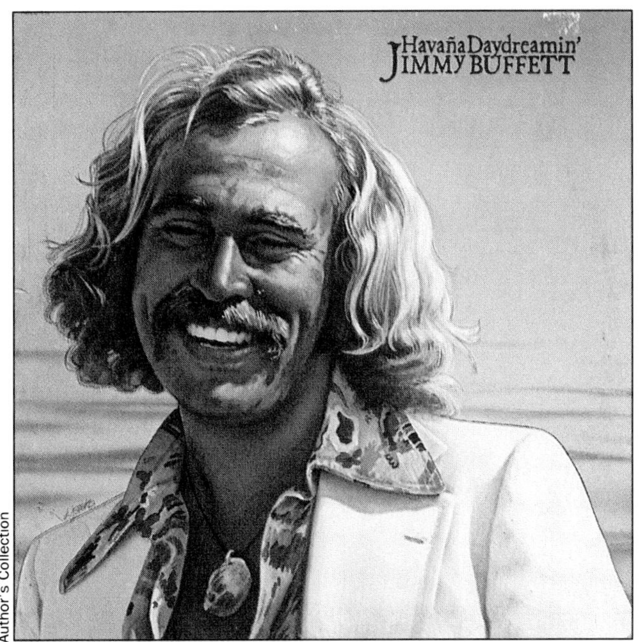

Author's Collection

Europe, Buffett's career was taking off in America. "Come Monday" appeared in *Billboard's* pop charts on May 18, and would eventually make it up to number 30. It was first heard on "easy listening" radio stations before being picked up and aired by country and mainstream pop radio. "I was in England when it hit," Buffett told *Rolling Stone*'s Judith Sims in 1975. "I went to buy a pair of shoes and heard it on the radio." Footwear played a role in Buffett's biggest pop hits—hush puppies in "Come Monday" and flip-flops in "Margaritaville." Britain's BBC initially balked at airing "Come Monday," since the song's mention of hush puppies was construed as free advertising!

"Come Monday" was written for Jane in the summer of '73 when Buffett was in L.A. for the Troubadour gig *Variety* favorably reviewed. In his *Parrot Head Handbook,* Buffett recalls "Come Monday" getting up to number 10 on the charts, but it got nowhere near that. Still, it was the hit ABC had been banking on, and his label would have been happy to hear more songs like it. However, "Come Monday" was one of a kind, more like a Glen Campbell record than typical Buffett, who felt embarrassment at being an "easy listening" artist. "It's kind of weird now with 'Come Monday' making the charts," Buffett told *Stereo Review's* Noel Coppage. "Even Middle America was playing the hell out of that."

Careful to distance himself from the squares, Buffett nonetheless enjoyed being noted by the hometown paper. RISING MOBILE SINGER APPEARS ON NATIONAL TV, crowed a *Mobile Press* headline of August 14, 1974. The brief story read: "Chances are good that many Mobilians—a good portion of them young—were glued to the tube last night when the Port City's native son vocalist Jimmy Buffett appeared on 'Your Hit Parade.' The mustachioed young man whose albums are climbing the national charts sang his biggest hit, 'Come Monday.'" The piece went on to briefly recap Buffett's career and note that he is "the son of Mr. and Mrs. J. D. Buffett of Mobile."

Like many high school misfits who made good, Buffett viewed success as sweet revenge on the jocks and prom queens who once made his life miserable. "... He's planning to use some of his free time to attend the tenth-anniversary reunion of his high-school class," Noel Coppage wrote in a

Harris Lewine Collection

Cuba before Castro: George Raft at the Hotel Nacional; the Marquis de Portago charging up the Malécon; Sepy Dobronyi's La Bodeguita del Medio; Veradero Beach; and the Shanghai Theater. Another kind of Havana daydreaming.

Frank Driggs Collection

I'LL SEE YOU IN C-U-B-A

by IRVING BERLIN

As featured in the Greenwich Village Follies

by "The JAZZ KING" TED LEWIS

1390

Harris Lewine Collection

Habana: Castillo del Morro.
Morro Castle.

Harris Lewine Collection

1974 *Stereo Review* profile. "'I'm just going to get real numb on something, go there, hang out, and *ob-zerve!*'" he says. [Janis Joplin "got back" at her high school reunion in Port Arthur, Texas.] "He pauses, fingering the lurid pink 'treasure-box' oyster shell he wears on a chain around his neck and swashing [*sic*] the ice around in his drink. 'Ought to be able to write a hellacious song about it.'" He didn't though. Under the headline, RISING SINGER PROUD OF CHILDHOOD HERE, reporter Natalie Crozier wrote in a July 11, 1974, *Mobile Press* profile: "Buffett's parents, Mrs. and Mrs. J. B. Buffett of Mobile, say there is only one thing their son regrets about his career so far. He will be leaving for a concert tour of England this week, and will be unable to attend the tenth anniversary reunion of his class at McGill."

While early interviews reflect Buffett as a sunny stoned wastrel, there was more to the picture. "Back then," recalls Chris Robinson, "he still had that business thing. He was determined to make it. He had that thing back there in his head, 'I'm gonna make it,' and as laid back as he was, he still had that sense.... When his popularity came on, he went and took vocal lessons and worked real hard to do what he's doing now."

Buffett ended his whirlwind summer of movie scoring and "easy listening" stardom back in Nashville, recording his third ABC/Dunhill album in August. Released in December, *A1A* took its title from the highway leading to Key West. The map of the Keys on the album jacket and the photos of Buffett (with and without God's Own Truck) looking breezily stoned underscored the Key West mystique more strongly than ever. So, too, did such songs as "A Pirate Looks at Forty" and "Nautical Wheelers." Stephen Holden's 1975 *Rolling Stone* review frames *A1A* in the context of its time: "Like his friend Michael Murphy, Jimmy Buffett belongs to the 'cosmic cowboy' school of country rock," Holden wrote. "In his best songs, Buffett evokes a man of the road: his special region is southern Florida, whose oceanic mythology entrances him. The album's high point, 'A Pirate Looks at Forty,' is a touching ballad that equates pirate legend with lost youth. The narrative songs, 'Migration' and 'Trying to Reason with Hurricane Seas,' detail more vividly the squalor and enervating languor of life between Miami Beach and Key West."

Even the big city bible of hip taste, the *Village Voice,* gave Buffett a nod in 1975. Under the headline, JIMMY BUFFETT'S OTHER AMERICA, Greg Waller wrote: "Buffett's form of 'country-rock' is a liberating synthesis rather than a proscriptive subgenre in Buffett's best material neither country nor rock loses anything in the musical shuffle—quite the contrary, an impressive freedom is gained.

"Jimmy Buffett is my personal pick for most

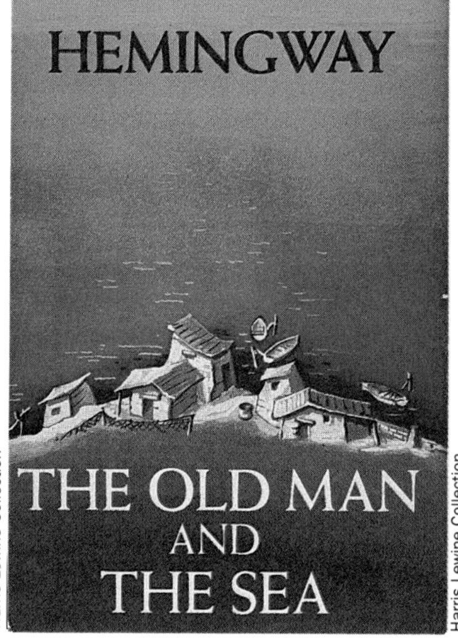

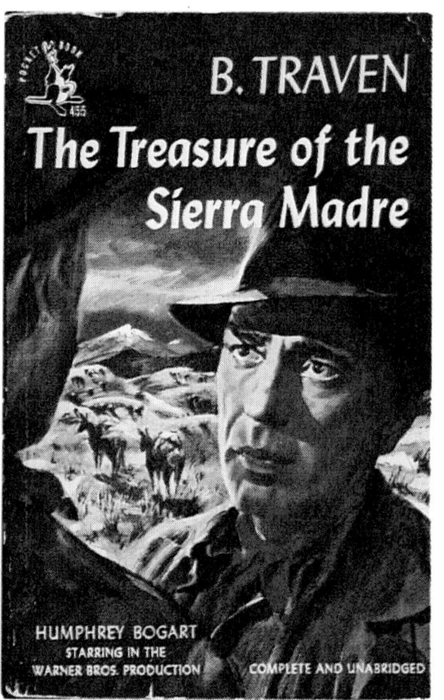

Buffett met the inspiration for Hemingway's "old man" in Cuba; Traven's jungle novels, set in Mexico also inspired him.

undeservedly overlooked troubadour of 1973-75. But his latest album,,*A1A*,' creates problems for even the most zealous partisan. Like A1A, a Florida highway, on this album Buffett travels for a while and then comes to a halt in Key West, satisfied with what seems suspiciously like a dead end: 'Gimme oysters and beer for dinner every day of the year.'"

If Key West looked like a dead end to New Yorkers, Buffett wasn't eager to swap places. "Cities are too fast a pace," he told Associated Press reporter Nat Yancey in 1975. "I've got lots of energy, but I don't want to have to spend it worrying about traffic or the air I breathe." Like John Denver's "Rocky Mountain High," Buffett's music represented a rejection of the urban fast lane, though Key West's bucolic lure was heavily drenched with booze at the beach, denoted by the popular expression, 'See the lower Keys on your hands and knees.'"

"Yeah, I guess I drink a lot," Buffett told *Rolling Stone*'s Judith Sims in 1975. "When you're onstage and the energy's going and the sweat's pouring out of you, you can drink a lot and it's all used up. What'll kill you is drinking at the same pace when you're offstage."

In the summer of '75, Buffett put together the first touring incarnation of the Coral Reefer Band. The ever-faithful "Fingers" Taylor played harmonica and keyboard, Roger Bartlett played lead guitar, Harry Dailey was on bass guitar, and Phillip Fajardo was the drummer. Touring caused Buffett to miss much of a major episode in the Key West boogie, the filming of McGuane's novel, *Ninety-two in the Shade.* "There was a large cocaine budget for that movie," laughs one observer. McGuane directed, Peter Fonda and Margot Kidder were among the stars, and Hollywood's glitterati and Key West's boogiers collided in what one participant likened to "a clusterfuck." Along with the cast and crew of *92 in the Shade,* Dennis Hopper descended on Key West: "It was a period of mass confusion," recalls Vic Latham, "just because there were so many new crazies in town." Everyone was high and, it seemed, in heat: tales of literati and starlets coupling in the bushes are still heard over drinks in Key West's bars. Buffett could have been in on the action but passed on writing music for *92 in the Shade* because he was upset with the producer of *Rancho Deluxe,* Elliott Kastner. "I just wanted nothing to do with movies right then," Buffett told an AP reporter. *92 in the Shade* may have been a better party than it was movie: audiences stayed away in droves and McGuane never directed again. The *New York Times*'s Richard Eder at least liked the writing: "Mr. McGuane captures the speech and style of young people who are funny and charming and empty and mean."

Encouraged by the success of "Come Monday," ABC released "Pencil Thin Mustache" as a single, a celebration of nostalgia which invoked Boston Blackie, Ricky Ricardo, Andy Devine, and "Sky King's Penny," a reference to the niece of rancher-pilot Schuyler J. (Sky) King in the 1951-54 kid's adventure series *Sky King.* It went nowhere. From *A1A*"A Pirate Looks at Forty" and the comic "Door Number Three" were picked as singles. Zilch. By the time Buffett waxed his fourth ABC album in November of '75, it was apparent that he wasn't really a singles act. But his album sales were decent, and he was developing the core of his cult following. Marketing demographics weren't as sophisticated as they have since become, but Buffett was already what MCA would later peg as "a lifestyle artist," and his albums shipped in the dead of winter as sunny postcards offering escape and a little auditory summer. *Havana Daydreamin'* was released in February 1976.

Stereo Review's Peter Reilly liked it a lot: "Perhaps the best here is the title song, 'Havana Daydreamin',' an ambiguous trip into B. Traven (you remember him—*The Treasure of the Sierra Madre, Death Ship*) territory. The story of a mystery man, apparently a Cuban exile, waiting—waiting to contact some equally mysterious person who will pay him a large amount of money to do ... what? Go back to Cuba to form yet another revolutionary army? To commit some sort of terrorist act? One is not quite sure, but the song, the lyrics, and the performance all have that kind of slumbering—daydreaming—menace under the blinding Caribbean sun that Traven, and Graham Greene as well, slipped so credibly between the lines of their novels."

Later that year, Buffett told Associated Press reporter Richard H. Lowe that he and McGuane were co-writing a screenplay for something called

"God's Own Drunk" and Burlesque's Own Hipster

"My lords and my ladies of the royal court," Lord Buckley would proclaim as greeting to a seedy bar populated with drunks and strippers. "People are the true flowers of life: and it has been a most precious pleasure to have temporarily strolled in your garden." No one had heard such a thing in such a place before, but Lord Buckley had a knack for combining the sacred and the profane: He regarded the bars and burlesque houses where he worked as churches, true gathering places of lost souls. Little wonder he officiated over *The Church of the Living Swing* (billed as "America's first jazz church") with a pair of belly dancers till the vice squad took an interest in its sacraments.

Richard Buckley was a California miner's son (born 1906) who worked in logging camps and oil fields till the Depression drove him to the shame of show business. He first worked as standup comic at the desperate marathon dances of the sort depicted in the film *They Shoot Horses, Don't They?* Chicago, he heard, was where the action was, and he settled there to clown for the underworld's royalty. (Al Capone supposedly called Buckley "the only man who could make me laugh.")

Buckley prospered in the Windy City, even presiding over a couple of clubs, Chez Buckley and the Suzy Q, in the 1930s. He listened with a loving ear to the "jive talk" of the black jazz musicians who played there, and incorporated their rhythms and accents into his emerging character, Lord Buckley, a mad aristocrat in a pith helmet who played with words as a jazz musician did with sounds. Buckley was doing "word jazz" long before Kenneth Patchen, another of Buffett's idols, or any of the other 1950s poets who self-consciously explored the idiom. For Buckley, life was a riff, and he honked on such topics as Jesus ("The Naz") and Shakespeare ("Willie the Shake") with gleeful abandon, a jazzy James Joyce of the strip clubs.

Author's collection

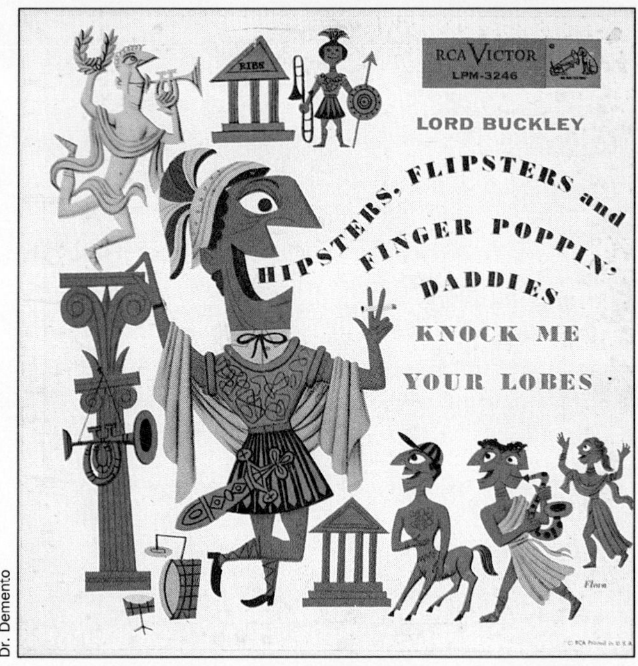

Dr. Demento

Ironically, the good times were already a dim memory for Buckley by the time we have record of his act, beginning with some monologues cut for the obscure Vaya label in 1950. He was then a worn vet who served as avuncular inspiration to Lenny Bruce, another strip circuit comic less inclined to poetry and more toward confrontation than Buckley, but who found the Lord's hipsterism (the onstage marijuana pipe) a gas.

Buckley thrived during the era of Prohibition, which inspired young Americans to overimbibe as protest and throw their Doors of Perception open to such lunacy as Buckley's. Had he taken better care of himself, Buckley might have become a Living Legend during the likewise flaunting great toke-a-thon of the late 1960s, but by then his liver (and the rest of him) had given out. Burlesque's great surrealist (he even looked like Salvador Dali) died at age fifty-four in 1960.

Buckley entered Buffett's consciousness during the era which should have cued the Lord's comeback, the smokin' sixties. "I been doing this particular song for about twelve years," Buffett told an Atlanta audience in 1978 when he performed Buckley's "God's Own Drunk" for his *You Had to Be There* album. "I learned it from two friends of mine down when I first went to New Orleans... I was about eighteen years old. Got down to Bourbon Street... It was written by the late, great Lord Richard Buckley, who I heard it off of a record one night at a friend named Bob Cook and Brent Webster's apartment. That song intrigued me to the point where I figured, 'Well, hell, this is really *great!*' Too many people have never heard Lord Buckley, who was an old humorist and king of the old jivers. So with much respect to Lord Richard Buckley, this is 'God's Own Drunk.'"

Buckley recorded "God's Own Drunk" at Los Angeles' Ivar Theater in 1959. Buffett first covered it in October 1973 for his *Living and Dying in 3/4 Time* album. Buffett's reworking of Buckley's piece bore a passing resemblance to the country genre of "comic drunk" recitations, of which Johnny Bond ("Ten Little Bottles") was master. In March of 1978, John Rockwell wrote in The *New York Times:* "Mr. Buffett emerged as a sort of folkie Southern boogier, and his cult still seems to regard 'God's Own Drunk' as his theme...." Buffett told Rockwell, a mite defensively, "People picked up on songs like 'God's Own Drunk,' which for me was almost like filler. I don't do that song anymore." Maybe in New York he didn't, but six months later he performed it con brio in Atlanta for his first "live" album.

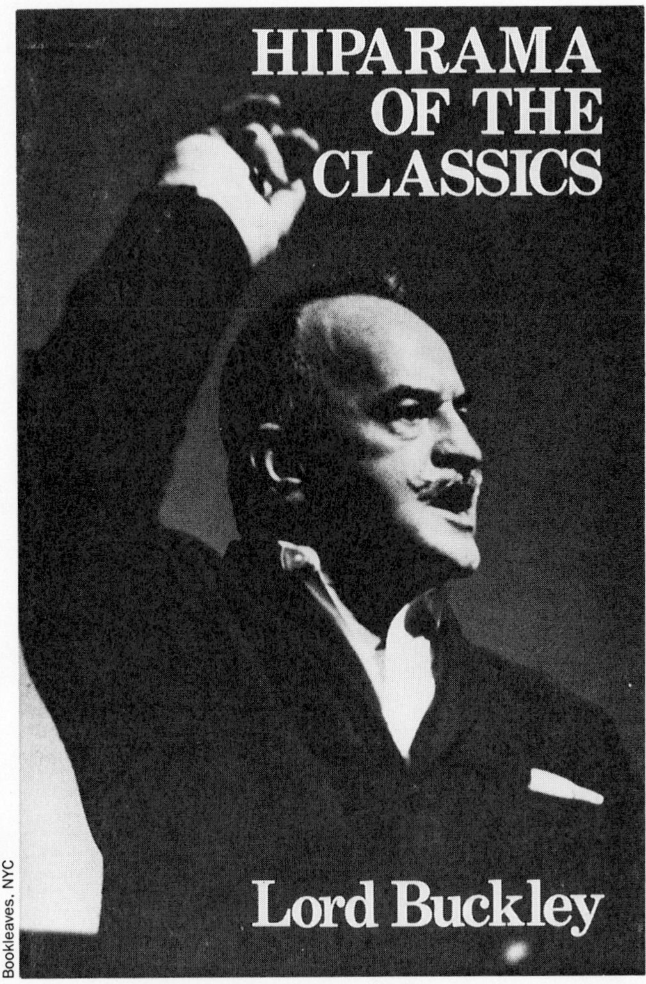

Bookleaves, NYC

BUFFETT SUED FOR USING LORD BUCKLEY'S MONOLOG was a headline in the August 31, 1983, issue of *Variety.* "According to the complaint," reported *Variety,* "Richard F. Buckley, Jr., alleges that, since August 30, 1981, Buffett has used the 1962 work as a featured selection without authorization. Further, he charges Buffett with 'willfully and maliciously mutilating and adulterating' the original version with at least eight instances of profanity or 'words and phrases of improper content and bad taste.' Plaintiff asks for $5,000,000 in actual damages and $6,000,000 in punitive and exemplary damages." There was no further mention in the trades of Richard F. Buckley, Jr.'s copyright infringement suit against Buffett. It's common practice for such matters to be settled out of court, often at a fraction of the amount sought in the suit.

Photo: Lawson Little

Photo: Lawson Little

Photo: Lawson Little

Windblown and chilled on a rare cold night in Key West, Buffett proved himself a trouper in a memorable Mallory Square performance, 1977.

Mangrove Opera. "It's set in the Everglades along Alligator Alley," said Buffett. "It's about these reprobates who run a reptile serpentarium and get involved in a cocaine smuggling operation." Buffett mentioned his screenplay in other interviews that year, though *Mangrove Opera* never made it to the big screen. But he was being increasingly frank in print about the role drugs played in his life and his music. The dope advocacy magazine *High Times* hailed Buffett as "the smuggler's favorite" and ran an extensive interview with him in December 1976. First, though, Buffett made sure interviewer Bob Anderson understood the ground rules: "A lot of journalists take a whole lot of fuckin' liberty," said Buffett. "That's why if you misquote me I'm going to kick your ass." As for drugs, he said, "I don't get stoned before shows. But afterwards, I get real high."

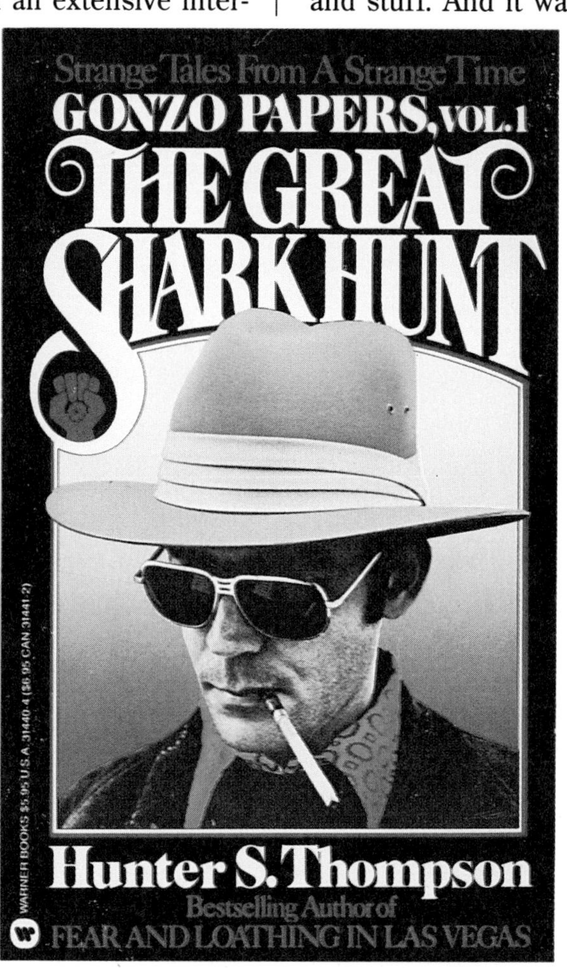

Strange Tales From A Strange Time
GONZO PAPERS, VOL. 1
THE GREAT SHARK HUNT
Hunter S. Thompson
Bestselling Author of
FEAR AND LOATHING IN LAS VEGAS

Phil Ahrens, Gotham Book Mart

Hunter Thompson perfected "Gonzo journalism" in the 1970s, displaying a dope-and-drink machismo Buffett admired. A Buffett crony in both Aspen and Key West, Thompson never let the business of writing interfere with an opportunity to party or live up to his over-the-top legend.

It was natural that Buffett would associate with people who were also famous and liked to "get real high." Many of them lived and played in Aspen, people with money from the movie and rock worlds. The writer Hunter Thompson had joined their ranks and become a celebrity from some good writing and much self-publicized substance abuse. He and Buffett became friends, and before Buffett bought a house in Aspen, he and Thompson swapped residences for awhile. "Jimmy had neglected to change the number on the phone," recalls Dink Bruce. "Hunter was in there for about a month, and ran up a $7,000 phone bill. And Jimmy's accountant paid it! There's no way in the world he'd ever get Hunter to pay back the $7,000. Hunter bought a boat, so Jimmy always claimed that the boat was half his."

"I had Hunter upstairs for a while," recalls Chris Robinson. "He was supposed to write a movie about scamming down here called *Cigarette Key.* I'd smoke that first joint with him about five in the afternoon. I learned you can't out-gonzo Hunter.... Jimmy got the JBL 100s [speakers] when they first came out. Louie's Backyard was next door, the *older* Louie's, it wasn't this Louie's as it is now. Hunter got mad at them, so he had this tape which was all these orgasms and whips and chains and stuff. And it was like prime dinner hour, 8, 8:30, and he cranked up Jimmy's stereo and there's all this UHHH! AHHHHH! OHHHHH! All these orgasms. Louie wasn't having a good time."

Buffett cultivated his party animal image on the road, though his idealist/entrepreneur side was drawn to Jimmy Carter, for whom Buffett played benefits in Oregon during the Bicentennial campaign year. He also found time to make a memorable appearance in Key West's Mallory Square. "It was one of those rare cold nights in Key West," recalls Vic Latham. "It was down to 45 degrees, and with the wind coming off that water, the wind chill must have been closer to 20. His hair was standing straight back from him. He stood there and did a two-and-a-half hour show, and did not walk off stage. He worked 'em as hard as I've ever seen him work. Under those totally adverse circumstances, he just worked like a trooper. He's got some of that Jolson, Garland thing in him where he needs the approval of and identification with the audience."

Buffett signed a new contract with ABC in 1976 and got a new producer in the bargain, Norbert Putnam. Noted as a session bass player,

Strider recores, NYC

Jimmy Buffett

JIMMY BUFFETT
Changes In Latitudes,
Changes In Attitudes

FROM THE HIT ALBUM
CHANGES IN LATITUDES
CHANGES IN ATTITUDES AB-990
featuring "MARGARITAVILLE"

Strider recores, NYC

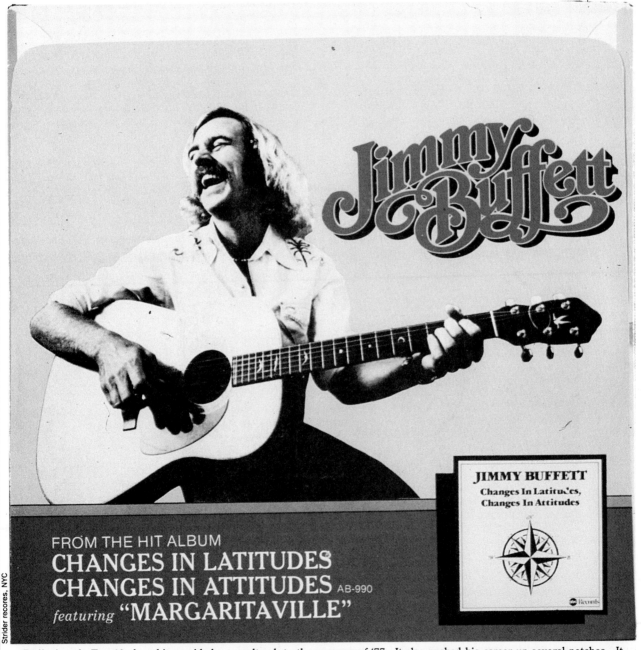

Buffett's only Top 10 chart hit provided a soundtrack to the summer of '77. It also pushed his career up several notches. It didn't hurt the sale of tequila either. Key West bartenders report margarita sales soared that summer and have only grown with the Buffett legend.

Cheeseburger in Paradise

Parrot Heads knew that Buffett was grappling with a sense of his own mortality when he confessed in *The Parrot Head Handbook* not that he was curtailing drink or drugs but that he was cutting down his cheeseburger intake: "I now treat a cheeseburger as a treat rather than a ration," he wrote. "Cheeseburger in Paradise" celebrated an all-American pleasure which is cheap and accessible to most everyone. Buffett wrote his song after one of his paradisiacal voyages turned sour as the boat icebox's ice melted, reducing Buffett and his crew to eating canned goods and peanut butter. The cheeseburger he found on the island of Tortola "tasted like manna from heaven," albeit burnt manna. And, as thanks, a song was born.

In 1959, Chuck Berry recorded "Back in the U.S.A." after an Australian tour where he suffered the dietary indignities of food boiled and mashed in fine British convict culture tradition. "I'm so glad I'm living in the U.S.A.," Berry sang when he returned Stateside, and one of the things that made him gladdest was his freedom to exercise his right to a good hamburger anytime he wanted one: "Lookin' hard for a drive-in, searching for a corner cafe, where hamburgers sizzle on an open grill night and day...."

Clearly the burger symbolizes post-World War II American consumer culture at its best. When Buffett recorded his song in 1977, the burger was under attack as being akin to cigarettes and driving without a seat belt: it was a potential health hazard. Buffett's song is a political statement: Cheeseburgers are one of his favorite pleasures of the flesh, and no amount of guilt about bludgeoned bovines or anxiety over carcinogens lurking in grilled flesh will curtail his indulgence. Squeamishness of that sort is un-American. The vegetarian is anemic, probably light in the loafers, and, at root, anti-American. Need proof? On a T-shirt with a plump and sensuous cheeseburger (seen in the display window of a shop selling jogging shoes) are these awful words: ANY NATION THAT WILL BUY THIS WILL SWALLOW ANYTHING. Altogether now: Boo! Hiss! Down in front!

Buffett also likes hot dogs, he tells us in *The*

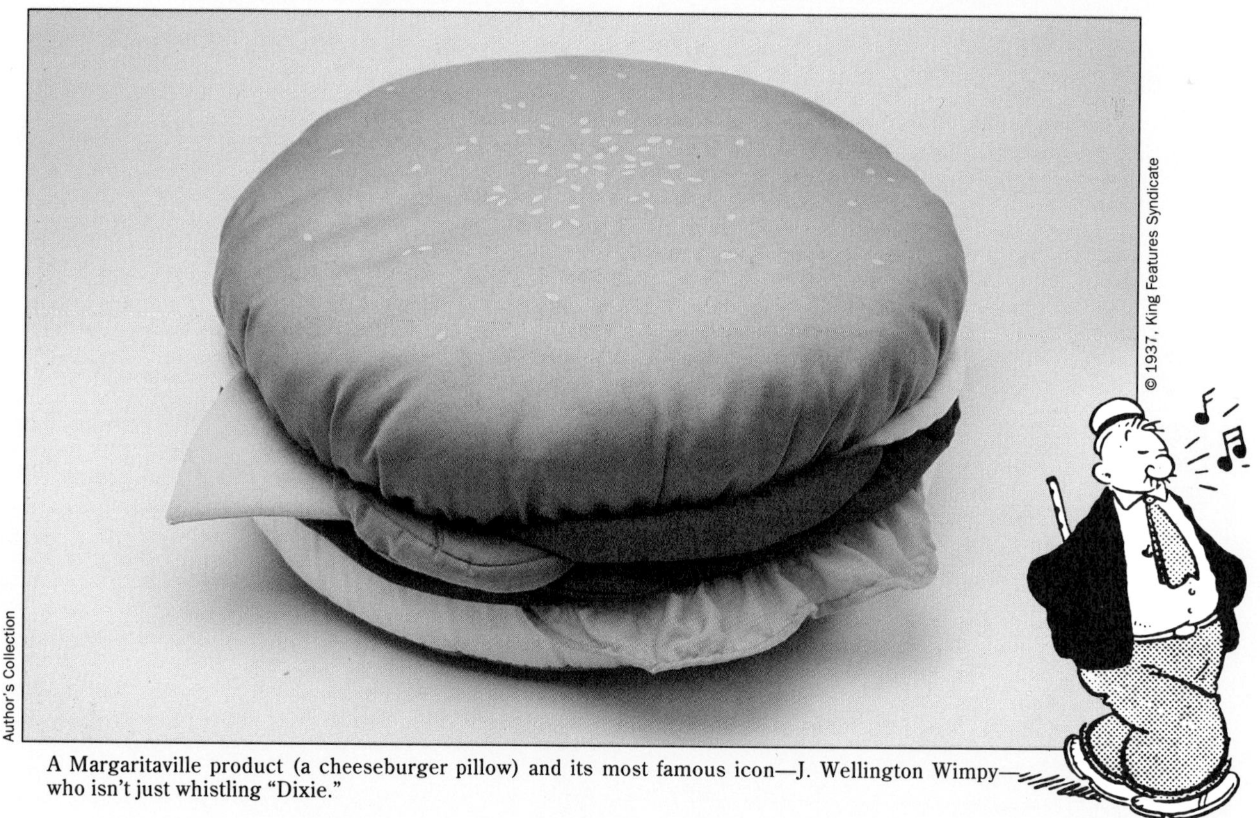

Author's Collection

© 1937, King Features Syndicate

A Margaritaville product (a cheeseburger pillow) and its most famous icon—J. Wellington Wimpy—who isn't just whistling "Dixie."

Parrot Head Handbook, especially the Demon Dogs in Chicago. He traces the evolution of his self-proclaimed "burger lust" from Mobile's Dew Drop Inn, now reputedly a yuppie lunch hot spot. From Mobile, he moves on in his burger tour guide to the Camellia Grill in New Orleans, and from there to Nashville and Rotier's. Like a nomadic beast driven by instinct to distant grazing lands, Buffett's life is tied to far-flung cheeseburgers: at Ruby's in the Bahamas or the Sky Way Drive in Akron or what he calls the Original Fat Burger in Hollywood. (The one Buffett mentions on La Cienega is actually the second in this Los Angeles area chain; the true original Fat Burger is at Western and Jefferson in a neighborhood blighted by the '92 riots. Sightings of pale pop stars chowing down there are rare. The one Buffett mentions may just be a burger stand, but it's a burger stand in the show biz "power lunch" district.)

Author's Collection

"There's an old burger joint on West Market Street in Akron," says Mark Faris, pop critic at the *Akron Beacon Journal.* "One of those little cruisin' drive-in places, the Sky Way Drive. They make all the stuff in there, and then they bring it out to the car. It's real popular with all the high school kids. Whenever he's in town, he always gets the cheeseburgers over there. He digs 'em big time. He orders a certain kind. As I under-

Author's Collection

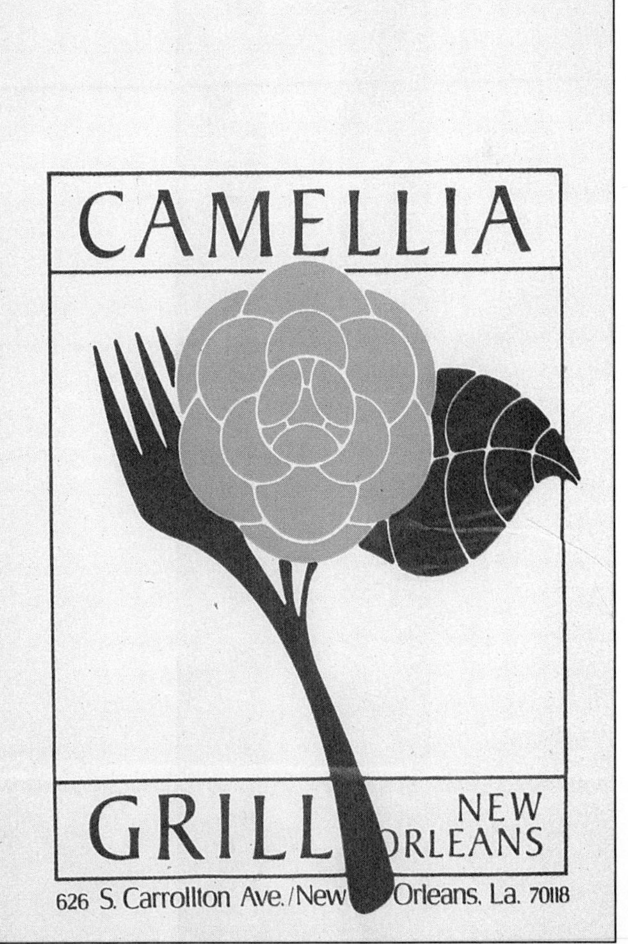

Author's Collection

stand it, he gets 'em for the whole crew."

Buffett is tremendously popular in Akron. "The people here understand rock music," says Faris. "It's good to develop a following here." Akron, you may recall, gave the world the sexy-tough Chrissie Hynde who formed the Pretenders in England, and the conceptual art disco band Devo were also Akronites. Devo's notion of "spud people" was deeply rooted in this midwestern rubber industry center. Before anyone heard of them, the Cramps briefly lived in Akron. It was a place, says Ivy Rorschach, that "made the crazy people even crazier."

But back to burgers. They have been with us many days and prepared in many ways. Stuart Berg Flexner offered a concise history in his wonderful *I Hear America Talking: An Illustrated History of American Words and Phrases* (Simon and Schuster, 1979): "*Hamburgers* have come a long way since the Tartars introduced eating shredded raw meat (we still call it *tartar steak*) into the Russian Baltic provinces. Germans picked up the dish from there and soon Hamburg, Germany, became famous for it, sometimes cooking it—and giving it its name. *Hamburg steak,* always cooked and served as a steak, appeared in the United States around 1884 and was soon called *hamburger steak,* then *hamburg* by 1903. Dr. J. H. Salisbury, himself a food faddist, helped popularize it and the term *Salisbury steak* at the turn of the century by recommending that it be eaten at least three times a day.

Author's Collection

Author's Collection

"By 1912 enough people were finally putting their hamburger steaks on a bun so that *hamburger* came to mean the sandwich. *Hamburger with the works* (with ketchup, mustard, and a slice of tomato, onion, and pickle) was first heard in the early 1930s, soon after hamburger began to overtake hot dogs as our most popular quick food. The meat shortage of World War II, and American postwar informality and backyard cookouts, increased the sandwich's popularity. The proliferation of names for hamburgers in the 1940s, depending on whim or public relations, was due to the explosion of the number of hamburger stands, advertising *beefburgers, wimpyburgers* (after the hamburger-loving J. Wellington Wimpy in the Popeye comic strip), *steerburgers,* and just plain *burgers* (cheeseburgers appeared in the mid-1930s). The term *hamburger stand* itself first became common in 1932, about four years after the White Castle and White Tower hamburger chains got started and some thirty years before most Americans had heard of *McDonald's,* the franchise chain with thousands of outlets and sales of billions of hamburgers, the hamburger mecca of today's children and a name heard over and over by America parents from children who wish to be dined there."

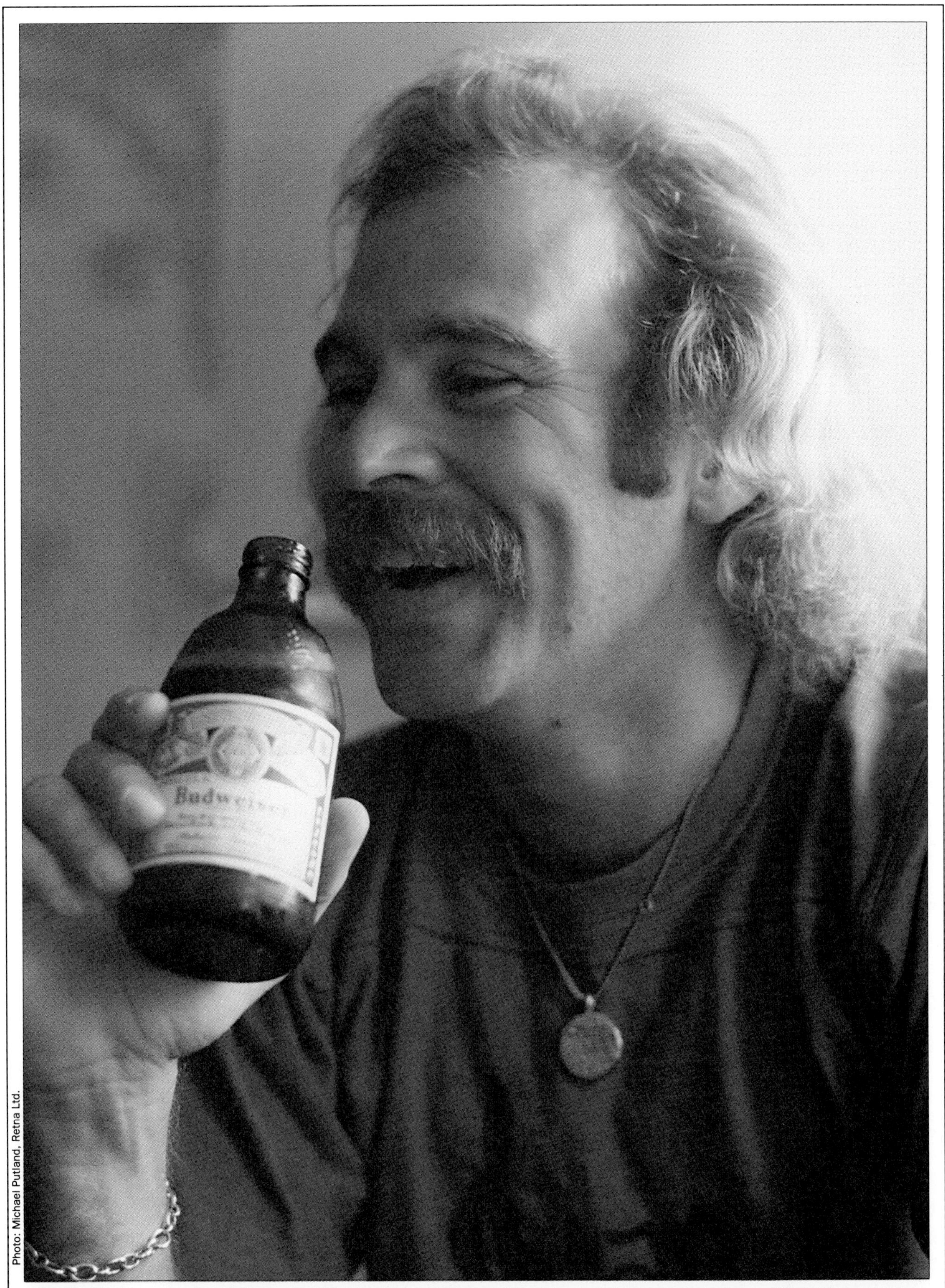

Photo: Michael Putland, Retna Ltd.

Buffett's 1970s style was laid back and irreverent without being confrontational. "I don't have any message," he said.

Putnam had also established a reputation as an "alternative Nashville" (read: not country) producer who had produced for the likes of Neil Young, the Flying Burrito Brothers, Joan Baez, and Dan Fogelberg. In November, Buffett was in studios in Nashville and Miami to record his fifth ABC album. *Changes in Latitudes, Changes in Attitudes* was released in February 1977.

Most critics applauded. Voice pop maven Robert Christgau called it "his most reflective album," and *Crawdaddy*'s Doug Wachholz predicted that it "should give Jimmy Buffett his day in the sun." England's *Melody Maker* raved, "There are no duff tracks. Positively therapeutic to play on a rainy day." Among the chorus of hurrahs, *Rolling Stone*'s Ira Mayer blew a raspberry: "The wry humor and carefully etched scenes that made Jimmy Buffett's *A White Sport Coat and a Pink Crustacean* so endearing have been slowly evaporating," wrote Mayer. "What remains three albums later are the occasional clever line and a lot of self-pitying drinking songs.... One can get away with one-liner songs if the picking and mood are right. Here, however, Norbert Putnam's overwrought production and arrangements milk each number of its potential charm.... A few loose country licks would have been more in order than the strings and flutes provided ...when it comes to this kind of laid-back (uptempo or down) drinking music, Jerry Jeff Walker'll play 'em all under the table any night."

The cheers outweighed the raspberries, however, and ABC decided to see if there wasn't a single worth promoting in the latest Buffett album. They picked a song he knocked off following a 1973 tour and then pocketed. "I wrote 'Margaritaville' in about five minutes at the end of a tour after having a margarita," Buffett told *Los Angeles Times* pop critic Robert Hilburn, "and it wasn't even a great margarita." After his Sport Coat promo tour, Buffett had returned to Key West to encounter "the first real influx of tourists that had come to the Keys." Nearly forty years after his prediction, Hemingway was finally right! "Everybody was shocked," Buffett told Hilburn, "the roads were packed. I was sort of sitting there in this great old bar called the Old Anchor Inn watching all this, and that's what drove me to

The Eagles, the 1970s California supergroup, brought diverse backgrounds in folk, rock, and even bluegrass to a sound which epitomized the mellow, hip lifestyle of the day. Buffett's tour with the land's then most popular band during the "Margaritaville" summer was a logistical coup.

write the song."

As with any success, timing was a factor in making Buffett's throwaway song a hit. "Margaritaville" entered *Billboard's* "Top 40" on May 7, 1977, where it would stay for a good fifteen weeks. The song peaked at number 8 on the chart, and was lapping at listeners' ears throughout the summer. If you were an American adult in May 1977, you may have been reading *The Hite Report* and probably had seen *Rocky,* the Spring "blockbuster" movie which would be eclipsed in the summer by *Star Wars.* You probably were among the 45 million Americans who watched former President Richard M. Nixon tell David Frost during an interview broadcast on May 4: "I brought myself down. I gave 'em a sword. And they stuck it in, and they twisted it with relish. And I guess if I'd been in their position, I'd have done the same thing."

Two days after "Margaritaville" first appeared on *Billboard's* "Top 40," Patty Hearst was sentenced to five years probation for her role in a Symbionese Liberation Army shootout which took place three years prior. Hearst, no less than Nixon, had become a curiosity left over from more passionate times. Americans were "wasting away," the young via drugs and everyone through our most pervasive narcotic, television. "Perhaps, as was often said, the country had been exhausted by the Vietnam War and the Watergate scandal," wrote James Reston in an overview of the national mood in 1977. "There was no sense of excitement, of urgency in the land...."

"It's not a debauched song," Buffett told Associated Press reporter Mary Campbell. "It's just a very light song about a person hanging out on the beach, not caring to do anything. The last verse goes, 'I blew out my flip-flop, stepped on a pop top, cut my heel, had to cruise on back home.' If you ever wore thong sandals and had somebody step on the heel, you know what it means to blow out your flip-flop."

Thanks to radio exposure of "Margaritaville," a million manana-minded record buyers made *Changes in Latitudes, Changes in Attitudes* "go platinum." Strangely, the single of "Changes ..." did better on the country charts (it made it to number 24 in October), than on the pop charts, where it only struggled up to number 37. Changes were plentiful for Buffett that summer: he opened shows for the Eagles, probably the most popular band in America then, and their powerful manager, Irving Azoff, took Buffett on as a client. Buffett visited the White House and had his picture taken with Carter and Mondale, but was especially jazzed to meet Admiral Rickover, "because he reminded me a lot of my grandfather." He played "Save the Whales" benefits. And on August 27, 1977, Buffett wed Jane Slagsvol in Aspen.

According to one source, it was Jane who had been altar shy: "I remember Jane saying before they were married, 'I'm only going to give him another year to become successful.'" A platinum record was a pretty convincing badge of success. Their wedding invitation read: "We are having a party on the 27th of August. It will begin at five in the afternoon and last until it is over. In addition to the usual eating, drinking, dancing and carrying on, we intend sometime during the evening to be married. Please come."

"The wedding was at Red Stone Mansion outside Aspen," recalls Chris Robinson. "They came up in a little carriage, and the Eagles played there. Those girls were awfully chilly that night when the sun went behind Red Mountain and they were in their little strapless gowns! It was fifty degrees. There was a bachelor party. Hunter was handing out acid to everyone. We were drinking magnums of Dom. I had a wonderful time. At the bachelor party, there was a girl, naked, covered up with food, and we were eating off her. I've forgotten what kind of food it was."

After the wedding, Buffett took his bride on an extensive Caribbean cruise on his new fifty-foot ketch, the *Euphoria II,* but not before dispensing with the annual business of making next year's album. In November, Norbert Putnam was again producer on sessions in both Nashville and Coconut Grove, Florida. The songs, Buffett told *New York Times* writer John Rockwell, were written the previous summer "entirely on his boat." His sixth ABC album in the can, Buffett could sail off on his honeymoon, perhaps taking his friend Tom Corcoran's profile of him for the December issue of *Crawdaddy* along to read. It concerned the romance of dope smuggling more than Buffett, and offered a fascinating glimpse of a still-active Phil Clark:

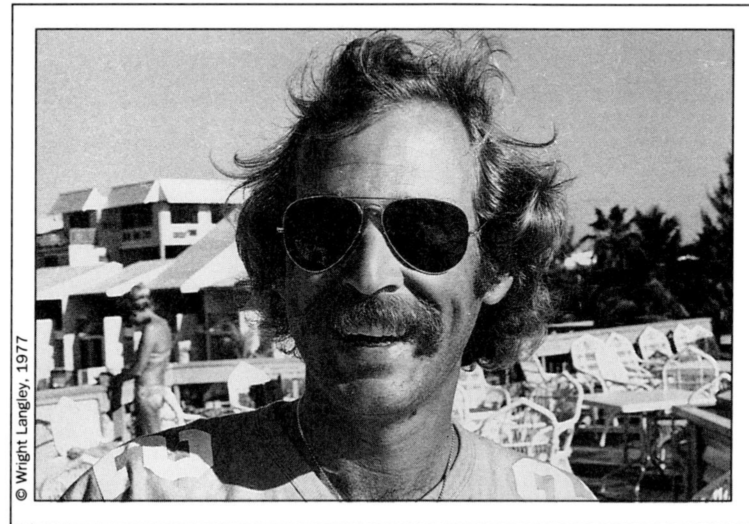
© Wright Langley, 1977

"The pirate who was turning forty when Buffett wrote the song is shrimping out of Tarpon Springs, Florida, right now, making good money and even saving some of it. And he's balling a parade of earthy nineteen-year-olds who became enthralled by his false Bahamian accent and the piece of treasure or fossilized shark's tooth, or brass turtle or whatever hangs around his neck on a chain this week. The pirate trolls with his ornaments. But since the bust at Immokalee Airport when a pilot turned out to be FBI, he has stayed out of the game for fear of something worse than twelve months' probation.

"He's too old for jail these days, yet every time Phil hears 'A Pirate Looks at Forty' on the jukebox, usually in a bar near the docks, he gazes off across the ocean, straining to see the sirens who call him to some untold scam. He yearns like an old soldier for the action and the fraternity ... he wants a salty caper beyond the sunset, where a gun in your boot and knowledge of navigation are your best insurance.

"Now Phil has eased back, another sentimental smuggler with enough stories to tell for a lifetime. But the stories don't get told often."

Son of a Son of a Sailor was released in March 1978, and shipped gold (500,000 copies). *Rolling Stone* liked this one: reviewer Frank Rose called it "one of those rare records that seek to capture the boisterous fellowship of the endless

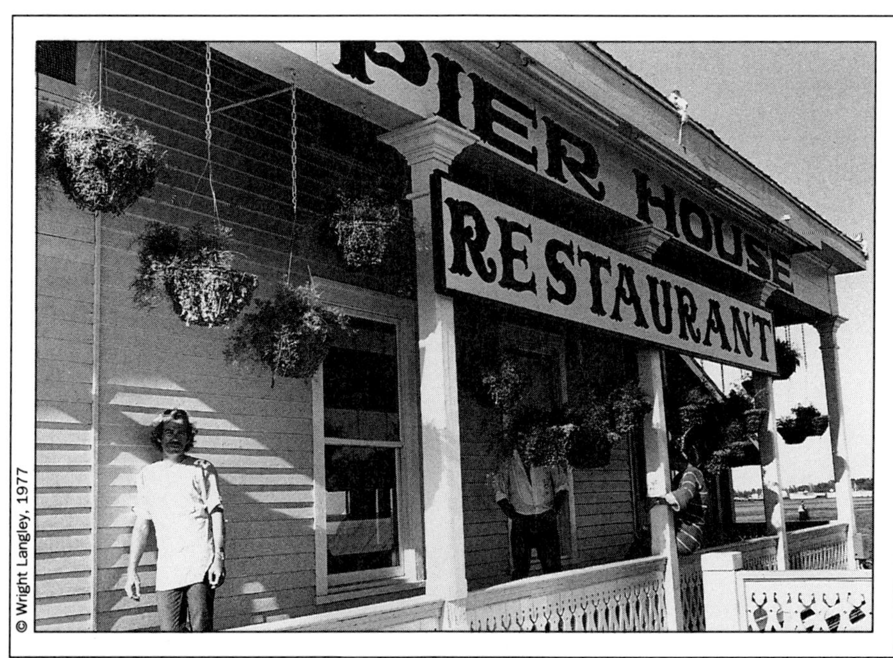

© Wright Langley, 1977

Buffett the star revisits one of his old haunts, Key West's Pier House, in November 1977.

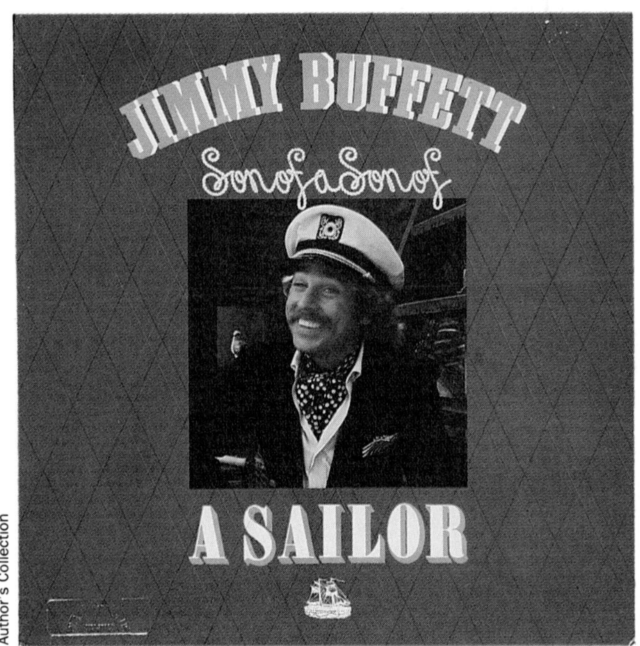

Author's Collection

party and the tingling brace of the sea." Buffett, wrote Rose, had "become the popular spokesman for an entire mellow way of life. His is the lassitudinous appeal of the vagabond on the loose in a sun-splashed, watery playland." Followers of Buffett's sun-splashed lifestyle could watch him perform "Margaritaville" at a fictional "Save the Whales" benefit in the movie *FM* that Spring, or tune-in whatever FM station might be playing the first single from *Son of a Son of a Sailor,* "Cheeseburger in Paradise." Improbably enough, country star Janie Frickie was one of the background singers on Buffett's hymn to beef and dairy products, which peaked at number 32 on the charts in time for his summer tour.

Buffett was gimped up that summer by a leg cast, souvenir of a May Palm Beach softball game. But the show went on, and he joked about the cast onstage, even changing song lyrics to point out that tour's comic foil. In August, recordings were made at concerts in Atlanta and Miami for a double "live" album, *You Had to Be There,* which appeared in November. As much as anything, the album documented a band committed to debauch. "We were one of the craziest bands on the road for awhile," "Fingers" Taylor would recall years later. "During the seventies with the band, it was a big party—it was a constant thing, but we held it together. We were young, we could rally—get drunk one night and wake up the next day and still fell alright." Buffett made several references to cocaine in the '78 concert recordings, a substance on which he perhaps leaned harder than usual with a broken leg to nurse. On *Havana Daydreamin',* a song co-written with Jane, "Kick It in Second Wind," equated "hope" with "coke." Thomas McGuane had by then married Buffett's sister, Laurie, and in his 1978 novel, *Panama,* a coked-up rock has-been returns to Key West to court "the beautiful South Carolina wild child" on which he is obsessively fixated. Purely fiction.

Buffett became a father in 1979 with the birth of Savannah Jane. He took time off both to adjust to his new role and to write songs for his next album. He needed atmosphere, so he sailed *Euphoria II* down to Montserrat: "I came down here to just sit on the boat and get into a schedule and write every day," Buffett told *Rolling Stone's* Chet Flippo. It was an opportunity to indulge his Caribbean fantasy to the hilt, including working with local musicians. "It's a misconception that all Caribbean music is reggae," Buffett told Flippo. "Most of the down-island stuff is more calypso, happy, good-time music. This band [the Woop-Wap Band] ... had a guy who played a long blowpipe and a banjo-uke player. The next day, I had about four working titles for the album, but none of them really grabbed me, and I was wondering, 'What the fuck can I call this record?' Then I looked out the window at the volcano [Montserrat has an active volcano] and I went *ding!* I'm gonna call the album *Volcano.* So I said, 'Now we got to

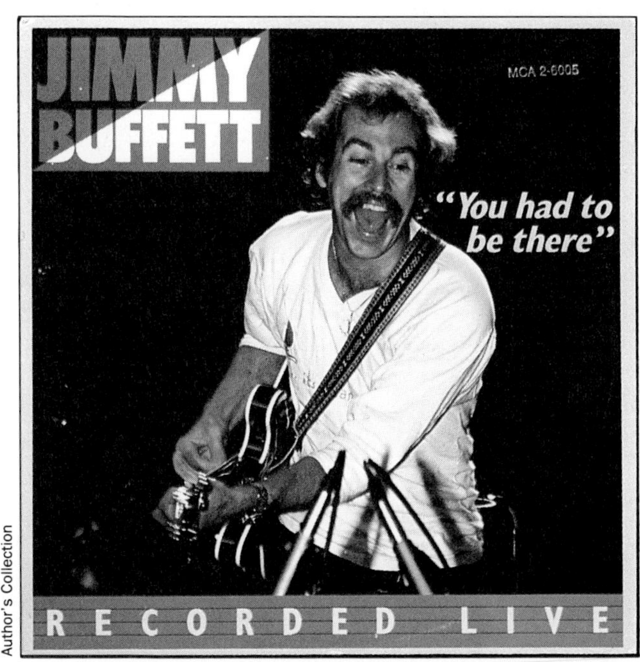

Author's Collection

write a song called "Volcano."' I went to the studio and Keith [Sykes] was fooling around, playing a little Caribbean shuffle, that little da da da ... So we wrote it and I said, 'Well, hell, let's go get the guys from the bar, we need the woop-wap sound to make it authentic.'... So we got the woop-wap band to come in and play and it was perfect. It just felt so godamned natural."

In his *Parrot Head Handbook,* Buffett recalls the writing and recording excursion to Montserrat as "one of the wildest times I've ever had in my career...." Flippo's October '79 *Rolling Stone* profile depicts a parade of stoned young women eager to bed Buffett (he discreetly didn't report any successes), including one who offered this striking opening line: "You know, Jimmy, you really oughta drink a lotta pineapple juice. It'll make your come taste *sweet!*"

Back in the States, Buffett began touring in August and promoted *Volcano,* which was released in September. "The material on Volcano is a lot stronger than the last few albums," Buffett told *Miami Herald* writer Bill Ashton. "If I can still enjoy it, after living with it for all those months, it's gotta have a lasting quality." Buffett was pumped up over *Volcano's* first single, "Fins." "'Fins' is my strongest thing since 'Margaritaville,'" he told Ashton. "'Cheeseburger' did okay, but nothing like what's happening with 'Fins.'" Actually, "Fins" flopped at number 35 on *Billboard's* pop chart, three positions lower than "Cheeseburger's" peak. "'Volcano' will be the next single," Buffett continued. "We sent tapes of the album out to [radio station] program directors before its release. The feeling was that 'Volcano' was a natural hit and that we might have to work 'Fins.' We felt if we could bring 'Fins' in, it would be easy to follow with 'Volcano.'"

Easier said than done. "Volcano" spluttered no higher than number 66 on *Billboard's* pop chart as 1979 was ending. *Rolling Stone's* Don Shewey wrote: "Buffett's album, unlike the volcano on Montserrat where it was recorded, is never in danger of erupting, and more's the pity." Shewey, however, liked "Chanson Pour Les Petits Enfants," writing "That Buffett manages to tap a child's sense of wonder and goodness without going smug, sentimental or religious might be the best thing about him."

"When his kid was born," recalls Chris Robinson, "he did his little lullabies. You can watch his life change through his music." Both Buffett and Robinson vacated the premises at 704 Waddell Street in 1979. The decade ended with Buffett making his most ambitious album, one that didn't live up to his commercial expectations. Buffett celebrated his thirty-third birthday that Christmas, little realizing that the majority of the songs for which he would be known were already written and recorded. No matter. He had business to tend to, a cult to cultivate. "We're just an old road-dog band," he said in 1978. "It's like anything else, when you put a lot of time in—I'm a veteran."

Author's Collection

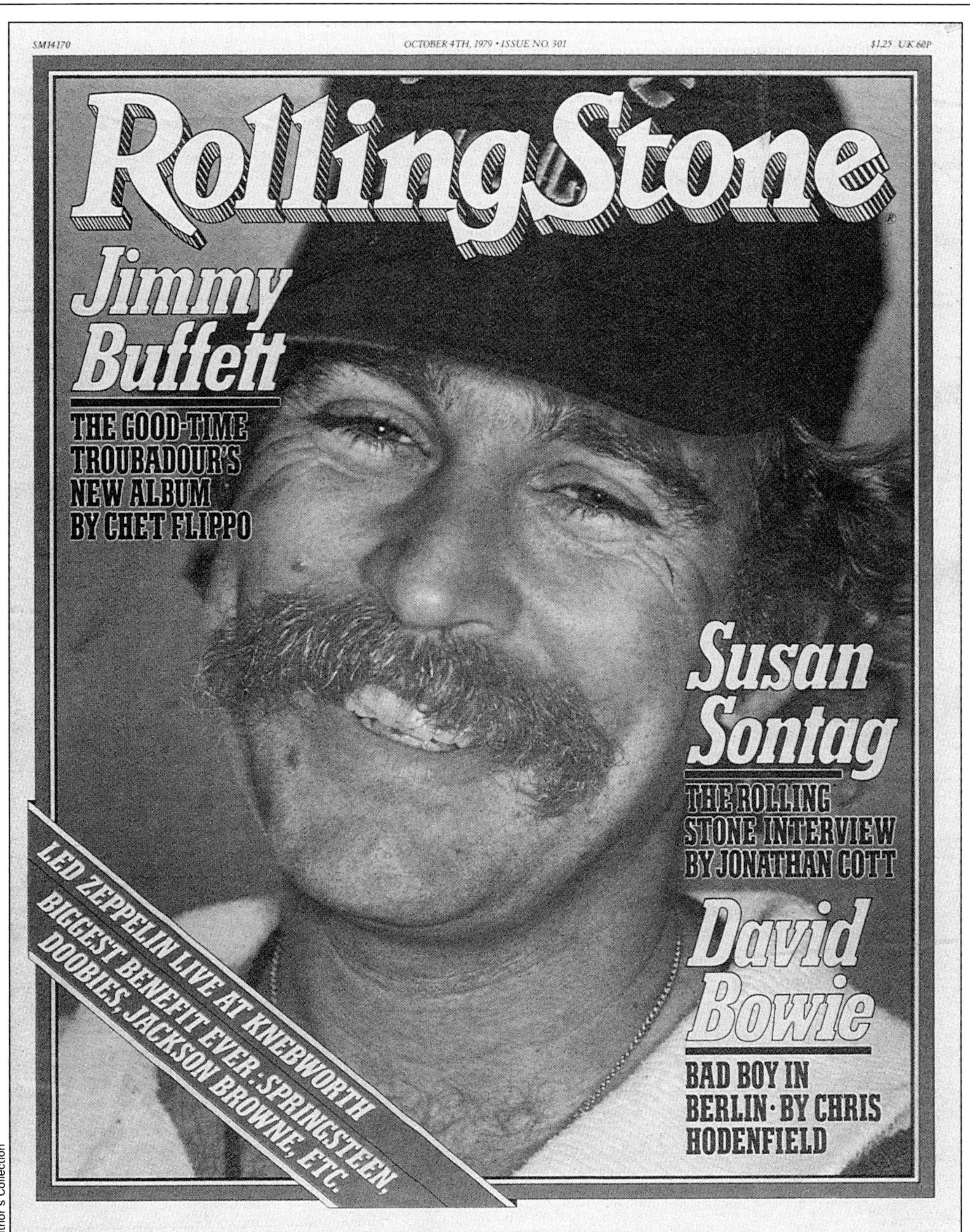

SM14170
OCTOBER 4TH, 1979 • ISSUE NO. 301
$1.25 UK 60P
RollingStone
Jimmy Buffett
THE GOOD-TIME TROUBADOUR'S NEW ALBUM BY CHET FLIPPO
Susan Sontag
THE ROLLING STONE INTERVIEW BY JONATHAN COTT
David Bowie
BAD BOY IN BERLIN · BY CHRIS HODENFIELD
LED ZEPPELIN LIVE AT KNEBWORTH
BIGGEST BENEFIT EVER: SPRINGSTEEN, DOOBIES, JACKSON BROWNE, ETC.
Author's Collection

Buffett was running in fast company (Susan Sontag and David Bowie) in *Rolling Stone,* October 4, 1979. Chet Flippo's "you-are-there-with-the-rock-star" cover story chronicled the recording of *Volcano* (along with a fair amount of drinking and toking). Don Shewey's review later panned it, and he wasn't alone. Buffett's most ambitious album wasn't the commercial smash either the artist or his manager, Irving Azoff, predicted. *Volcano* signaled the start of a long doldrum in Buffett's recorded voyages.

Buffett's Caribbean Soul

CALYPSO KING TO REIGN HERE, blared a 1985 Chicago Sun-Times headline announcing an upcoming Jimmy Buffett concert. A 1988 *Southern Magazine* cover feature on Buffett offered this insight from author Pat Jordan: "Jimmy would do for black Caribbean music what Elvis Presley did for black rhythm and blues: He'd make it white and respectable." The headline and the comparison to Elvis exaggerate Buffett's use of Caribbean elements in his music: he's skimmed the top for atmosphere rather than engaged in a deeper dialogue with Caribbean culture. But coming as he did from the era of backyard Limbo parties, that was only natural. Atmosphere, be it Tiki torches or straw hats, was as deep as most Americans cared to go with "exotica." As with much else in Buffett's music, his Caribbean spices are a postcard from his childhood in the fifties.

"I guess this is a Harry Belafonte inspiration," Buffett drawled to Whoopi Goldberg before playing a song on her talk show. "He was one of the big inspirations on me, his calypso shirts tied above his navel. In Mobile, Alabama, that was very risque." Belafonte, no less than Elvis, was a sensation in 1956, singing "Day-o" and scintillating "exotica" fantasies for white women in a rigidly segregated America. Belafonte's Calypso album soared to number one on *Billboard*'s pop album charts for thirty-one weeks. In fact, Calypso ranks just below the South Pacific soundtrack as the fourth most popular album of the LP era.

The New York-born Belafonte was essentially a singer-actor playing a role as calypso singer. The real stuff came from Trinidad, and had been popularized in America by Wilmoth Houdini, who first recorded in New York in 1927. (Nearly a quarter of black Harlem's residents at the time were of West Indian descent.) Calypso's roots integrated African, Hispanic, French, and British elements, and it was already a flourishing art in the nineteenth century. "The calypso was without a doubt fairly well known locally under its present name, or a version of it, in 1859," wrote John Storm Roberts in *Black Music of Two Worlds* (Original Music, Tivoli, New York, 1972). "That was the year a luckless U.S. ornithologist, William Moore, was unwise enough to claim that calypso was nothing but variations on British ballads. Moore immediately experienced a full-blooded Africanism—the use of song for public and embarrassing rebuke—when a singer named Surisima, or Sirisima, the Carib turned up outside his hotel with a large, vociferous crowd and sere-

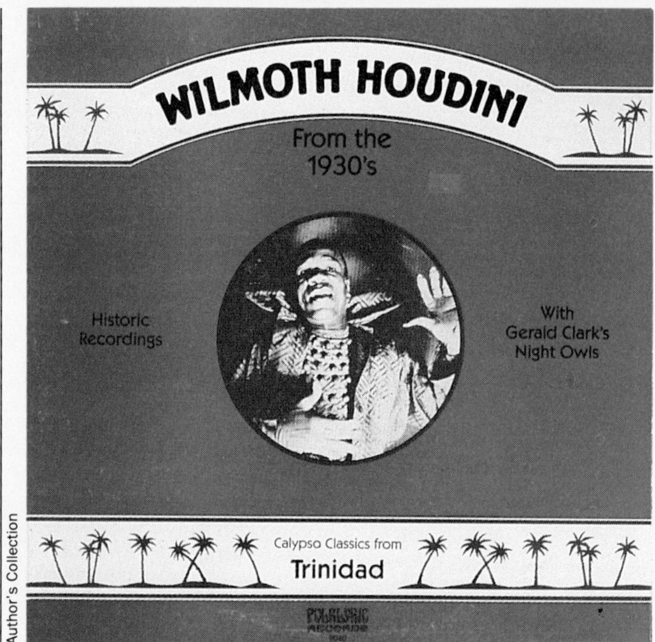

Author's Collection

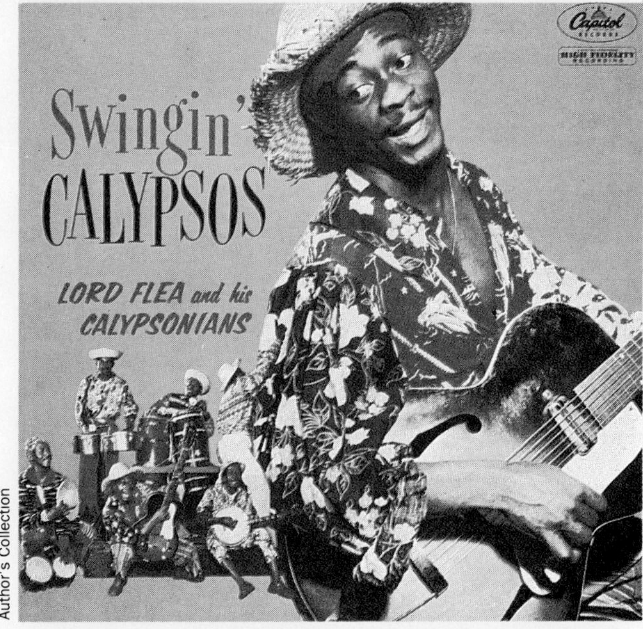

Author's Collection

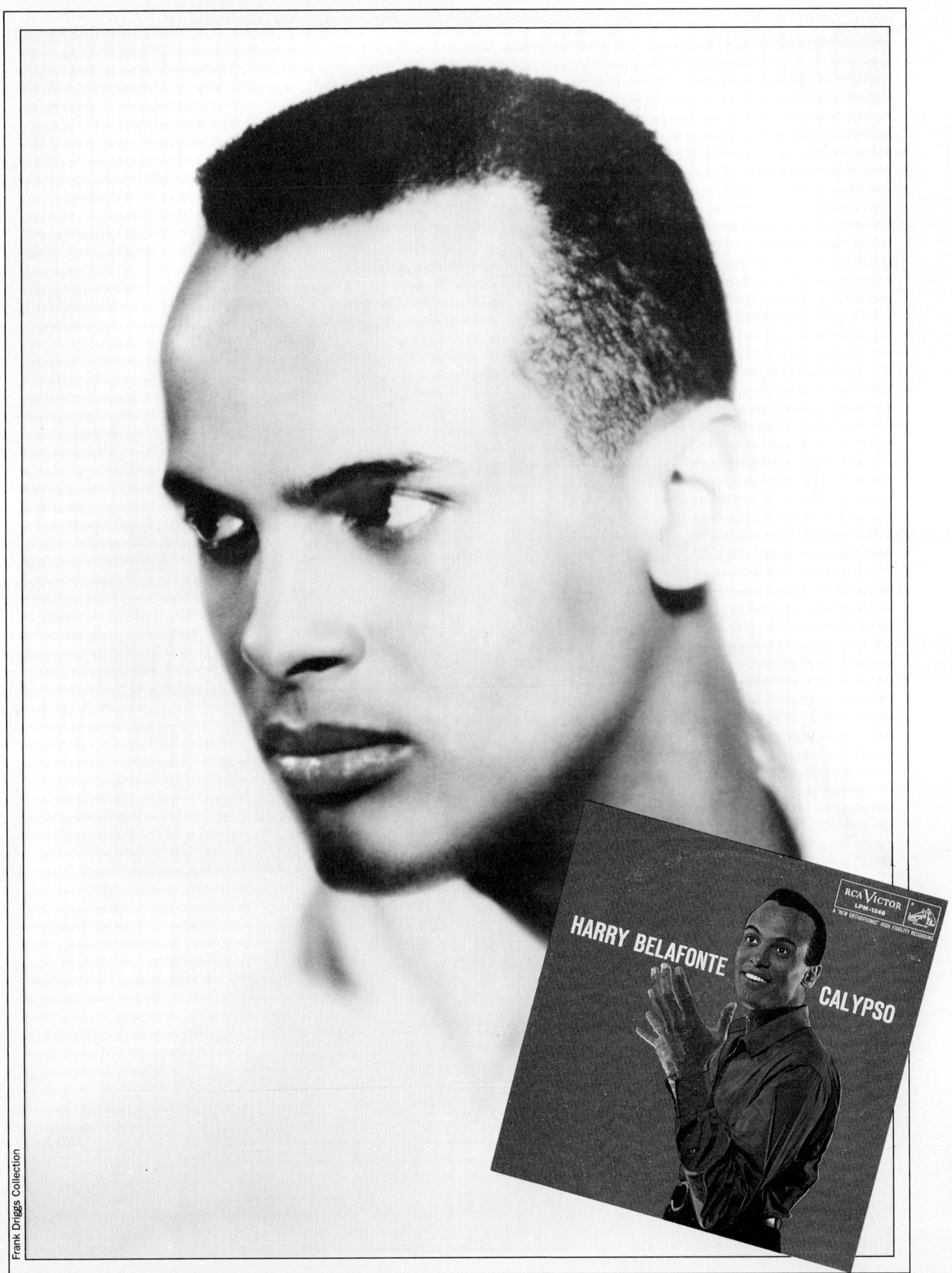

Frank Driggs Collection

naded him in call-and-response fashion, the spectators in African style providing the responses:

> Surisima: Moore, you monkey from America,
> Crowd: Tell me what you know about we cariso!

"Another Africanism, the dynamic use of repetition, also came into play, and a lengthy good time was had by all but one until the police finally broke up the party."

Calypsos were associated with carnival, and calypso singers were flamboyant men with names to match: Atilla the Hun, Lord Invader, the Executor, the Growler. Like the "dissing" of rival rap artists today, calypso singers would square off in "wars": "The man who gives out the biggest insults is the winner," Wilmoth Houdini explained to Joseph Mitchell for a 1939 New Yorker profile. "I was so insulting in my first 'war' the other men congratulated me. Since then I maintain my prestige and integrity as Houdini the Calypsonian. I got a brain that ticks like a clock. I can sing at any moment on any matter."

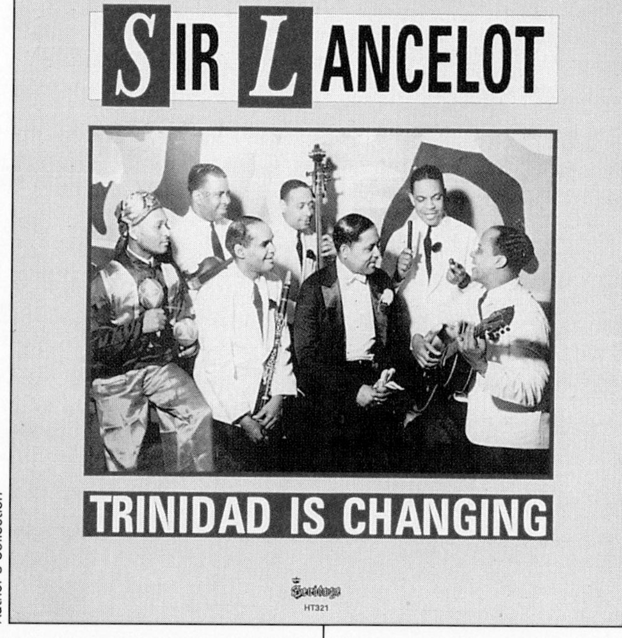

Author's Collection

Sex was a matter on which calypso singers often sang, but songs with political bite were also common. Topics like black pride, Marcus Garvey, the Depression, and oilfield strikes in Trinidad appear in calypso recordings of the 1930s. As recently as the early 1980s, political calypsos played a role in the revolution in Grenada which the Reagan administration squashed.

Calypso blended music and cultural motifs from Africa and Europe at birth, and experienced further synthesis as many of its performers moved to America. Sir Lancelot couldn't find any Trinidadians to accompany him in Los Angeles, so the recordings he made there in the early 1950s featured Cuban trumpeter Chino Ortiz's band, resulting in spicy Cuban-tinged Calypsos. Lancelot supplied songs to such Hollywood epics as *Tarzan and the Mermaids* (1947) and, in a non-musical role, portrayed the boat-hand Horatio in 1944's *To Have and Have Not.*

Along with Calypso, Buffett has assimilated another sound of Trinidad's carnival, steel drums. Robert Greenidge has played steel drums on record and on tour with Buffett for years. The instruments are recycled oil drums which echo ancient African xylophones. They evolved as a replacement for the "tamboo bamboo" seen in carnival parades until the dual use of these long bamboo sticks as both percussion and weapons caused them to be banned.

Steel drums began appearing in carnival parades in the 1930s, and today sophisticated bands compete in festivals and for tourist dollars. "There are five steps," says the *Grove Dictionary of Musical Instruments,* "in making a (steel drum) pan: sinking (pounding the head into a concave shape), grooving (marking the position of each note with a steel punch), burning (tempering the metal), cutting the drum-barrel to the required length, and tuning (making the final adjustment for each pitch with a small hammer). The note layout is not consecutive; each unit gives off to some degree the pitch of its neighbors, and therefore contiguous units are tuned, when possible, to octaves, fifths and fourths. Pan sticks are rubber-headed. Pans can be slung from the player's neck, mounted on racks or wheels for carnival, or on stands for stationary concert performances."

Steel drum bands were among the pre-concert entertainment at Buffett's "Primo Parrot Head Party" in New Orleans during his 1993 Chameleon Caravan Tour. Even so, Buffett's status as "Calypso King" is a mite exaggerated. Don't expect to read he's won any "wars" down in Trinidad.

CHAPTER SEVEN

COCONUT TELEGRAPH

I'm one of the few living legends left.
—Jimmy Buffett, 1987

Basically, Jimmy's saying, "Be who you are, like who you are, and just have fun." That's why he's more than just a musician. He's one of the great philosophers of our time.
—Parrot Head at 1987 Miami concert

Nineteen eighty—Buffett and the world had a brand-new decade to reckon with. It turned into an era that was "full tilt" in a very different way from the seventies, with the investment banker replacing the rock star/dope smuggler as its glamour idol. The eighties were an era of greed — feeding frenzies — in which a few Americans made a killing and many others (figuratively at least) got killed. Buffett would end this decade a very wealthy man, because as it wore on from one Republican administration to the next, Americans needed a *Fantasy Island,* a "Margaritaville," more than ever. Buffett, to quote an entrepreneurial axiom, found a need and filled it. By the end of the eighties, the old Key West "boogie" had taken on mythic/Edenic overtones. But as the decade dawned, Buffett was scrambling to keep his *Volcano* ignited: the album he felt sure would reach number 1 had peaked at 14 on the charts.

The touring and promoting begun late in summer 1979 started its second leg in early 1980. Buffett played a benefit for the victims of Hurricane Frederic before 8,200 homefolks at the Mobile Municipal Auditorium on March 4. "Benefits I've done in the past have been a real pain in the ass," Buffett groused to *Mobile Press* entertainment editor Tom Mason, who noted a "strong raggae [*sic*] influence" in the song "Volcano." "I can write a Buffett song better than anybody," boasted the singer/songwriter, who complained of recent imitators. He accused multi-tattooed "outlaw" singer/songwriter David Allan Coe of stealing a Buffett tune for a song called "Divers Do It Deeper." "I would have sued him,"

Author's Collection

Author's Collection

Harris Lewine Collection

Harris Lewine Collection

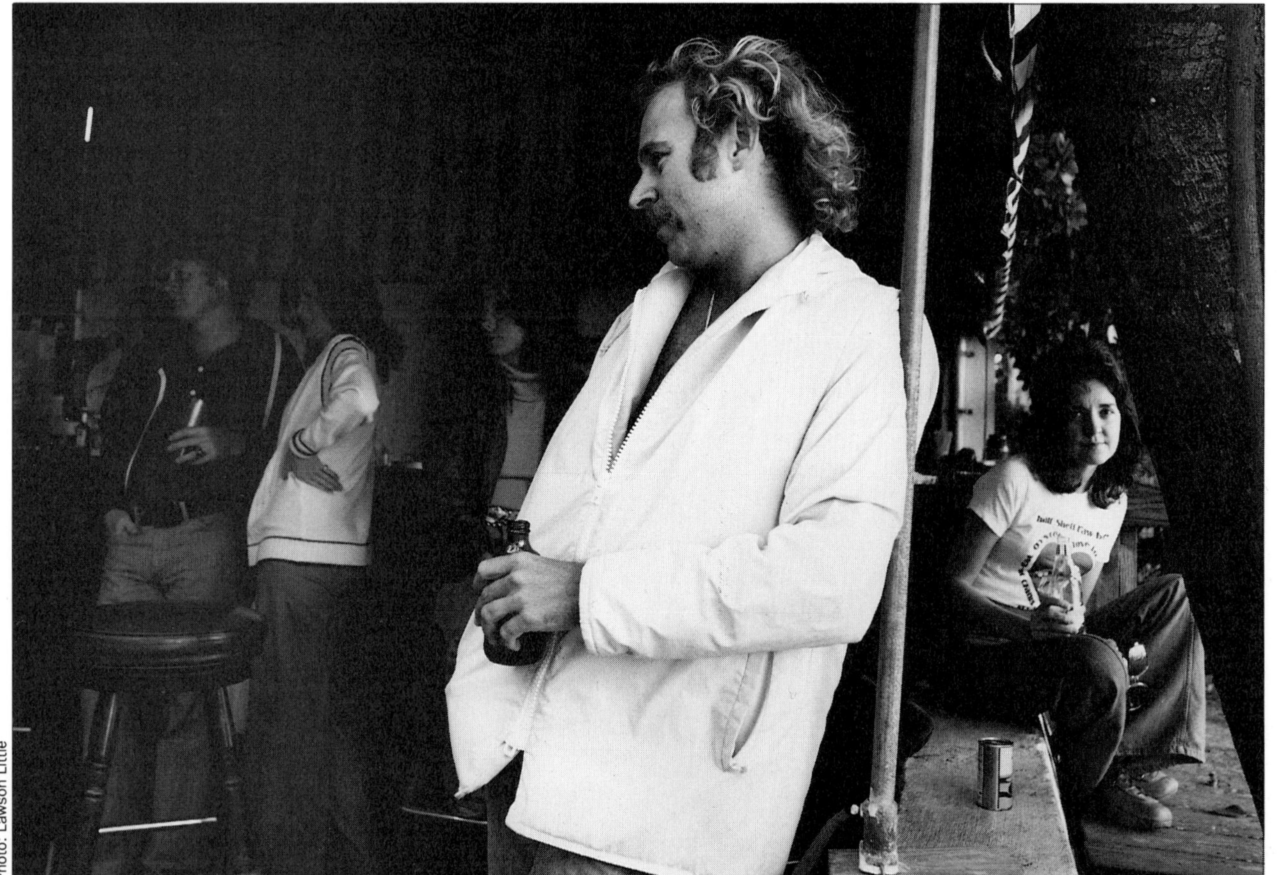

Photo: Lawson Little

After "Margaritaville," the raffish image of the mid-1970s (opposite) was replaced by an eternally blissed-out countenance. "This," Buffett seemed to tell us, "is living!" Still, he contemplated mortality (John Wayne's) and nostalgia on the 1981 album *Coconut Telegraph.*

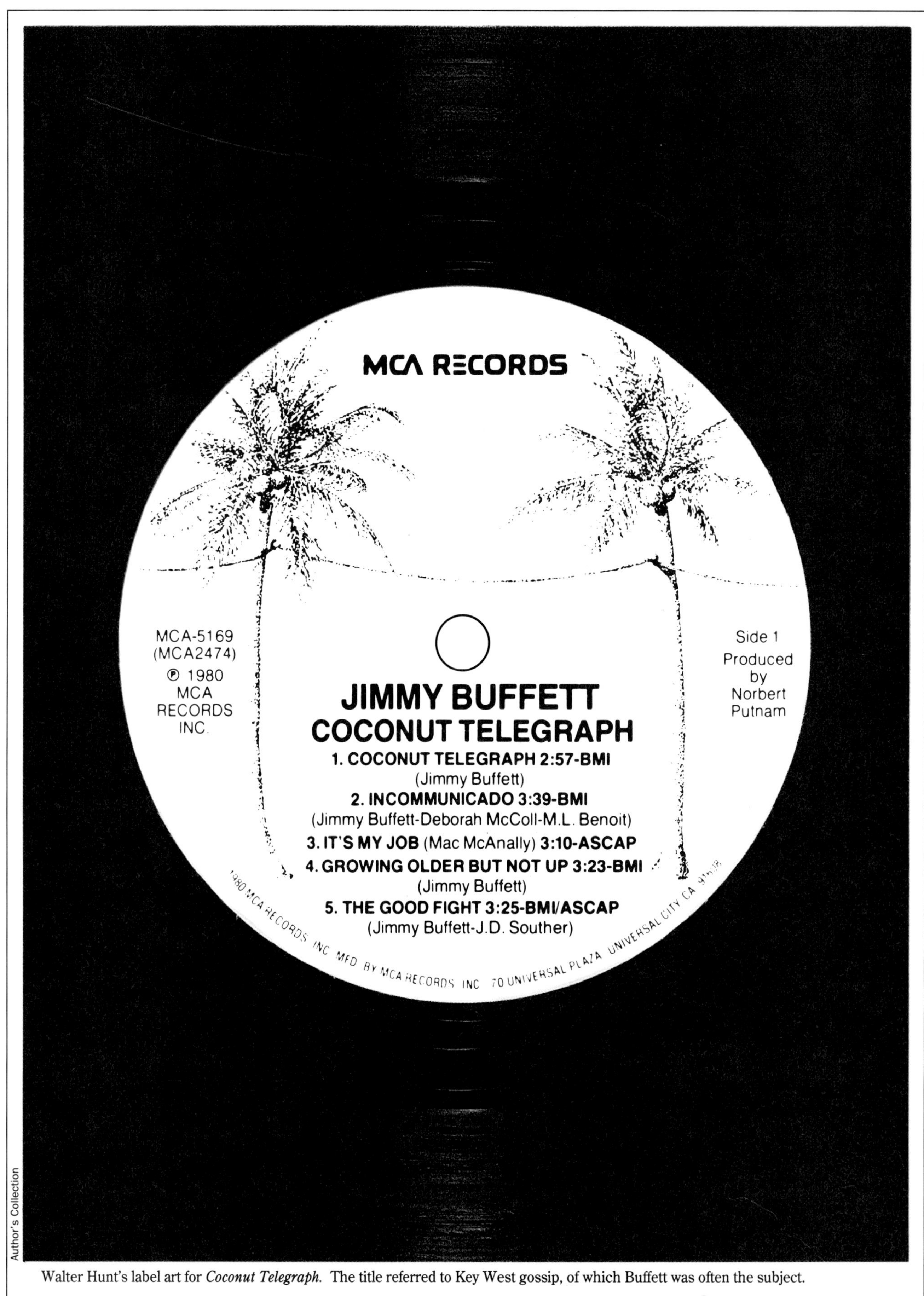

MCA RECORDS
MCA-5169
(MCA2474)
℗ 1980
MCA
RECORDS
INC.
Side 1
Produced
by
Norbert
Putnam
JIMMY BUFFETT
COCONUT TELEGRAPH
1. COCONUT TELEGRAPH 2:57-BMI
(Jimmy Buffett)
2. INCOMMUNICADO 3:39-BMI
(Jimmy Buffett-Deborah McColl-M.L. Benoit)
3. IT'S MY JOB (Mac McAnally) 3:10-ASCAP
4. GROWING OLDER BUT NOT UP 3:23-BMI
(Jimmy Buffett)
5. THE GOOD FIGHT 3:25-BMI/ASCAP
(Jimmy Buffett-J.D. Souther)
1980 MCA RECORDS INC MFD BY MCA RECORDS INC 70 UNIVERSAL PLAZA UNIVERSAL CITY CA
Author's Collection

Walter Hunt's label art for *Coconut Telegraph.* The title referred to Key West gossip, of which Buffett was often the subject.

said Buffett, "but I didn't want to give Coe the pleasure of having his name in the paper." And the benefit concert? "Buffett's music, always laced with images of getting high and sailing on some artificial euphoria, was ideal for the rock concert crowd," Mason wrote. Buffett dedicated "Son of a Son of a Sailor" to his dad, who was in the audience that night.

The tour plowed northward into bad weather and mishaps. "We got snowed in last week at the Naval Academy in Annapolis," Buffett told New York *Daily News* reporter Mark Liff two weeks after the Mobile benefit. "And in Washington, Fingers Taylor, my harpist, broke his collarbone. He just walked out of the hotel and slipped on the ice. He was stone-cold sober." The tour's road manager "started passing kidney stones on the bus and we had to take him to the hospital." Buffett's Palladium appearance was his first in New York in nearly two years. (He promised "no new wave, all old wave.") *Village Voice* reviewer Geoffrey Stokes damned it with faint praise: "Neither a passionate nor hardrocking performer, Buffett is almost totally dependent on verbal felicity and wit to cut the sentimentality his storytelling often risks. Without that edge, his weirdness shades into triviality." Buffett's latest *Volcano* single, "Survive," Stokes dubbed "a real stinker, with a chorus carved from caramel." (Buffett had told Chet Flippo "Survive" was a stab at writing a Billy Joel song; it lurched no higher than number 77 on *Billboard's* pop charts.) It was surely with great relief that, at tour's end, Buffett sailed away from his troubled *Volcano* aboard the twenty-six-foot boat named for the new lady in his life, daughter Savannah Jane. He would make his next album in the fall, and the need to write fresh material coincided neatly with watery escape.

In September, Buffett was at Muscle Shoals Sound Studio in Sheffield, Alabama, with producer Norbert Putnam to record *Coconut Telegraph.* The title song was a humorous look at island gossip, applicable to Key West (or, for that matter, many a small town). "There was an old saying," recalls Chris Robinson, "'You can fart on one side of the island and you're gonna hear about it on the other side before the smell gets there.' People talked, they told stories, but it wasn't like *The Harper Valley PTA.* Nobody condemned or condoned you for what you did, they just told it as a good story."

Buffett's stories on *Coconut Telegraph* addressed John Wayne's passing ("Incommunicado"), daddy's little girl ("Little Miss Magic"), and his attitude toward adulthood ("Growing Older But Not Up"). He even saw fit to wax a chestnut from 1934, the Mitchell Parrish and

Harris Lewine Collection

Harris Lewine Collection

Buffett completed a script entitled "Evening of Margaritaville" on the table William Faulkner used to write the classic *Absalom, Absalom!* Buffett dedicated the song "If I Could Just Get It on Paper" to Faulkner.

Frank Perkins tune, "Stars Fell on Alabama." *Coconut Telegraph* was released in March 1981, with Walter Hunt's warm pointillist graphics (extending even to the record label) making it the most visually appealing Buffett album. It rose only to number 30 on *Billboard*'s album charts.

Nineteen eighty-one's summer tour brought Buffett to Radio City Music Hall, and *New York Times* critic Stephen Holden wrote: "One of Mr. Buffett's virtues as a performer is that he knows his artistic limits and exactly how far to push them. His songs, which detail an easygoing life in the coastal cities of the Caribbean and the Gulf of Mexico, celebrate both the pleasures and the foibles of the flesh, especially drinking, with a hearty good humor spiced with wisecracking philosophical commentary. Mr. Buffett could never be accused of pretentiousness. Lyrically, he might even be pop music's most convincing chronicler of a hedonistic style of life that suggests a posthippy Ernest Hemingway."

Author's Collection

Like Hemingway, Buffett was much on the move, as Kathleen J. Hargreaves reported in a November 1981 profile for Key West's *Sun Life:* "A man with many homes, including one in Colorado and another on an island off the coast of France, Buffett said he came to Key West because he 'had to get back to the sea.... A lot of people have the misconception that when I came here I stayed in a house in a rented room and stayed drunk for ten years and became a star. That's absolutely not true. Most of the time I stayed here those ten years I literally spent maybe a month at my apartment here because I was quite vigorously on the road doing concerts.... Everybody will tell you they knew me. Only a few of them do. I haven't deserted Key West. I haven't deserted anybody. People leave Key West and where they go next they have to find out for themselves. I know what suits me best. I'll always come back to Key West. That's for sure."

Buffett returned to play a benefit on November 28 for the Tennessee Williams Fine Arts Center. It was exactly ten years since he had first come to Key West, he informed the five hundred fans who packed the theater at $25 a seat. After singing his most famous song, he said, "That's for all you citizens of Margaritaville."

The annual fall recording session found Buffett back in Nashville with producer Norbert Putnam. Their harvest debuted in early 1982 and earned two-and-a-half stars from *Rolling Stone:* "*Somewhere Over China* is a pleasantly accomplished set of easy-rolling rock with a taste of the tropics," wrote reviewer Parke Puterbaugh, who went on to comment: "To Buffett's loyal listeners—that peculiarly American brotherhood of sailboat cowboys, resort-town drifters and gonzo highlifers—these flights of fancy will undoubtedly strike a resonant chord. The question is, does he really intend to break new ground or is this simply the wanderlust of the armchair hedonist? The answer never arrives."

Somewhere Over China stalled at number 31 on the *Billboard* album charts. Buffett, no armchair hedonist, didn't hang around wondering where his momentum went. He made two trips to Tahiti in 1982, and visited the annual Faulkner and Yoknapatawpha Conference at the University of Mississippi in Oxford. "I came to this Faulkner conference because I am Southern and I am originally from Mississippi," Buffett told the Associated Press. "And as a writer, I see a lot of analogies between what I am writing about and what Faulkner wrote about. Faulkner drew most of his themes from the world around him and that is what I try to do with my songs. Basically everything I write about is drawn from everyday experiences."

Buffett chose the Faulkner conference to

announce that he was working on a movie script called *Evening of Margaritaville.* In October, Buffett told *Miami Herald* reporter Frederick Burger that he had finished his *Margaritaville* script at the Faulkner conference "on the same table Faulkner used to complete *Absalom, Absalom!*" The table, however, did not inspire further similarity. "I play myself currently as the narrator, looking back ten years at a bar in Margaritaville," said Buffett. "It's roughly Key West in 1971 but other than a few episodes or stories, it's not autobiographical. It's going to be more of a thinking movie than *Animal House,* but it's going to be funny."

Wide World Photos

Margaux Hemingway and a big fan of her grandfather's ham it up in Key West, 1983.

Buffett also had a collection of stories, poems, essays, and recipes in mind, to be called *My African Friend and Other Stories.* "It'll just be a small book," he said. "This will be a good preliminary thing to do before I hit forty and try my major work."

Buffett garnered good press in March 1983 for his efforts on behalf of his feathered friends (not, in this case, parrots). "An unlikely coalition of the Audubon Society, Walt Disney Productions, and singer Jimmy Buffett is trying to save an endangered sparrow species by mating the last survivors—five males with a compatible cousin," announced an Associated Press story. There were only five dusky sparrows left, though they had "once thrived in the marshy grasslands of the east-central Florida coast. But highways, coastal damage and a postwar population explosion from Jacksonville south to the Kennedy Space Center drastically altered its habitat.... Disney will pay about $55,800 of the experiment's $64,300 first-year cost, and plans to exhibit some of the duskies' offspring at the [Walt Disney World's Discovery Island Zoological] park in December. To raise its $9,500 share of the project's initial expense, the Audubon Society has enlisted entertainer Jimmy Buffett for a March 20 benefit to be held in Miami."

Later that year, Buffett helped his old pal Vic Latham by playing at the opening of the new Full Moon Saloon in Key West. "He played for free," recalls Moon bartender John Hellen. "Best night we ever had, even to this day. Best night the bar next door ever had, too. People couldn't get in, so they'd go next door and buy beers." Those determined to hear Buffett simply squeezed through the packed Full Moon's windows.

Buffett now had a home in the French Antilles, a house in North Florida on the Suwannee River, and the ever-changing boat collection boasted an eighteen-foot mahogany speedboat from 1932 named *Runamuck.* He maintained an expensive lifestyle as he cruised through his thirty-sixth year, which found him smiling and signing autographs at Nashville's Fan Fair in June. Country music's annual "meet the stars" promotional love-in seemed an improbable place to find Buffett, who had always aired a contempt for country. But he had also done most of his recording in Nashville and, through the years, maintained business contacts in Music City. As this pirate looked at forty, he was not the only seventies singer-songwriter who felt bewildered by the MTV generation (the Buggles' "Video Killed the Radio Star" was MTV's premier video in August 1981). Compared to the cold world of techno-pop, Nashville looked downright friendly to an old hippie like Buffett. And he was mapping his new Southern strategy with an important ally: Irving Azoff, Buffett's manager, was now president of MCA, Buffett's label.

"I decided to come back [to Nashville] since I'm staying on the label," Buffett told reporter

Birth of a Parrot Head Nation

"The name was created a couple of years ago," Todd Everett wrote in a 1986 *Los Angeles Herald Examiner* piece, "when bassist Timothy B. Schmit looked out at a particularly wildly bedecked [Cincinnati] concert audience and exclaimed, 'Look at 'em squawkin'—they're Parrot Heads!'"

"For some reason," Buffett confirmed, "the Ohio Parrot Heads can combine colors of more outlandish fabrics in more creative ways than any other people who come to our shows. Cincinnati was the right place and time, and the name typified what was out there. It gave 'em an identity, and it struck."

Larry Nager is pop music critic at the *Commercial Appeal* in Memphis. He was formerly pop music critic at the *Cincinnati Post,* where he covered the Birth of a Parrot Head Nation. "I saw Buffett more times than any other journalist in Cincinnati. The first time in 1983. That was at the time he had just moved to the King's Island Timber Wolf Amphitheatre. Open air. Bench seats. It holds about 10,000. At that point he was comfortably selling it out, but not much more than that. You started seeing the whole Parrot Head phenomenon there with people dressing up and bringing inflatable animals, the umbrellas and the drinks and the leis and the Hawaiian shirts. It was very much a natural progression. Every year you saw more stuff and people tried to outdo the year before. It got a little crazier. The show was starting to sell out faster and faster. People were dressing wilder and wilder and bringing more and more stuff. They added an additional show. Then he went to two nights at Riverbend. At the time of the change, Riverbend was at 16,000 capacity. It has since become 18,500. It may even be up to 20,000. This year Buffett's doing six nights there.

"There's a little of the disease everywhere, but it's a full plague in Cincinnati. There's no place like it, though apparently Atlanta's supposed to be big. It's a massive phenomenon in Cincinnati to this point. It's a seasonal promotion for stores. You're seeing things like Buskin Bakery, this little neighborhood chain in Cincinnati, and when Buffett comes to town, they bake special parrot cookies. You would see seasonal promotions in a lot of the stores. I think some department stores started doing Buffett windows. It became the weirdest phenomenon I've ever seen in Cincinnati. Like Halloween is a season, and Jimmy Buffett concerts are a season there. It was all-pervasive.

"It had gotten a little too crazy, a little too drunken there for a while. You had things like, there were complaints a couple of years back of guys getting so drunk they were pissing in their beer cups and spraying the crowd with it. This is out on the lawn where there is no law. TV people are always interviewing 'the press' journalists, because we would be the ones in the trenches there. 'What is this? Why Cincinnati?' The line, of course, is that, in the land of perpetual Lent, everybody needs a little Mardi Gras. And Cincinnati is a real uptight little town. It's Procter and Gamble; it's very corporate. You can see certain things like, you remember the Mapplethorpe case where the sheriff arrests a museum director on obscenity charges? It's white and uptight. That's Cincinnati. So every year this is an excuse to get loose, get drunk, and go out and party.

"I've interviewed people like sixty-one-year-old engineers from Procter and Gamble. And these guys would say, 'Well, I'd always wanted to be a beach bum. I'd always wanted to sail around the world.' All these Walter Mitty dreams coalesce at the Buffett shows. They dress crazy. These guys'll wear the tit hats, which are charming things which have two artificial breasts on the front of a baseball cap. They are among the many decorations you'll see at a Buffett show.

"You've probably seen the boxed set [Boats, Beaches, Bars & Ballads]. Remember the one guy with the broken neck? This is amazing. His wife was like eight months pregnant. And he had a broken neck. And the decorated neck brace. And they were out there to see Buffett.

"My background is anthropology, and that fit

right in. I've always liked the subcultures which appear in music, whether it's the women's music thing that started cropping up, or the Dead Heads. The Parrot Head thing was kind of fascinating, because it was a subculture that was very much like golf. It was totally white-bread, and it was a lot like golfing. They're not ashamed to wear these idiotic clothes on the links. These same people were wearing these idiotic clothes to Riverbend. You talk to these folks, and they're going to go back to Procter and Gamble tomorrow, but tonight, they're living out their fantasy. It really was like Mardi Gras in the most literal sense. These people live these Catholic, Lent-like lives all year long, and then one night a year or four nights a year or now six nights a year, they were able to just go totally mad, Carnival in Rio, and then go back to the office on Monday."

Revelers at the Primo Parrothead Party entering "Margaritaville."

Sacher Nature Collection

Photo: Syndey Byrd

Buffett as the King of the Krewe of Clones, Mardi Gras, 1983.

Sandy Neese of Nashville's *Tennessean.* "I think Irving will make a big difference. He's a dedicated man. And country music's the only thing that's making money for MCA.... I've done eleven albums and been through five regimes at the label. Nobody knew what to do with me. They'd fight me on what singles to release and I got no tour support. I've survived for fifteen years in this business, and I thought I should be listened to." Buffett said he hadn't recorded anything in two years (a slight exaggeration), but that his next album would have "some potential country things on it."

Country radio didn't touch anything from *One Particular Harbor,* and Buffett's cover of Van Morrison's "Brown Eyed Girl" was only a minor blip on the pop screen. But the Southern strategy continued. In April 1984, a Nashville margarita party was the stage for Buffett announcing that one of his oldest Nashville cronies, Buzz Cason, would manage the publishing of Buffett's song catalogue, Coral Reefer Music, through Cason's Southern Writers Group USA. The occasion was a good excuse for Buffett to sound off on his "kiss-and-make-up" attitude to *Tennessean* reporter Robert K. Oermann. "I don't think I've changed that much, but Nashville sure has," said Buffett. "Before, when I was here, there really was no place for me to go.... There's more room for versatility than there ever was before, more room to fluctuate musically than in any other form of music right now." And, demographically, Buffett saw country as open to an artist of his vintage. "I'm thirty-seven," he said. "I'm not nineteen anymore. And I felt it, too, this month when I was out doing 'Solid Gold' and lookin' at the 'Solid Gold' dancers and the audience. I said, 'What in the hell am I doin' here?' They were talkin' to me about hosting the show and said, 'We wish you were a little younger.' And I said, Well, I'm *not!* So I'm goin' to Nashville. The audiences twenty-five to forty are right here. All I'm doin' is following my market, you know? I am as old as the people that like me. All kinds of people are coming back into this town, from musicians to producers to writers. And you can't tell me that's not healthy for the business. It shows. This is where I belong."

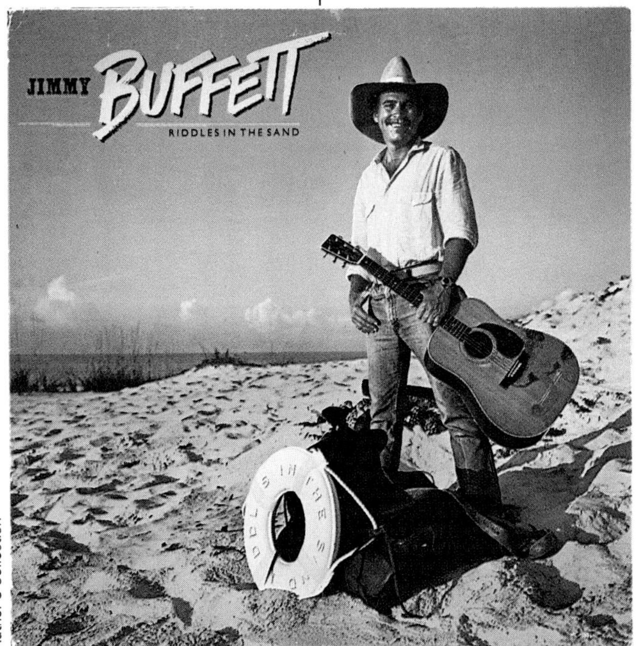

Author's Collection

To underscore the message, MCA paired Buffett with "boss hoss" country producer Jimmy Bowen and posed him with a horse and an oversized cowboy hat for the cover of his 1984 album, *Riddles in the Sand.* Three of *Riddles'* songs squeaked into the country charts ("Who's the Blonde Stranger?" made it to number 37 in March 1985, his best chart action since "Fins" in 1979), and the breezy "Ragtop Day" introduced a new icon into the Buffett mythology. Reading between the lines of *Riddles'* dedication, there were hints of trouble in paradise: "This album dedicated with much love to Jane Slagsvol Buffett, who over the years, has been, and remains, the ultimate riddle in the sand."

Nineteen eighty-four, the year of Buffett's reconciliation with Nashville, was also the year John Morthland's *The Best of Country Music* (Doubleday, 1984) offered this on-the-money overview of him: "Buffett is one of those singer-songwriters who built up cult followings in pop and around the fringes of country before finally busting out all over with the 1977 'Margaritaville,' which faithfully translated the Jerry Jeff Walker style into something the masses could appreciate. Because Buffett was once a journalist, he wrote literate songs; because he was a Southerner, who wrote of Southern people and places, his initial audience came mostly from below the Mason-Dixon line. Because he was a sailor, many songs had nautical themes, dealing with pirates, smuggling, banana republics, and the like in ways that had surface appeal no matter how romanticized they became; because he was also a rogue, many were irreverent and witty.... I've always considered Buffett something of an overachiever, a talented folk-rocker capable of providing small pleasures who arrived at just the right time—when Southern pride, wordy singer-songwriters, and absorption in beer 'n' drugs as a way of life were all peaking."

By mid-1984, Buffett was beginning to joke about his age. "I'm so old," he told *Mobile Press Register* reporter Eddie Menton, "I can remember when [Alabama Attorney General] Charlie Gradick used to play in a rock band." With a heavy hitter like his record label president at his side, Buffett's Southern strategy was bound to see some success, but he also knew that it was time to hedge his bets. He designed a clothing line with the help of Jane and Florida designer Michael Latona and signed a licensing agreement with United Shirts of America. He was thinking business.

Encouraged and helped by an old friend from the seventies, Sunshine Smith, Buffett opened Key West's Margaritaville on January 28, 1985. Mayor Richard Heyman came by for the ribbon-cutting ceremony, and christened the store with a bottle of tequila. Margaritaville sold out its initial stock (including $700 worth of T-shirts) on opening day. Buffett enlisted Carol Shaughnessy's help in creating a newsletter-advertiser, *The Coconut Telegraph,* which kept Buffett's fans apprised of his doings while offering them his Caribbean Soul T-shirts, each skewed graphically to the theme of a Buffett song. The first *Coconut Telegraph* appeared in February 1985, and tantalized its 650 recipients with a description of the Margaritaville Store as "... a cheerfully shabby place, with its weathered front porch, well-used rocking chair, and lobster-trap display cases." Buffett celebrated the opening by hosting a "Key West film festival" at the Strand Theatre which featured such "classics" as his early ABC promotional short, a video of *One Particular Harbor,* and Count Valdene's tarpon fishing film.

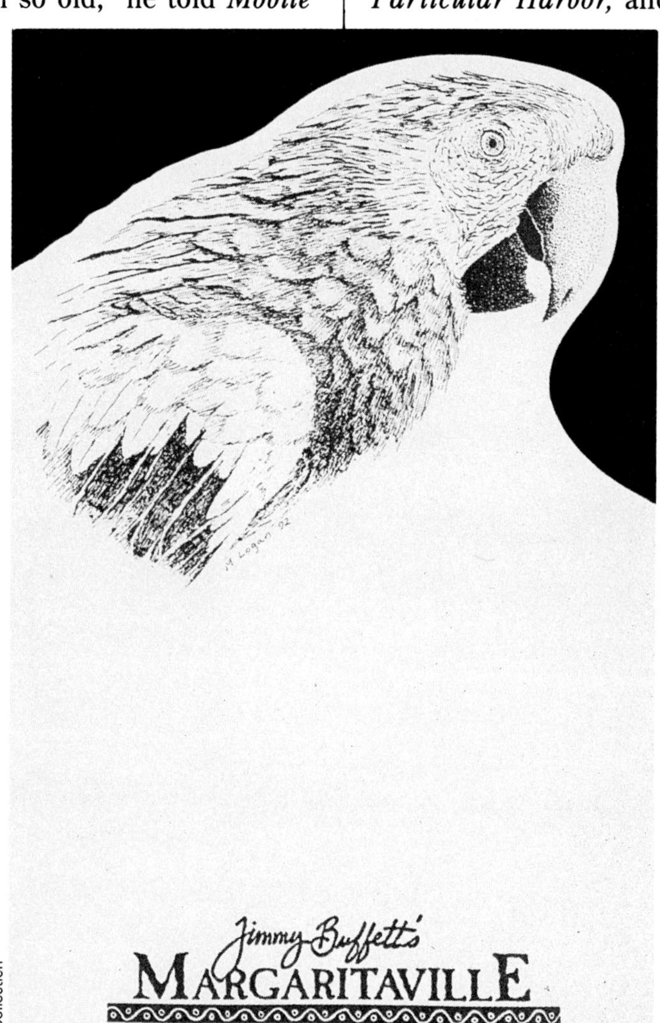

Author's Collection

Buffett was clearly enjoying his new role as self-promoting entrepreneur. His *Coconut Telegraph* solicited entries in a "Perfect Margarita" contest (the winner got the complete line of Buffett's Caribbean Soul T-shirts). "Parrot Head" as a description of Buffett's fans first appears in the April 1985 Telegraph, and was picked up by the press that summer as Buffett toured to promote his new *Last Mango in Paris* album. The album had an entry form for a "Last Mango Cruise" which would take five couples on an expense-paid trip to Key West during its October Fantasy Fest. Seventy-five thousand entered, and helped Buffett build up a mailing list for his *Telegraph* while committing him to give ten of them a private island concert laden with margaritas and cheeseburgers. "I was going, 'Please, God, don't send me any assholes,'" Buffett told the *Miami Herald,* adding tactfully that He didn't.

Mango was less skewed to the country market than *Riddles in the Sand,* but it ironically yielded Buffett his first Top 20 hit in any format since "Margaritaville" when "If the Phone Doesn't Ring,

Author's Collection

Buffett's business drive kicked in with the 1985 opening of his Key West Margaritaville store. He was right on the money with the hunch that Parrot Head paraphernalia would find a ready market.

It's Me" made it to number 16 on the country charts in the fall of 1985. MCA released the "Best of Buffett" album, *Songs You Know by Heart,* at that time, and business at Margaritaville was humming.

"What Jimmy projects is very precious to a lot of people," says Carol Shaughnessy. "It was the Margaritaville mystique that we were selling, not the Margaritaville T-shirts. Through the letters of his fans, it became clear that the Parrot Heads were bringing up another generation of Parrot Heads. We'd get letters from them saying, 'My baby smiled for the first time when she heard a Jimmy Buffett song,' or, 'My three-year-old is the most animated she's ever been when we play Buffett and she dances around the house,' or, 'The first word that my child said was *cheeseburger.*' We consistently got that kind of letter and that kind of call."

In March 1986, MCA Home Video released the eighty-seven minute *Jimmy Buffett—Live by the Bay.* "I wanted something people would be able to repeat," Buffett told the *Hollywood Reporter.* "If they're in Minneapolis in February and it's twenty degrees, I wanted them to be able to have a 'Margaritaville' party and play that video." In *Music Video: A Consumer's Guide* (Ballantine Books, New York, 1987), Michael Shore wrote: "Jimmy Buffett's obsessively tropical mellowness can get a bit precious at times, but Mr. Miami Nice sure does have his fans, and if you're one of 'em, you should definitely settle back and enjoy this. Buffett's on his home turf at Miami's Marine Stadium (a former boat-racing facility), and he and his Coral Reefer Band easily charm an audience that's both in the stands and on the water. The very smooth direction (by Jack Cole) and production complete the pretty picture."

"Three hours before Jimmy Buffett's concert at the Miami Marine Stadium, the parking lot was filled with the sound of Jimmy's greatest hits coming from stereos in the parked cars of his Parrot Head fans," wrote Pat Jordan in a 1988 *Southern Magazine* profile of Buffett. "The fans were all wearing Hawaiian shirts and Shark Fin or Parrot Head caps and were all partying in the Jimmy Buffett style: Beer. Peanut butter sandwiches. Hot dogs. Cheetos.... The Miami Marine Stadium is a concrete bandshell covering concrete bleachers that face a barge on Miami Bay, where Jimmy's band was already setting up their instruments. There were only a few people in the band shell, but the waters surrounding the barge were packed with boats of every description and Parrot Heads in bathing suits. It looked like something out of *Animal House,* only the revelers were people in their late twenties and early thirties. They were firing water balloons from boat to boat, Nerf footballs, Frisbees. Most of them were already drunk in the hot sun. They fell off their boats into the bay and then paddled on rafts from boat to boat. A few of the girls took off the tops of their bathing suits to the cheers of the men. It was a waterlogged bacchanal whose only excuse for being was Jimmy Buffett's music.

"Each new generation, it seems, is tuned to the Jimmy Buffett of 'Margaritaville,' and in his concerts that is the Jimmy Buffett he gives them.... No one really comes to a Jimmy Buffett concert to hear *him* sing. His fans come to hear themselves. *They're* the concert. Jimmy's just the vehicle for them.

"He ended the show with a rendition of 'Margaritaville.' Florida Senator Bob Graham came on stage to join him. The fans were all singing and swaying in the sunlight like shafts of colorful wheat. Some were so drunk that they fell off the barge into the dirty water, and security men tried to drag them out. But before they could, Jimmy, to solidify his communion with his fans, dived into Miami Bay. He swam around touching his fans in the water, reaching up from boat to boat to touch everyone's hands, and then he was pulled back onto the barge by his security guards. When some fans tried to climb up after him, they were pushed back into the water. It looked like a scene in a lifeboat after the sinking of the *Titanic.*"

Despite his separation from Jane, who, with Savannah Jane, had moved to New York, 1986 was an up year for Buffett. He was a big winner on the tour circuit, and felt cocky about it. "I'm not necessarily yearning to have another big pop hit single," he told *Chicago Tribune* pop critic Lynn Van Matre. "What I really would like is to have a battle of the bands. Or a battle of the bands video. I'll take on anybody." He told Pat Jordan in a *Southern Magazine* profile: "I know I'm just a mediocre singer and writer, but I am a great performer and

Authro's Collection

The Coconut Telegraph newsletter has been apprising Parrot Heads of Buffett's exploits and offering his wares since February 1985.

The Coconut Telegraph
MARGARITAVILLE JUL-AUG 1992 VOLUME 8, NO. 4

FAR FROM WASTING AWAY

JUST FOR THE RECORD, THE MARGARITA THAT INSPIRED JIMMY BUFFETT'S MOST FAMOUS SONG WAS DRUNK IN AUSTIN. OR SO HE SAYS.

By John T. Davis. This article originally appeared in the Austin-American Statesman.

But no one, not even Buffett himself, is entirely sure where in the city the fateful beverage was quaffed. It might have been at Castle Creek, a dearly departed place on Lavaca Street that was next to the equally-defunct Capitol Oyster Bar.

That's where I saw Buffett for the first time, back in the mid-1970's. He pulled up just before showtime in a station wagon, yanked his guitar out of the backseat, and walked inside to play for a relative handful of strangers. It was successful, as far as such things go, and when, on the break, the singer announced he was going next door for a dozen raw, about half the tiny audience elected to join him.

"I've played every junior college in the entire state of Texas," said Buffett on a recent trip to Austin, speaking of his scuffling days. "And that's where my affection and love for the people of Texas and their appreciation of music - which is really unique in all the travels that I've done - was formed.

"When you were hitchhiking in Texas with a guitar case, it wasn't treated like an AK-47, it was treated as something that was admired."

Buffett plays the Erwin Center these days, when he is playing at all. He has lately re-cast himself as a mini-mogul, with a career in fiction, and a retail store and a restaurant, and several real estate investments that compete for his attention. The amiable, drifting-with-the-tides facade in display for concert-goers conceals a restless intelligence and eclectic curiousity.

That footloose sense of experimentation is manifested these days in **Margaritaville Records**, an independent label that has been created, seemingly, out of a notation on Buffett's long lifetime wish list. Based in Nashville, the label has signed two new artists (New Orleans rockers the **Iguanas** and **Evangeline**, a Cajun-esque female band) and has released a boxed Buffett retrospective.

Anyone who has been around the music industry for a while has come across star-driven vanity projects before; ego-gratifying custom labels in which the artist dabbles until the new wears off. And then one day, the phones are disconnected and there is a lot of leftover letterhead stationery, and the star is off on some new and more fashionable tangent.

But that is not the case with this endeavor, insisted Shellie Erwin, who, along with English music veteran Bob Mercer, makes up Margaritaville's entire staff. "He's always wanted to have a record label that is artist oriented," she said. "(But) he's very quality oriented. He's really conscious about things that have his name on them."

Buffett remains an MCA recording artist, but, according to Erwin, he has a hand in every stage of the projects initiated in the Margaritaville offices, from finding the talent to guiding them in the studio to administering their song publishing (in itself a potentially lucrative business) to creating a marketing image. The resulting products will be distributed by MCA, beginning with Evangeline's debut effort and Buffett's box set, *Boats, Beaches, Bars and Ballads*.

For a variety of personal and professional reasons, the musician himself has moved back to Nashville. The move may come as a surprise to fans who have grown up with Buffett's salt-cured, Gulf

(continued page 6)

Photo: Suzanne Hitchcock

Author's Collection

The Coconut Telegraph
MARGARITAVILLE, FEB. 1986 VOLUME 2, NO. 2

TRUE TALES OF THE SNAKE PIT

By Tom Corcoran

Many characters in Jimmy Buffett's lyrics seem to live in Key West or unpredictably pass through. Fifteen years after "I Have Found Me a Home" and "Nautical Wheelers," they are here in spirit and in person. But things change, and they no longer congregate in any single place. One thing we post-Woodstock crazies and nautical vagabonds thought would last forever was the infamous "Snake Pit," The Old Anchor Inn.

In the early '70's, hanging out at the Anchor was like living in a wacko film. It was episodical, a street opera, a circus where at center ring all performances were tolerated. The mysterious Club Mandible congregated there in purple shirts and inspired Jimmy's irreverent "My Head Hurts, My Feet Stink, and I Don't Love Jesus."

The Anchor was so funky the State tried to close it on principle. It finally shut down when the revolving credit plan spun out of control.

Bud MacArthur ran the place. A highly decorated war hero, "Budman" had a heart of gold and a tolerance for offbeat behavior. A large laughing man, always holding a glass of wine and accompanied by his wife Dorothy, Bud lorded over the Anchor in a jovial, gentle way. The MacArthurs were parental figures, psychologists, money lenders, and everyone's common conscience.

Somehow The Old Anchor Inn's presence didn't sit well with the authorities. There were strange odors: ganja in the backyard, faulty plumbing in the men's room, last night's beer under the floorboards.

Inside were dozens of Monkey Tom's paintings: psychedelic shrimp-boats and witches' eyes. The jukebox was a music salad: Hendrix, Cocker, Joplin, Clapton. After every third song came the house favorite: "I Can't Get Started" with Bunny Berigan's trumpet solo.

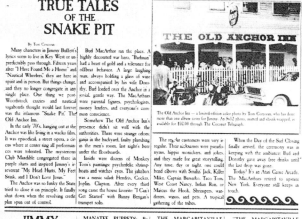

The Old Anchor Inn — a limited-edition color photo by Tom Corcoran, who has done more than one album cover for Jimmy. An 8x12 photo, matted and shrink-wrapped, is available for $32.00 through The Coconut Telegraph.

The regular customers were very irregular. Their nicknames were pseudonyms, hippie monickers, and jokes, and they made for great storytelling. Any time, day or night, one could bend elbows with Smilin' Jack, Killer Mike, Captain Berserko, Taco Tom, West Coast Nancy, Indian Ron, or Marcus the Hook. Shrimpers, wanderers, winos, and pets. A tropical gathering of the tribes.

When the Day of the Sad Closing finally arrived, the ceremony was in keeping with the ambiance: Bud and Dorothy gave away free drinks until the last drop was gone.

Today? It's an Atari Game Arcade. The MacArthurs retired to upstate New York. Everyone still keeps in touch.

JIMMY BUFFETT'S MAIL ORDER!

"THE COCONUT TELEGRAPH": Read about all the latest Buffett doings. $2.00 for a year's subscription.

Yes, you can still order from Jimmy Buffett's Caribbean Soul T-shirt Line. Choose from the following designs: Cheeseburger in Paradise, Son of a Sailor, Changes in Latitude, Hurricane, Fins, Migration, One Particular Harbour, Margaritaville, and Why Don't We Get Drunk and Screw. All shirts are $12.95, and come in S, M, L and XL.

THE OFFICIAL PARROT HEAD SHIRT: Proclaim your allegiance to Jimmy Buffett's Parrot Head Club. $12.95.

TROPICAL LIZARDS: The official mascots of the Conch Republic, in vivid cotton prints. These little guys can really climb the walls! $10.00 apiece.

MANATEE PUPPETS: Be-whiskered friends—because we're growing older but not up. $13.00 each.

"SONGS YOU KNOW BY HEART": The best of Jimmy Buffett on one cassette tape. $8.98.

THE MARGARITAVILLE STORE SWEATSHIRT: Snuggle into it—a splashy Margarita decorates the front. Sweatshirts come in white or grey—S, M, L, XL. $16.95 apiece.

JIMMY BUFFETT'S PARROT HEAD CLUB

Join the Club with this Official Parrot Head Club T-shirt.

"THE MARGARITAVILLE COOKBOOK": A collection of island recipes by a couple of long-time residents of Margaritaville. $12.95.

"IMAGES OF THE PAST": Joan and Wright Langley's book offers a glimpse of fascinating Old Key West—highlighted by photographs of the era. $10.95.

BOAT DRINK TUMBLERS: Let a boat drink chase away those cold-weather blues. Acrylic glasses are $8.00 apiece.

MARGARITA GLASSES: Large, long-stemmed glasses engraved with Jimmy Buffett's signature. $10.00 apiece.

To order, send your check or money order to T-SHIRTS, The Margaritaville Store, P.O. Box 1459, Key West, Florida 33041, or call 1-305-296-9981.

There is a $3.00 SHIPPING AND HANDLING CHARGE for orders of 6 items or less, $5.00 for orders of over 6 items. The shipping charge for any glassware order is $3.50. Florida residents, please include sales tax. Please allow 4 to 6 weeks for delivery.

Author's Collection

PARROT HEAD CLUB
MARGARITAVILLE

Author's Collection

Nostalgia for the sleazy Old Anchor Inn and membership decals are offered in Buffett's *Coconut Telegraph,* tip sheet and fan magazine for Parrot Heads. Buffett often contributes to it.

Children of Parrot Heads can join the Parakeet Club; T-shirts expressing the Buffett world view are popular items.

that counts. I saw Frank Sinatra play fifty-four minutes to old ladies who were his fans, and they didn't give a shit that he was flat. They just reminisced and went away feeling good. As an artist, you could nail him, but as a performer, you had to respect him. I understand that. I put on a good show for my fans. I sell them Jimmy Buffett. They appreciate that. Even if I'm never on radio again—and I think I deserve to be—it won't bother me. I still have my fans. I'm one of the few living legends left."

Buffett's 1986 summer tour generated a lot of press, and that year's album was *Floridays.* He was seen in the right company—actors Jack Nicholson and Harrison Ford were pals—so the celebrity magazine *Interview* did a Q&A with Buffett. In it, Buffett likened performing to sailing ("At any given time the bottom could fall out"), and said he always checked his crowds for "drunk spots." He told of a show in Atlanta "at a place called Cahstang Park, a beautiful setting where everyone brings their lunches out ... there's nothing that really takes the heart out of you like seeing a fight in the audience. It's so contrary to what I'm trying to do up there.... We're playing 'Margaritaville,' the very last song in the set. I look over and I see a guy coming out of stage left who goes straight and sucker-punches another guy. He misses the one he aimed for—but misses him totally—and hits a kid in the head and knocks him out.... I *heard* the punch and it was a real foul blow. And I wanted to stop the show and go out and beat the shit out of the guy because I saw him running. So I stop the show and yell, 'Get the son of a bitch! He's got a red shirt on, goin' left!' And they tackled him and got him. Locked his ass up. And I filed charges against him."

Buffett continued to talk about the *Margaritaville* movie ("pure escapism," he would say), voicing frustration at his inability to get Hollywood backing. In November 1986 he was back in Margaritaville proper, playing a benefit for the ponds, marshes, and uplands across the Key West airport known as the salt ponds. "We're trying to preserve a little piece of this island so it doesn't look like the rest of Florida," said Buffett.

Buffett was sighted partying Down Under in January 1987, playing the America's Cup Ball before 2,500 guests who paid $300 a head. (Lionel Richie and Elton John also performed.) Buffett had been invited to write a "fight" song for the Stars & Stripes challenge as the Yanks sought to win back the America's cup. "It has been a real challenge," he told the Associated Press. "We will play it for the first time when the boat is towed out Saturday. Right now, I'm working on the sound mix so the music will win out over the engine noise.... I can't tell you much more about the song other than that I do a Popeye imitation. It will really make you get up and convert to our cause." The song, "Take It Back," appears on Buffett's *Boats, Beaches, Bars & Ballads* boxed set.

Nineteen eighty-seven's summer tour took the whimsical name, "A Parrot Looks at Forty," though Buffett claimed age didn't phase him. "I think I've done more at forty than most people have done at eighty," he told *Chicago Sun-Times* reporter Dave Hoekstra. "I don't have time for a

Author's Collection

Author's Collection

midlife crisis. I've had those but they've come in mini-spurts since I was eighteen."

As his forty-first birthday approached, Buffett came home to where it all began for him—Pascagoula. SKIPPER JIMMY BUFFETT LOOKS OVER THE SHIP was the headline for the following bylineless story in the September 15, 1987, *Mobile Press Register:*

"The honorary captain of the *Governor Stone,* singer Jimmy Buffett, saw his charge for the first time Sunday.

"'I think's it's great what you're doing here,' Buffett said. 'It's a great cause. I think it's essential to keep your traditional roots and values.'

"The ship, a schooner built on the east bank of the Pascagoula River in 1877, was given to the city by John Curry of Tarpon Springs, Florida. The ship was brought to its new home last month.

"Buffett said the schooner 'looks great' for a 110-year-old vessel. He said he was glad to have received a letter about the schooner.

"'The project comes at a good time,' Buffett said, because his father, J. D. Buffett, is retiring from his position at the Alabama State Docks in Mobile.

"J. D. Buffett has been named port captain and general manager of the *Governor Stone.*

"The singer said that some of his friends in the world of sailing, connected with sailing twelve-meter boats in America's Cup competition, might be able to lend a hand with refitting the schooner.

"Buffett has been sailing since he was a boy in Pascagoula, and has owned several sailboats.

"One of the suggested uses for the schooner has been for training Sea Scouts. Buffett himself was a Sea Scout, and said it was a 'great idea' to involve the organization.

"'We didn't have a boat then,' Buffett said. 'It would have been better if we had had a boat.'

"Buffett autographed posters of the *Governor Stone* for sale, and offered some advice on fund-raising.

"'You've got to start locally,' Buffett said. 'You can sell crew memberships, and apply for state and federal restoration grants.

"'A cause like this is not controversial and has no down sides.'

"Buffett came to Pascagoula from New Orleans, where he saw Pope John Paul II, and gave a concert attended by about 7,000.

"Buffett, who flies his own plane, landed at the Jackson County Airport. On his way back to Key West, Florida, where he lives, he flew his plane past the *Governor Stone* and its supporters, wigwagging his wings in salute."

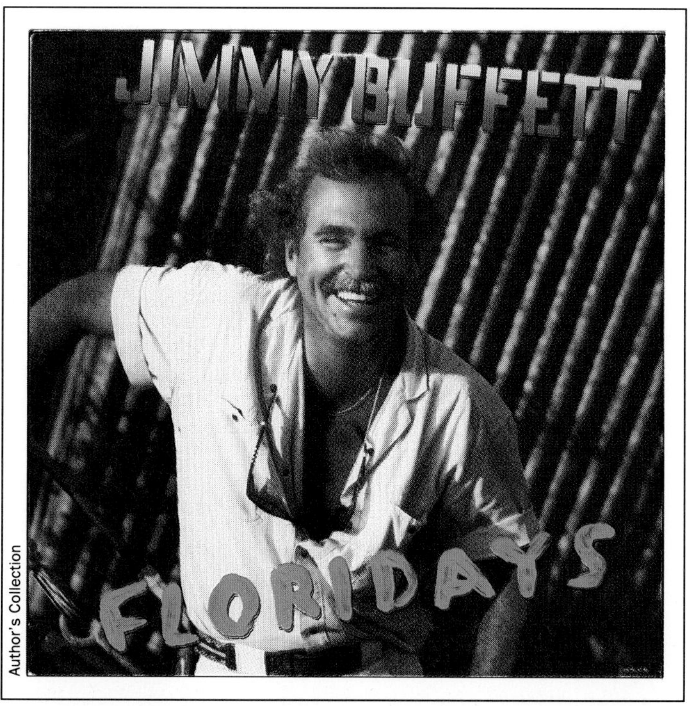

Fit at forty, Buffett embodied his sunny lifestyle on the 1986 *Floridays* album cover.

Of Man and Manatee

December 1981. "Signs warning boaters to slow down will be put up in manatee areas of Florida's waterways, courtesy of country singer Jimmy Buffett, who gave Florida $35,000 for that purpose," reported an Associated Press story from Tallahassee. "What is a manatee area, you might ask? It is an area populated by manatees, the large docile water creatures sometimes called sea cows.

"Buffett, a Floridian who has taken an interest in the endangered animals, presented a check to Natural Resources Director Elton Gissendanner in ceremonies Thursday. The money, which will pay for 365 signs, came from proceeds of two of Buffett's recent concerts.

"Governor Bob Graham, a fan of Buffett's music, asked the singer earlier this year to help lead the state's effort to protect the animals, which are sometimes injured or killed by boats in bays and rivers."

1986: Buffett explains his interest in manatees in the April *Interview:* "Well, the manatee sort of reminds me of what I want to be when I get old. Fat, swimmin' around in warm water, and just eatin' all the time. They used to be all up and down the coast. Now all but a thousand of them have been killed off. I figure if you can't save the creatures of the habitat, it doesn't say much about the survival of the human species. And if I could get people to take a little care about the manatee, then it would be the domino theory in reverse. They'd start thinking about other things. About the rivers and how to develop the land without destroying the real reason why everybody came down there [Florida] in the first place."

1987: Gregory Spears, Washington bureau reporter for the *Tallahassee Democrat,* writes the following in an April 8 feature headlined BUFFETT SINGS THE PRAISES OF ENDANGERED SPECIES ACT: "Buttoned-down Washington took a quick trip Tuesday to Margaritaville as balladeer Jimmy Buffett testified on behalf of his mellow friends, the manatees, at a Senate hearing on the reauthorization of the Endangered Species Act.

"Buffett—the singer-songwriter usually seen bicycling around his hometown of Key West in jeans and a floral shirt—wore a suit to the hearing, where he was hailed as a role model for his work to save the manatees.

"'We live on a big round time-share, and if we as humans want to assume the role of landlord then we have to take care of all the tenants,' the deeply tanned Buffett told a handful of senators and a standing-room-only audience. 'We are the reason that endangered species exist....'

"Buffett, perhaps best known for a song about downing tequila and getting 'wasted away again in Margaritaville,' was appointed chairman of Florida's Save the Manatee Commission in 1980 by then-Governor Bob Graham. At Senator Graham's invitation, Buffett told the Environmental Protection Subcommittee on Tuesday that money provided by the act has helped establish sanctuaries for the manatee, whose deadliest enemy is man.

"The Endangered Species Act extends federal protection to the manatee and 925 other plants and animals near extinction. Sen. George Mitchell (D-Maine) introduced legislation reauthorizing it with a budget of $56 million next year, but the Reagan administration proposes spending only $28.6 million.

"Buffett said the higher spending level 'will for the first time give us a good grip on the tools we need to ensure the survival of the manatee in Florida.' The manatee population has stabilized at roughly one thousand, Buffett said, although about fifty of the docile animals are killed each year in collisions with boats.

"'We still face the day-to-day problems of irresponsible boat operators in our waterways and developers only interested in profits, not responsibilities,' Buffett said. 'But the tide, I feel, is changing.... The manatee symbolizes the quality of life we all seek—to go about our daily lives in the most pleasant surroundings.'

"But Buffett's role as a sober-minded environmentalist did not hold up long under questioning.

"'Can you tell me more about manatees—we

MARGARITAVILLE
PARROTHEAD
Save the Manatee
92C-0784

Author's Collection

don't have many in Montana,' said Sen. Max Baucus (D–Montana).

"'They hang out in bars in Montana,' Buffett cracked, flashing a toothy smile."

1993: The March issue of *Sky Magazine* has a feature on the manatee in which Claire D. Hughes writes: "Save the Manatee Club, established in 1982, acts as a kind of public voice for the other groups, leading the way in manatee education, public awareness, and lobbying. The group produces public-service announcements starring singer/songwriter Jimmy Buffett, chairman of the club's governing board. They distribute educator's guides, a newsletter to more than 32,000 members around the world, and 'Caution: Manatee Area' signs free of charge to the Florida Marine Patrol and dock owners.

"... On the positive side, last year's estimated mortality figures were lower than those of the previous three years, and just thirty-eight manatee deaths were attributed to watercraft strikes by the Florida Department of Natural Resources as of December 1992, compared to fifty-three in 1991. Excluding cold-related deaths in 1990, last year was the first in ten years in which boats were not the primary cause of mortality."

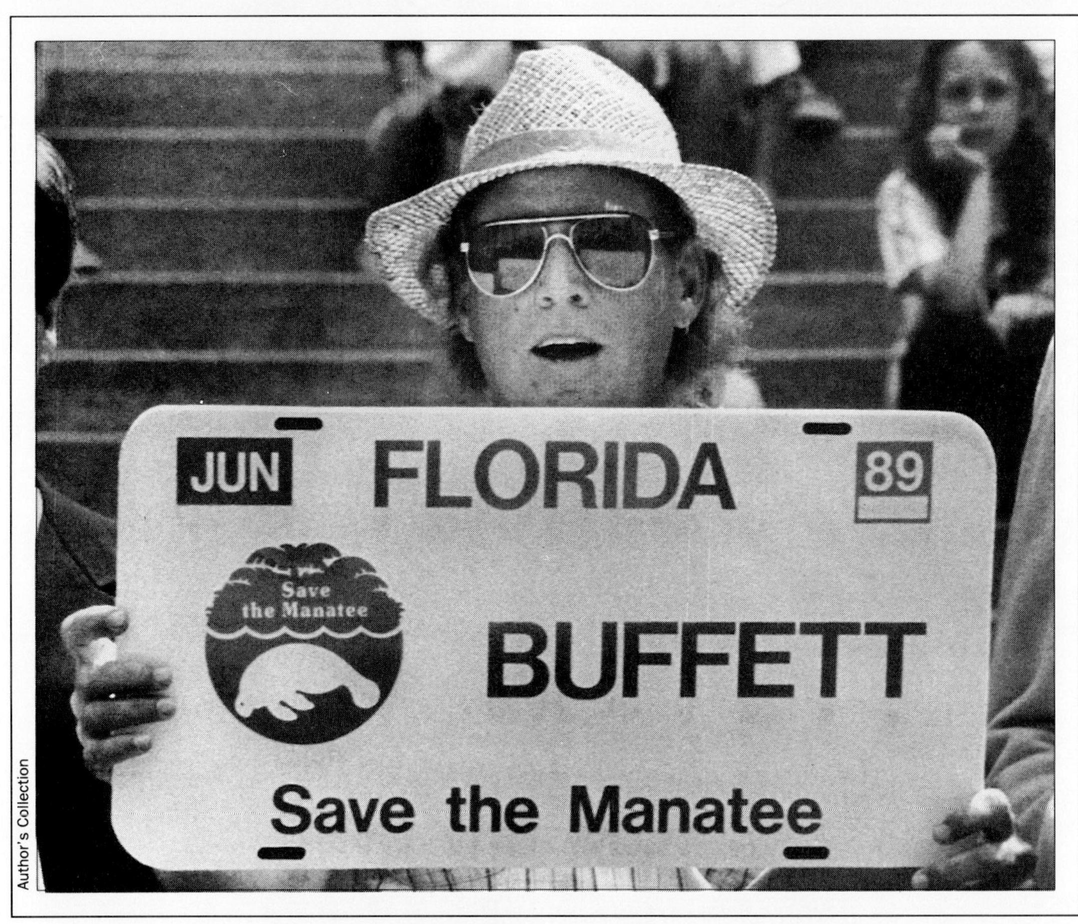

Author's Collection

CHAPTER EIGHT

QUIETLY MAKING NOISE

It's basically selling snake oil and I don't deny it a bit, but it's pretty good snake oil.
—Jimmy Buffett, 1985

Success turned Jimmy Buffett into a human tourist attraction...
—*The Rolling Stone Album Guide*

If the real me were ever known, my entire image would be shot.
—Spike Jones, Buffett's boyhood idol

In August 1986, Buffett told *USA Weekend* reporter Craig Modderno: "When I hit forty, I'm gonna travel around the world in eighty days and take $50,000 with me. I'm gonna write a script or a book or a bunch of songs about the experience. I'm gonna start in New Orleans on a ship my grandfather used to captain and then I'm gonna head for Rio and then turn right. I never planned on living until forty, so I figured I owed this to myself. It's going to be my birthday present to myself."

"He always had the idea of doing this tramp steamer trip around the world," recalls Buffett's Key West crony Dink Bruce. "He always wanted to just sit and write on a steamer and go around the world. I think he's kind of outgrown that one."

What Buffett did not outgrow was a goal: in his forties he would settle down to carve his niche in the literary world. A voracious reader from childhood, Buffett's heroes were less musical than literary, and he loved to litter his album sleeves with quotes from (and references to) his favorite authors. When interviewed, Buffett quoted Hemingway and mentioned Mark Twain. More than musicians or fellow songwriters, he sought out literary pals, among them Tom McGuane, Jim Harrison, and Pat Conroy, whose *Prince of Tides*

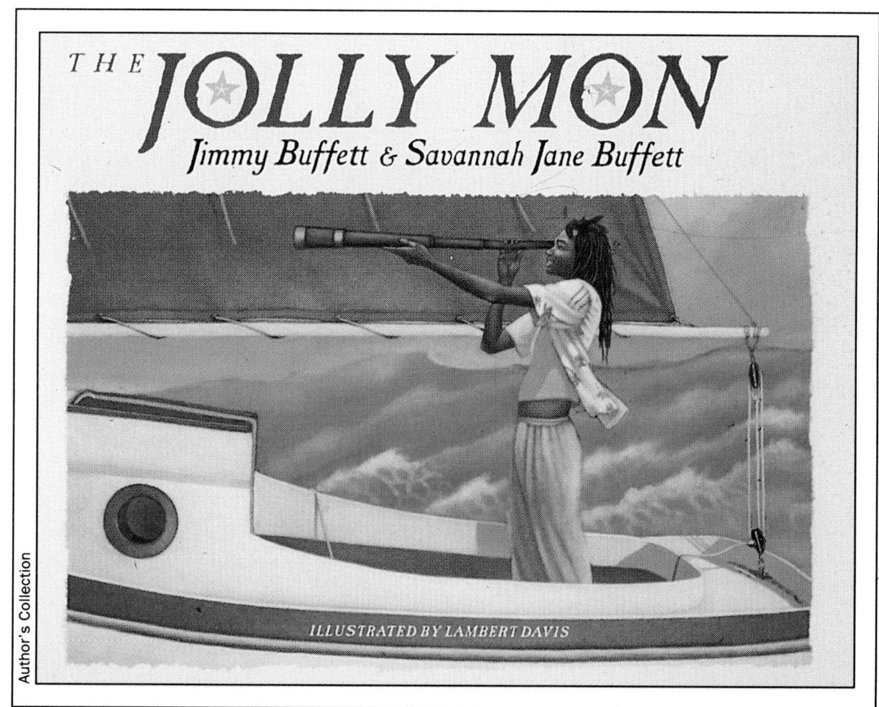

Inspired by a Caribbean folk tale, 1988's *Jolly Mon* was Buffett's first book in print, a collaboration with daughter Savannah Jane.

inspired Buffett to write a song of the same name. "I always knew I was good enough to be on their turf but nobody else did," he told the New York Times News Service. "I was just the singer."

Despite his aspirations to be taken seriously as an author of adult fiction, Buffett's literary career began modestly (but successfully) with a children's book cowritten with his daughter, Savannah Jane. *Jolly Mon* was a delightful retelling of a Caribbean folk tale which Buffett had first used for the song "Jolly Mon Sing" on 1985's *Last Mango in Paris* album. The book was dedicated "to all the people of all the Islands in the Caribbean and to all the dolphins in the sea below."

Meanwhile, there had been no new Buffett album in stores for two years (1986's *Floridays* was his last). Frustrated by what he saw as MCA's unwillingness to promote him to radio and retail, Buffett had been sitting on an album's worth of songs for some time. *Hot Water* finally came out in time for Buffett's 1988 summer tour. "If I make a conscientious effort to do anything," he told *Milwaukee Journal* reporter James Plath, "it's to make damn sure that something on that record is funny. What I want them to do is go 'Oh no, not another one of those!'"

Stereo Review's Parke Puterbaugh wrote that Buffett's *Hot Water* successfully conjured a "tropical fantasy world [where] the days are golden, the nights are long, the margaritas are served in goldfish bowls, the women are willowy and willing—and Buffett is the troubadour who paints this largely untroubled paradise in words and music."

Before his summer tour began, reporter James Plath caught up with Buffett down in Margaritaville. "Interviewed on his Key West back porch," wrote Plath, "the forty-one-year-old Buffett was as laid back as he is onstage, meeting you halfway down a flight of wooden steps and wearing shorts and a khaki shirt, with a loose bandanna tied around his neck. He says that after the interview he's going tarpon fishing, then, barefoot, leads you through a sparsely furnished interior to a deck that faces the Gulf of Mexico. Grinning like a child on Christmas morning—which coincidentally is Buffett's birthday—he points proudly to a huge telescope he bought to view Halley's comet....

"'I should have been a PT-boat captain in World War II, or a steamboat captain. I am definitely a romantic, and I love these periods,' says Buffett, a history buff whose grandfather was a South Seas sailing captain.

"He confides that he carries two books with him at all times—*Hemingway on Writing* and *Elements of Style* by Strunk and White—and when

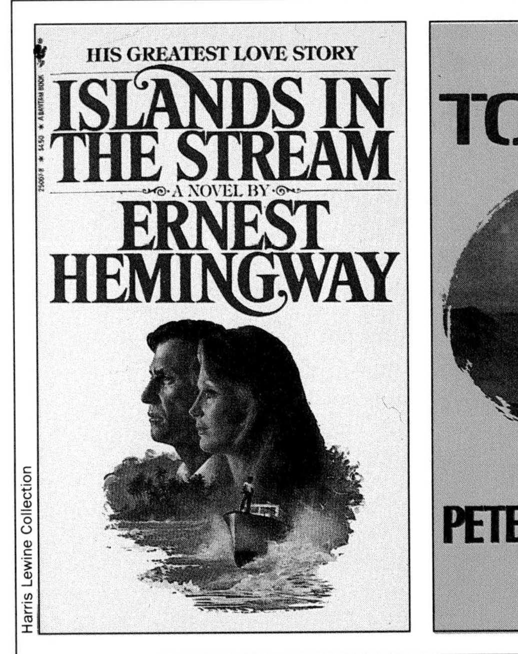

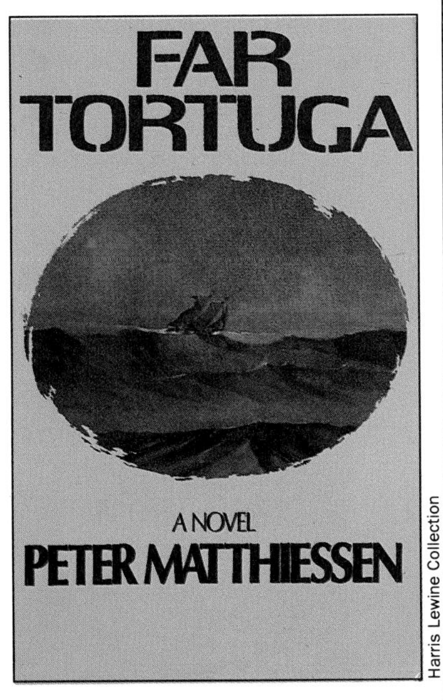

Edmund Wilson called *Islands in the Stream* "some of the best of Hemingway's descriptions of nature." William Styron called Peter Mathieson's *Far Tortuga* "a wonderful tone poem about man, sea, and destiny . . . a work of great beauty." Buffett admired these books too.

you ask about the rhythm of one song, he says, 'It's a tap song. I take tap dance. Really. I took it up when I thought I was going to be doing a Broadway show. That fell through, but I kept up the tap. I still enjoy it.'"

Buffett's public soft-shoe routines generally met with applause, though *Houston Post* critic Bob Claypool was a hard sell when he reviewed a 1988 Buffett appearance at the Houston Livestock Show and Rodeo. "Jimmy Buffett is like some preppie version of a country rocker," Claypool groused, "a musical dilettante who makes occasionally cute 'Caribbean music,' but who, in the end, strikes me as a monotonous bore. Buffett's songs never aim very high or sink very low—they just ooze along, providing quirky little jokes and very little real emotional substance."

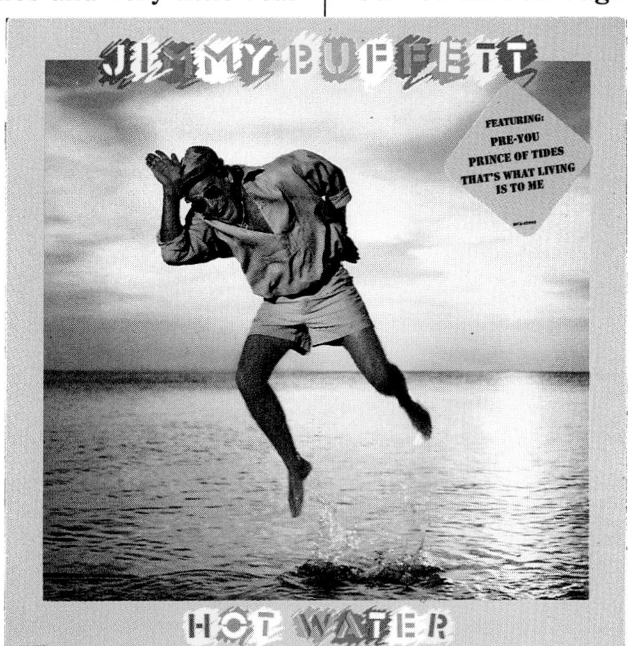

Author's Collection

Nearer the norm was Gerry Wood's review for *Billboard* of an appearance at Nashville's Starwood Amphitheatre: "Buffett, for three shining hours, turned Nashville into 'Margaritaville,' where one could almost hear the whir of the mixer and the roar of the ocean."

That sound was real and constant at Buffett's Key West Margaritaville Cafe, which opened in 1987. "Location-wise," says John Hellen, "it's never been a real good location. There's no parking, and it's basically passers-by. There's been five or six different incarnations of bar or restaurant in there. But as soon as he put his shingle out there, name recognition, it's kind of like 'Hemingway's favorite bar,' that type of thing. Buffett's Margaritaville, it's packed consistently since the day it opened. It's a destination-type thing now. You gotta go there when you're in Key West." Business wasn't bad at Buffett's Margaritaville store in 1988, either. It netted $2 million in its fourth year of business.

There were new worlds to conquer, of course. Buffett and comic Bill Murray became part owners of the Miami Miracles baseball team: "Mr. Buffett has even been known to show up at the ballpark and take a turn at the stadium organ," reported the *Atlanta Journal-Constitution*'s Kathy Hogan Trocheck. In 1989, Buffett was again talking up his *Margaritaville* movie, as well as a Broadway musical, *Rules of the Road,* about a touring country rock band (ex-Eagle Glenn Frey was also involved). Buffett told Trocheck he was writing a novel called *The Black Bean Expansion,* "a story of caviar theft, overweight, and murder." While nothing came of those projects, 1989 was a productive year for Buffett anyway. Encouraged by the success of Hot Water, he released *Off to See the Lizard* in time for that year's summer tour. (*Lizard* would be Buffett's last LP, a format which served him through twenty collections of his songs from 1970 to 1989.) In the fall, his collection of short stories, *Tales From Margaritaville,* hit the bookstores.

Back in 1976, Buffett had discussed the relative merits of rock stardom and fiction writing with *High Times* interviewer Bob Anderson. "I get that instant feedback," he said. "But you writers, there are thirteen fucking critics in New York that run your life. They can make you slash your wrists in the bathroom, depending on what they say about you in the *New York Times Book Review.* You spend maybe a year writing a book, and then you wait a month for ten people to decide whether it's good or bad."

Buffett surely breathed an audible sigh of relief when the dreaded *New York Times Book Review* praised his *Margaritaville* characters' "exuberant antics" and their creator's "lighthearted endorsement of adventure," in the words of reviewer Janet Kaye. Less influential but nonetheless encouraging was *Houston Post* critic John Voland's praise of the book as "a tribute to Buffett's storytelling skills and his essentially sunny, mañana-influenced world view." Closer to home, *Sun-Sentinel* reviewer Chauncey Mabe called *Tales From Margaritaville* "an amazingly adept debut from a rock star who wants to be a writer," adding, "Buffett aspires to be with these stories a regional humorist in the manner of his idol, Mark Twain." A rare raspberry came from Clark Perry at the *St. Petersburg Times:* "Jimmy Buffett," Perry wrote, "who is regarded by many in this state as the ultimate laid-back demigod, has put together an uneven, unpolished collection of writings called *Tales From Margaritaville: Fictional Facts and Factual Fictions* ... his fans will love this book. Buffett's personality and beach-bum outlook dominate every page." His fans did love the book, making it a bestseller. (As 1990 closed, there were three hundred thousand copies in print.)

Buffett ended the eighties an extremely successful and wealthy man. His record-breaking appearance at Nashville's Starwood Amphitheatre (17,200 attended) wasn't an isolated case, and underscored the ironic fact that this one-hit wonder (and his hit was twelve years in the past) had become one of the biggest draws on the summer outdoor "shed" circuit. His Margaritaville Store and Cafe were raging successes; 20,000 Parrot Heads were paying subscribers to his *Coconut Telegraph* newsletter/advertiser. And—the sweetest icing on the cake—he had become a bestselling author of adult fiction. Not bad for the self-described "professional misfit" of the early seventies. Now if only he could get his personal life together....

Author's Collectiom

"Jimmy Buffett, the rock star known for his hit song, 'Margaritaville,' and his wife, Jane, have divorced," Suzy Knickerbocker reported from New York in March of 1990. "The split becomes final in a few weeks. No one is terribly surprised. They've lived more or less separate existences for the past five years. Jane is living the clean life in Malibu, exercising and all that, while Jimmy tours and performs." The divorce did not become final, but it must have been bewildering for Buffett to contemplate the "Miss Jane" who was the mother of his daughter and to whom he'd dedicated so many albums becoming just another memory of the seventies.

If there was trouble in paradise, you'd never know it from Buffett's 1990 summer extravaganza. "'Jimmy's Jump Up' tour is his most theatrical and elaborately staged to date," wrote Tom Walton in the Toledo *Blade.* "The Blossom Music Center stage was converted into a tropical island complete with thatched roofs and flaming tiki torches. A rear-projection screen cast a full moon and a sky full of stars behind the performers. But Buffett saved the best for last. For his encore piece, 'Volcano,' a twenty-five-foot volcano arose from the stage, erupted right on cue, and showered the crowd with sparkling ash while the multitudes sang along with the boss...."

Moira McCarthy reflected both on the "Jump Up Tour" experience and Buffett's audience in her review for the *Brockton Enterprise:* "Watching Jimmy Buffett perform is not a practice in metaphysics. Neither is it an evening of musical wonder. It's more like a giant happy hour, the way they used to be.... It's probably no surprise that Buffett's fans, like himself, are watching their hairlines recede daily. For what Buffett offers to fans is an escape, for an hour or so, back to the days of college dorms, spring breaks, and summer vacation. And who more than those of us well into real life could get into that?

"... A highlight in the evening was the silly giant shark that floated over the fans as Buffett belted out his popular 'Fins.' Another shark was inflated ... behind Buffett onstage as he sang."

Recordings of "Jimmy's Jump Up Tour" dates in Atlanta and Cincinnati comprised the *Feeding Frenzy* album, which welcomed Buffett to the era

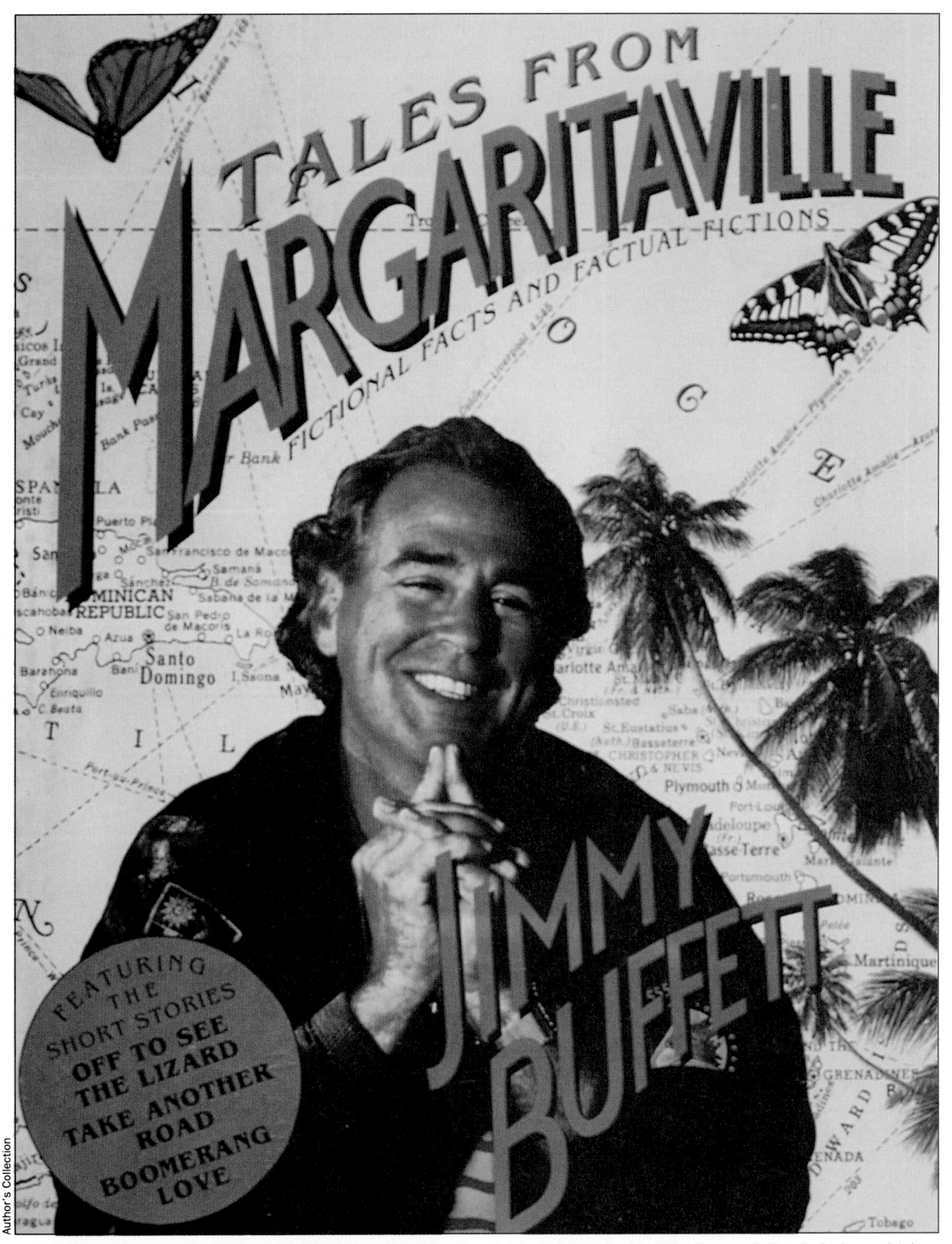

Author's Collection

Tales From Margaritaville (1989) was Buffett's first adult fiction though it included stories like "The Pascagoula Run," which are plainly autobiographical. From Heartache, Wyoming, to Graceland to Heatwave, Alabama, Buffett's stories portray a southern and western world that's neither "hick chic" nor "cornpone."

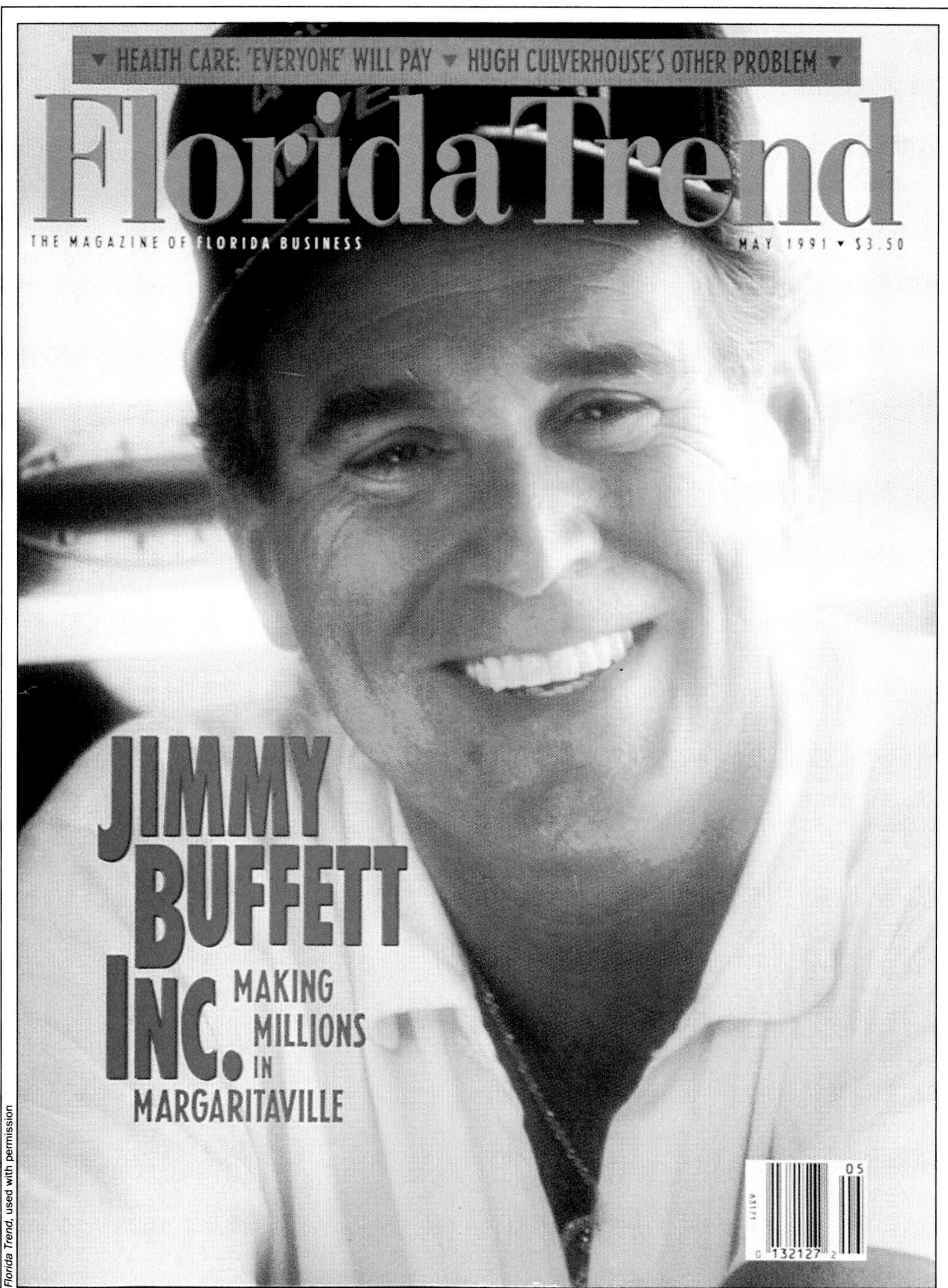

▼ HEALTH CARE: 'EVERYONE' WILL PAY ▼ HUGH CULVERHOUSE'S OTHER PROBLEM ▼
Florida Trend
THE MAGAZINE OF FLORIDA BUSINESS
MAY 1991 ▼ $3.50
JIMMY BUFFETT INC.
MAKING MILLIONS IN MARGARITAVILLE

Florida Trend, used with permission

Move over, Paul McCartney. Buffett's business acumen impressed the editors of *Florida Trend,* which made him its May 1991 cover subject. The article applauded Buffett's diversity and sure sense of marketing his myth.

of the compact disc. Cajun rocker Zachary Richard, who opened for Buffett on that tour, remembers it as "totally pro; people were very considerate, everybody did his job, and there were really no assholes on this tour. The thing about Jimmy, I have this theory that we're all victims of our own particular myth, we create these stories about ourselves and spend our lives trying to prove that they're true. And I think that he's got the whole pirate mentality, and going off on a Buffett tour is kind of like going off on a pirate ship in a way. The captain always takes care of his crew on a successful voyage."

The slickness of Buffett's elaborately-staged "theme" tours of recent years is a quantum leap from the loose "boogie" of the late seventies: for audible evidence, compare his two live albums, 1978's *You Had to Be There* with 1990's *Feeding Frenzy.* Even though the band's name remained a hokey dope joke, Fingers Taylor would tell an interviewer that, in the Coral Reefers of the nineties, drugging was a firing offense. And their boss? Clean as a whistle. Up at eight, working out with his personal trainer.

And when not working out, Buffett was writing. "My intention, being the good Catholic schoolboy that I am, was to write every day on the road," Buffett told *Publishers Weekly* reporter Beth Levine. "It just didn't work out that way." Still, he was well on his way to completing a novel, and independently negotiated a deal with Harcourt Brace Jovanovich for a six-figure sum that *Publishers Weekly* described as 'handsome.' Buffett recalls that there were many agents interested in representing him, but he decided in the end that he didn't need one. "It doesn't take much to add up the numbers, does it? You'd have to be a dummy not to see that if 20 percent of the people who buy half a million of my record albums a year buy a book, that's a substantial sale."

Buffett had become very good at adding up numbers. The Florida business magazine, *Florida Trend,* reported that "his various ventures grossed an estimated $30 million in revenues" in 1990. He would do even better in 1991, when Buffett gave the venerable Grateful Dead and the upstart Guns 'n' Roses a spirited run for scarce concert dollars with his Outpost Tour: Those three acts were the summer's top draws. *New York Newsday* reviewer Steve Zipay noted that Buffett's tour had "taken wing" on an aviation theme: "Buffett and his eleven-member Coral Reefer Band 'deplaned' in the 'Margaritaville Clipper,' a huge mock-up of a thirties-style flying boat. The

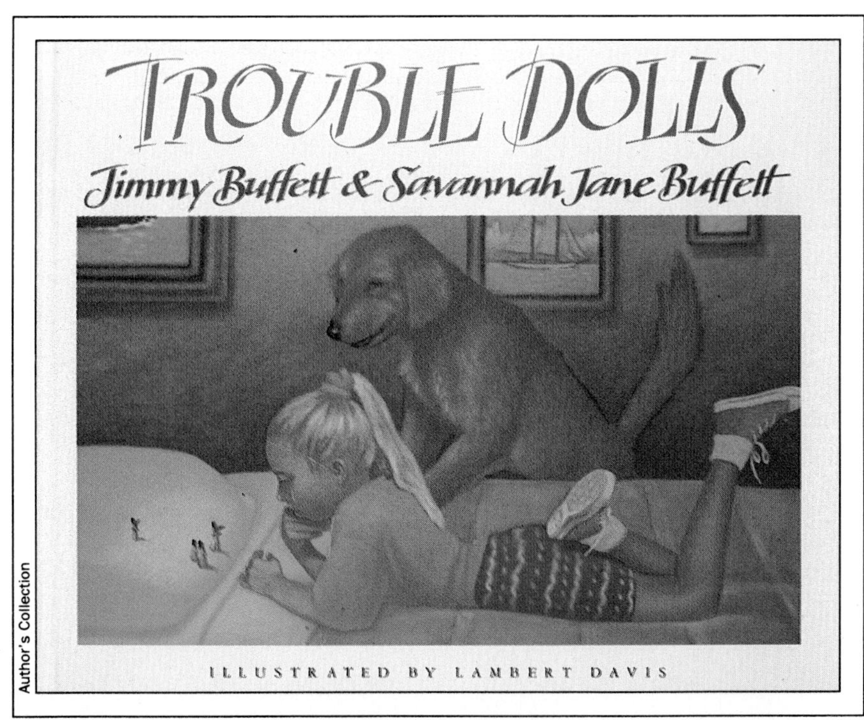

Buffett's second collaboration with daughter Savannah Jane, *Trouble Dolls* (1991), had a precocious little girl as heroine. (Following spread) Buffett calls himself one of the last living legends, and Parrot Heads nationwide agree. Buffett onstage in Los Angeles, 1992.

Photo: Susan Watts, Retna

'landing' took place on a stage framed by palm fronds, tiki torches, a smoking volcano, and a backdrop of billowing clouds in an azure sky. And during the two-hour set, a black-and-white newsreel-style short featured Buffett and the Reefers winning dogfights against the enemy forces of DRAL (Disco, Rap, and Lip-Synch) and a cameo by Harrison Ford's Indiana Jones."

It was a good summer: Buffett's three days at Cincinnati's Riverbend Music Center alone grossed over $1.2 million. While he played the carefree party animal onstage, Buffett was all business elsewhere. "Over the past six years," Elizabeth Willson wrote in *Florida Trend,* "as his hair has thinned and the crow's-feet have lengthened, Buffett has developed the offstage persona of a hard-driving, self-styled CEO with a savvy sense of marketing." Willson described what must have been, to a member of the Mouseketeers generation, an especially satisfying offer: "He has even resisted the ultimate marketing seduction—a courtship by Walt Disney Company. Disney is eager to add a Margaritaville restaurant and club to Pleasure Island at Walt Disney World. 'Yeah, it's pretty hard to turn down the Mouse,' Buffett says in his smooth Delta drawl. 'It didn't feel right. Disney is creating myths and we are one. They're still calling us.'"

Buffett's second children's book, cowritten with Savannah Jane, appeared in 1991. *Trouble Dolls* concerned a young girl's rescue of her "famous environmentalist" father when his seaplane is lost in the Everglades. Buffett's three published books and the six-figure advance for *Where Is Joe Merchant?* were making the book business a factor of significance in his financial empire. "With royalties and advances," wrote Willson, "the books already have added $1 million to Buffett's earnings and easily could have reached $2 million. And then there's the Corona Beer endorsement. Corona Extra beer helps bankroll Buffett's summer concert tour in exchange for stage props and Jimmy's endorsement. That could be worth $500,000 or more, say entertainment lawyers.

"How much does Buffett take home? Buffett won't say; he guards his finances as diligently as

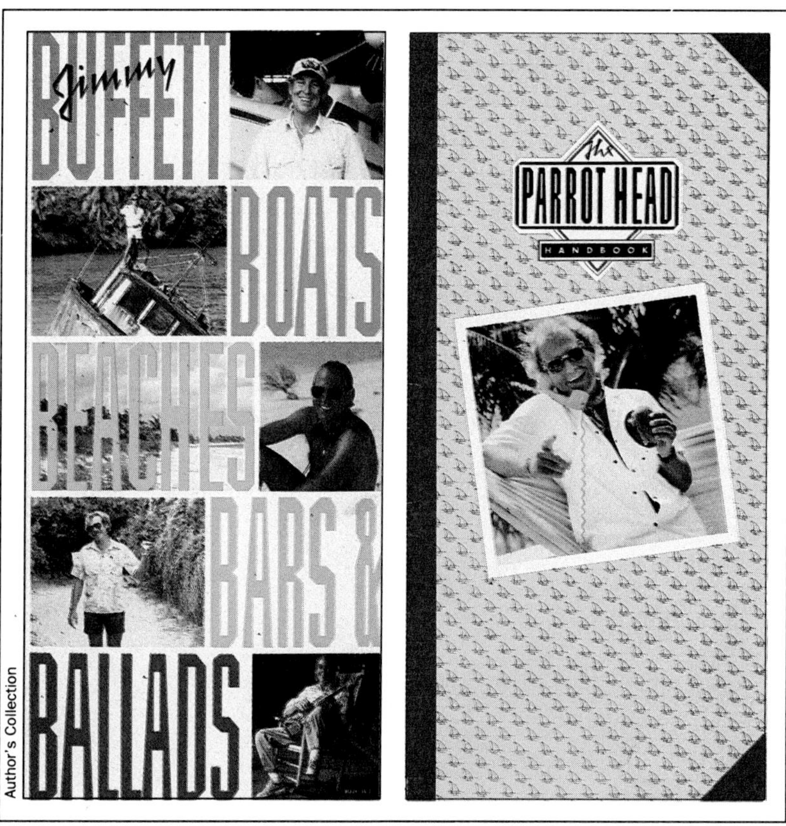

The 1992 Buffett box had little music his fans hadn't heard hundreds of times, but they bought it anyway to hear it on CD and to read *The Parrot Head Handbook* Buffett wrote for the faithful. Many were inspired. It became MCA's bestselling boxed set.

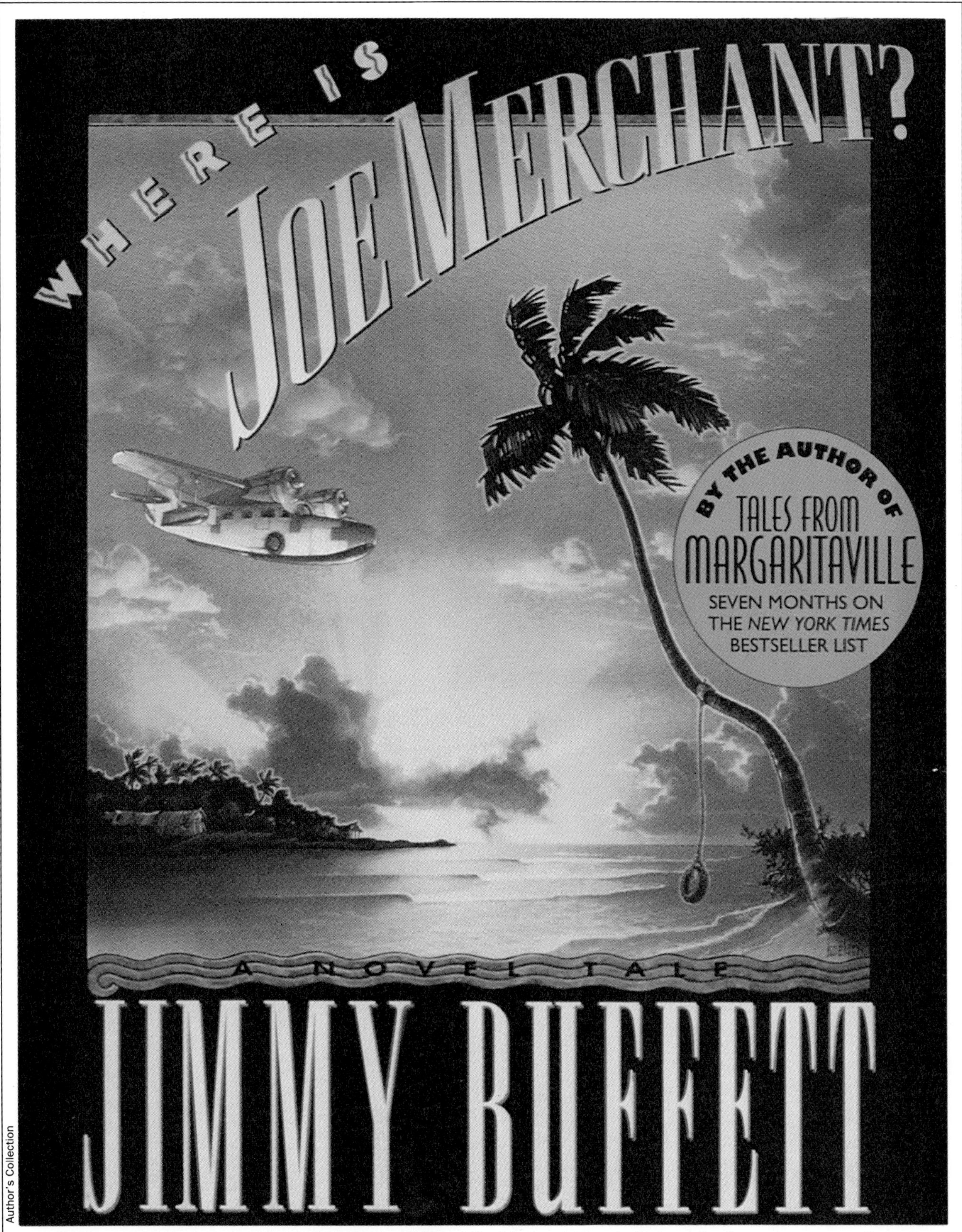

Author's Collection

Buffett's most ambitious prose to date is the 1992 novel *Where Is Joe Merchant?* It made the bestseller lists and was reportedly among the books Bill Clinton took on vacation with him in August 1993.

Play It Again, Joe

If Buffett's *Where Is Joe Merchant?* makes it to the big screen, there are two groups of show-biz professionals who will be left out of the usual moviemaking process. The first: song pluggers—people who work at music publishing companies and whose job it is to scan the trades for word of forthcoming productions and then pitch songs from their company's catalog which they hope will fit a film's mood, theme, and era. Second: music supervisors—free-lance "ears" hired by productions to ferret out the songs you hear with movies. Music supervisors are the usual targets of song pluggers' pitches. But *Joe Merchant* won't need either, thanks, since Buffett preempted both pluggers and supers when he wrote the novel. The songs which are background to specific scenes are already written into the text.

Not everybody thought that was a great idea. "Buffett takes some unfortunate shortcuts," wrote *Chicago Tribune* critic Mark Caro in his review of *Joe Merchant.* "He often tries to establish atmosphere simply by naming what song is playing in the background...." But the songs do help set Buffett's scenes, especially in bars, and offer insight into the songwriter-novelist's musical taste. It should come as no surprise that many of the songs he "plays" simply by mentioning their titles were popular in the late sixties and early seventies and call up powerful memories among Buffett's contemporaries, the Parrot Heads he calls "war babies."

If you remember fringe jackets and patchouli oil, Buffett effectively pushes your buttons merely by mentioning Crosby, Stills & Nash singing "Suite: Judy Blue Eyes" on the jukebox at Key West's Bobalou. ("On the bar, a bouquet of flowers lay slumped over in an iced-tea pitcher.") A couple of pages later, Van Morrison's "Tupelo Honey" comes through a radio: "The music set the mood for the stormy afternoon." A later scene introduces Charlie Fabian over a beer at

Strider records, NYC

Strider records, NYC

Strider records, NYC

Strider records, NYC

Charleston's Equator bar, and we hear Al Green's aching 1972 testimonial, "Love and Happiness," "flow out of the speakers behind the bar...." At a disco, the Rolling Stones' 1980 hit, "Emotional Rescue," is heard. Buffett's only other reference to music of the Reagan era is Prince and the Revolution's 1984 "Purple Rain." Most of the songs he "plugs" to provoke an emotional twitch in "war baby" readers were hits between 1969 and 1972: "Let the Sunshine In" from *Hair* (the Fifth Dimension's *Hair* medley, "Aquarius/Let the Sunshine In" was number one for six weeks in 1969), Santana's 1970 hit, "Black Magic Woman," and Derek & the Dominos' "Layla."

Derek, of course, was Eric Clapton, and "Layla" was one of his first triumphs after the disbandment of the legendary British rock "power trio," Cream. Edited to under three minutes, "Layla" staggered up to number 51 in *Billboard*'s pop charts in 1971. But, in a reversal of "edited-for-radio" successes, "Layla" was rereleased in its full-blown seven-minute glory, and made it up to number 4 on the charts in June 1972! Stranger still, Clapton would rerecord his blazing guitar anthem ("Goddamn, man, that is a rock-'n'-roll song," writes Buffett) as an acoustic folk-blues for his 1992 *Unplugged* album, and his laid-back "Layla" became a hit twenty years after the original.

The Stones' "You Can't Always Get What You Want" from 1969's *Let It Bleed* so impressed Buffett that he mentioned it both in Tales From Margaritaville and again in Joe Merchant. It seems ironic that a millionaire with an abundance of yachts and seaplanes takes solace in a song about not getting what you want (and gratitude for having only what you need), but there it is. "You love it because it says what you can't," Buffett writes of the song.

Since *Joe Merchant* has plenty of action in the Caribbean, its author (the Calypso king) mentions a lot of Caribbean music, right? Well, he invokes Jamaica's Jimmy Cliff ("Many Rivers to Cross") and Sam Cooke's 1959 "exotica" era goof, "Everybody Likes to Cha-Cha-Cha." Buffett tells us, "Bob Marley was the St. Jude of the third world," but nothing of Marley's music. A cartoon version of Afro-Cuban music is depicted when a character named Fernando believes himself to be the reincarnation of Ricky Ricardo: "... he would

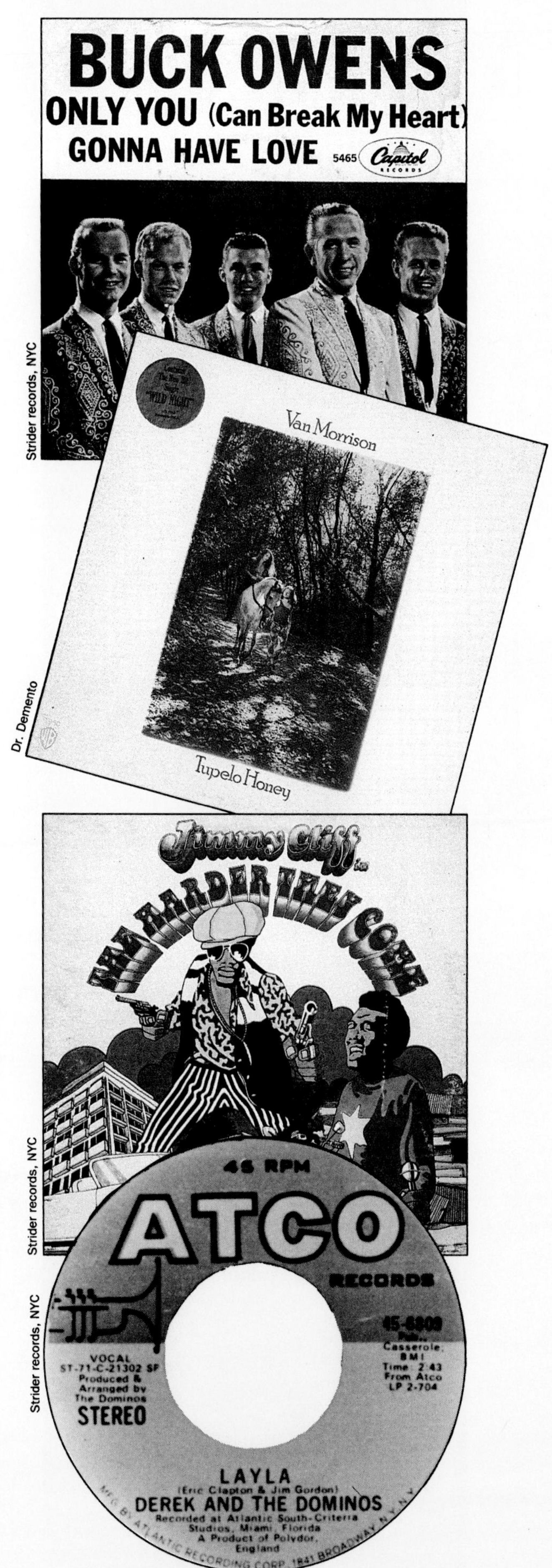

Strider records, NYC

Dr. Demento

Strider records, NYC

Strider records, NYC

Frank Driggs Collection

Sam Cooke

Golden Disc, NYC

play his conga drum and sing 'Babalu' as if it were a religious experience." The song was rooted in African ecstatic religion, and Desi Arnaz's cover of Margarita Lecuona's "Babalu" had been a hit for Arnaz in 1946 before becoming a "war baby" gag via its exposure on I *Love Lucy*. ("He's Ba-ba'd his last lu," Lucy to teenager smitten by Ricky.)

Buffett naturally gives his own songs plenty of play in *Joe Merchant.* He subheads chapters with his song titles ("Changes in Latitudes") or lyrics ("Fins to the Left, Fins to the Right"). He quotes his most familiar lyrics with a wink ("I realized Rudy was just wasted away again") and christens a cruise ship *Havana Daydreamer.* Sizable chunks of Buffett songs, among them "Boat Drinks" and "Sending the Old Man Home," appear in such a way that, if *Merchant* becomes a movie, the songwriter Jimmy Buffett will clearly be getting a piece of change along with Buffett the novelist. You can bank on that.

Having a song in a hit movie is a lucrative business, especially if the song plays in a key scene excerpted in a music video promoting the movie, which may catapult the song into a hit independent of the movie. Buffett has prior experience at the song placement game. "Volcano" was used in the 1982 Sean Penn (remember Mr. Madonna?) comedy, *Fast Times at Ridgemont High.* The song was retitled on the soundtrack as "I Don't Know (Spicoli's Theme)." In 1990, *Always* used "Boomerang Love," a track from 1989's *Off to See the Lizard,* which shared its title with one of Buffett's *Tales From Margaritaville.* In the summer of 1993, Buffett's decade-old recording of Rodney Crowell's "Stars on the Water" could be heard in the Tom Cruise vehicle *The Firm.* According to a press release on *The Firm*'s soundtrack, director Sydney Pollack "picked Jimmy Buffett's bluesy 'Stars on the Water,' with lyrics that capture the natural beauty of the South, to go with a scene that takes place at a truck stop." Such placement links Buffett with the dreaded country music, dismissed in *Joe Merchant* as good pigeon repellent and little more: "Country music ... kept the pigeons from roosting in the rafters and shitting on the planes.... There was something about country music that made them stay airborne." Does that mean we won't be hearing Garth Brooks on the *Merchant* sound track?

his privacy (he rarely grants interviews). But even estimating a 10 percent gross profit (earnings before taxes) from his enterprises, Buffett would easily be a $3-million-a-year entertainer."

As reminder that not everyone shared his good fortune, Buffett found a group of Cuban refugees docking in his backyard in 1991. Kermit Patison filed the following report at the *Key West Citizen:* "Perhaps tempted by notions of living on spongecake and watching the sun bake in Margaritaville, four Cuban refugees landed at the home of musician Jimmy Buffett early Wednesday.

"The refugees motored their eighteen-foot boat up to the Riviera Canal-side home of the musician, who wrote the Key West tune 'Margaritaville' and owns a Duval Street bar by the same name.

"'They came up for the concert, who knows?' said Lt. Jeff Karonis of the Coast Guard Operations Center in Miami. 'Just another day in Margaritaville.'

"After two men and two women landed in his backyard, Buffett reportedly invited them in for refreshments and offered a few souvenirs.

"'He came out and gave them all tapes and gave them all drinks,' said Lt. Tom Criman of the Coast Guard Operations Center in Key West.

"Buffett telephoned the Key West Police, who transported the refugees to the Coast Guard Station. They were later processed by Immigration and Naturalization Service Officials."

On his 1993 tour, Buffett would tell this story, adding that one of the men, in hopes that he could stay, told the INS officials that he had a cousin in Miami. "I said, 'I think I hear a song in this,'" and Buffett wrote the salsa-flavored "Everybody Has a Cousin in Miami," which he promised would be on his next album.

Author's Collection

"The Good Life for Men" certainly describes Buffett's style. Like his idol, Hemingway, he combined sports with prose in a 1992 *Esquire Sportsman* feature on quail hunting, "Everything in the Woods Wants to Eat a Quail (Including Me)."

Empire building and visiting aliens aside, the significant event of Buffett's life in 1991 was his reconciliation with Jane. "We were both basically living different lives," Buffett told *USA Today*'s Ann Trebbe in 1992. "Living Aspen to Key West to St. Bart's and it was great. I did a lot of hard living. And Janie did, too.... We stayed in touch and we were good friends but not lovers. It came right up to the point of getting a divorce.... I found myself in Bora Bora going, 'What the hell am I doing here? I've come all the way to this magical place and I'm not here with anybody!'... If it hadn't been for Janie, I'd-a quit and become a bachelor and gone to live in the woods with my dogs." The Buffett's second daughter, Sarah Delaney, was born in April 1992.

The reunion with Jane and its implications were also on Buffett's mind when he spoke with *Los Angeles Times* pop critic Robert Hilburn in 1992. "I did some therapy myself when I went back with my wife," he said, "and one thing this guy pointed out to me was that performance is part of your life but your life is not a performance. That rang true because I had been trying to live my personal life like a performance.... My performance had always come first. Everything was about Jimmy's job, what Jimmy wants. Everything else was secondary. All of a sudden, I'd say, 'I've got to go to Tahiti and do research' or 'I've got to work on a record,' and everybody else had to stay in the background. But it eventually catches up with you, and I realized I was missing something [during the separation in the eighties]. I was about to lose the woman I really loved and who was my soul mate. We were very close to getting a divorce. We had filed the papers and everything, but I finally had a heart-to-heart with

Ran into a chum
With a bottle of rum,
And we wound up
Drinking all night.

We've lived in Washington, D.C. for most of our lives but have never been very active in politics or it's surrounding affairs. That is until we heard that Jimmy Buffett was performing at the Tennessee Ball; one of the official inaugural celebration balls President Clinton would be attending.

Being true Parrot Heads, we had to find a way to witness this historic event. Not having tickets (which started at $175.00) made this somewhat difficult, but not impossible. Having an inside connection at the Washington Hilton, and with a local company providing the lighting at this event greatly enhanced our chances.

We showed up early Wednesday (Jan. 20) evening, underdressed in jeans and "*If we weren't all crazy we would go insane*" T-shirts, and naturally stood out from the rest of the revelers outfitted in rental tuxes and evening gowns.

We discovered that Jimmy was not scheduled to perform until midnight, so we decided to head back to Georgetown. We found ourselves at Champions Bar standing next to Ted Koppel doing an **Nightline** interview with a member of the Young Republican Party while his cronies chanted "Quayle in '96!" [Insert comment here.] At any rate, we got our picture taken with Ted Koppel, had a couple of beers for courage, and headed back to find Buffett.

We found our contact person and proceeded to our vantage point, sandwiched between the sound system and the stage lights, overlooking the entire ball. It was very cramped and hot as hell from the heat of the spotlights.

Paul Simon began performing "You Can Call Me Al", prompting Vice-President Al Gore and his wife Tipper "Watch Those Lyrics" Gore to jump on stage and show all America their own version of the Tennessee Waltz.

After a brief intermission, Jimmy Buffett & The Coral Reefers finally took the stage.

Is this a great country or what. Where else can you see the president jamming with Jimmy Buffett?

It was a definite surprise to see Jimmy dressed in a black tux with a Telecaster hanging around his neck. It was no surprise, however, when he tore the bow tie from around his neck and tossed it into the crowd.

The big moment came when President Clinton appeared and announced to all that, "Yes, Jimmy Buffett is a friend of mine!" Jimmy then brought his family on stage to meet the first family, and segued into the most appropriate "Changes in Latitudes, Changes in Attitudes." It was then that the President of the United States of America, the leader of the free world, and arguably the most powerful man on the face of the earth, grabbed a saxophone and jammed along with Jimmy to the roar of the crowd. Certainly a moment in Parrot Head Madness that will long be remembered.

By The Mayr Brothers - Ingo & Andy

Jimmy & The Reefers at the Tennessee Ball. *Photo: J.L. Jamison*

Author's Collection

myself. I never knew what marriage really was ... how to be a husband. I never really gave it a shot, and I thought that if I didn't give it an honest effort, there would be a real hole in me. I could have all the success in the world, but there would still be something missing."

"All the success in the world" continued to be Buffett's. He launched Margaritaville Records (in association with MCA) in 1992 with the four-CD career retrospective, *Boats, Beaches, Bars and Ballads,* which quickly 'went platinum' and became MCA's best-selling boxed set. Margaritaville Records enables Buffett to make his own music his own way (and in his own good time) while supporting hungry up-and-comers like Evangeline and The Iguanas.

As had been the case for several years, the crowds just got bigger in 1992 for Buffett's summer Recession Recess Tour. And as if a four-CD boxed set weren't "product" enough for one year, Buffett's novel, *Where Is Joe Merchant?* was published in early September. Buffett knew it would be a bestseller. "Here's how I figured," he told Hilburn. "If you are selling 400,000 albums and playing to 700,000 to a million people a year, you ought to be able to sell 100,000 books, which should be enough to put you on the bestseller list. But it took off well beyond anyone's expectation ... 400,000 in hardback sales."

Where Is Joe Merchant? weaves three or four subplots around seaplane pilot Frank Bama and the title character, a Jim Morrison-style rocker turned mercenary fighter. Reviews generally gave a "thumbs up" to Buffett's 382-page novel. "Buffett has a storyteller's gift," Mark Johnson wrote in the *San Jose Mercury News,* "honed in a thousand tropical barrooms." The *San Francisco Chronicle* said, "Buffett's episodic novel moves quickly and readably from one adventure to the next, stirring every new character neatly into his narrative jambalaya." At the *Orlando Sentinel,* William McKeen likened Buffett's novel to "listening to one of his albums—pure pleasure, with a dash of insight."

"If I were quail hunting," Joe Merchant coolly announced after killing two people, "that would be called a double." Along with fishing, flying, and sundry other activities, quail hunting had become one of Buffett's passions, and he wrote about it in the autumn 1992 *Esquire Sportsman* in a piece entitled "Everything in the Woods Wants to Eat a Quail (Including Me)." In it, Buffett paid tribute to his old pal Guy de la Valdene ("... taught me most

Wide World Photos

Along with a reunited Fleetwood Mac and other stars of the 1970s, Buffett was among the entertainers at the Clinton inauguration in 1993. Clinton became an honorary Coral Reefer, blowing sax behind Buffett. We don't know if First Lady Hillary Clinton has followed the precedent set by Rosalynn Carter, who reportedly enjoyed wearing a Jimmy Buffett T-shirt in the White House (Buffett campaigned for Carter in 1976).

Photo: Gary Gershoff, Retna Ltd.

The self-proclaimed "spokesman for the bald spot generation" still loves performing for his fellow "war babies" and their children. "I like to see forty-year-old people standing on their seats dancing," Buffett once told *USA Today.*

of what I know about quail hunting") and to a golden retriever named Cheeseburger. Buffett hunts quail on Springhill Plantation in South Georgia, space rented in an ever-changing global real estate portfolio: a Paris apartment, homes in Sag Harbor, Long Island ("it's a natural northern extension of Key West"), Key West, and Nashville. With time, some residences are likely be history and others may fill their place. Given such abundance, it's reassuring to know that Buffett has performed at benefits for the homeless in New Orleans.

Buffett began 1993 in high-celebratory style at President Bill Clinton's January 20 inauguration when he and the Coral Reefers performed at the Tennessee Ball. Ingo and Andy Mayr of Washington, D.C., described the festivities in the March issue of the *Coconut Telegraph:* "It was a definite surprise to see Jimmy dressed in a black tux with a Telecaster hanging around his neck. It was no surprise, however, when he tore the bow tie from around his neck and tossed it into the crowd.

"The big moment came when President Clinton appeared and announced to all that, 'Yes, Jimmy Buffett is a friend of mine!' Jimmy then brought his family on stage to meet the first family, and segued into the most appropriate 'Changes in Latitudes, Changes in Attitudes.' It was then that the President of the United States of America, the leader of the free world, and arguably the most powerful man on the face of the earth, grabbed a saxophone and jammed along with Jimmy to the roar of the crowd. Certainly a moment in Parrot Head Madness that will long be remembered."

With spring Buffett's empire expanded again as a second Margaritaville opened in New Orleans.

MARGARITAVILLE NEW ORLEANS SPECIAL ISSUE

Once upon a time there was a big bang. Gasses swirled, galaxies were created, the planets formed. One we call Earth gradually cooled, the oceans were formed and separated the land masses. One particular land mass in the western hemisphere near the Tropic of Cancer became known as the Florida Keys. The last of this stretch of islands was called Key West, and it was here that Jimmy Buffett planted the seed that would grow into Margaritaville.

Key West, or Cayo Hueso as it was known 200 years ago, was first given to mercenary Juan Pablo Salas by the Spanish crown for "deeds and services performed." In the first documented Florida land scam, Salas sold the island...twice! In keeping with this creative real estate tradition, John Strong, one of Salas' original dupes, also sold the island twice. A rather inauspicious beginning for Key West. It took 5 years and an act of Congress to straighten everything out.

Lt. Matthew C. Perry, sent by the U.S. government on a fact finding in 1822 reported that "...heretofore, the Florida Keys have been the resort of smugglers, New Providence wreckers, and in fact of a set of desperadoes who have paid but little regard to either Law or Honesty..."

The more it changes the more it stays the same. Key West's history is an economic roller coaster, from being the richest city per capita in the nation, to being surrendered to the federal government as a result of 80% of it's population being on relief. Through it all the illicit activity referred to Lt. Perry continued. Prohibition, the bane of the 20's, passed relatively unnnoticed in Key West. Smuggling; guns and rum, was a popular pastime. Tourism came and went, then came and went again defeated by hurricanes and WWII.

In a 1978 interview with the **Miami Herald**, Jimmy Buffett said, "Key West goes through phases. It's been proven in history too many tines. She's been up and down too many times. If it's going too pretty now, something will come along and change it."

The Margaritaville Store opened in January 1985, in Land's End Village, Key West. A small store in a good location (surrounded by bars) that served it's purpose and is fondly remembered by Margaritians everywhere.

In October, 1987, the Margaritaville Store burst it's seams and was forced to find more suitable accommodations. Unable to contain the constantly changing merchandise, much less the hundreds of Parrot Heads who visit daily, we moved to 500 Duval Street, the main

Jimmy has long and strong ties to the Crescent City. Jimmy's first public performance took place in New Orleans - on Bourbon Street. Literally, on Bourbon Street. You'll recognize many of his favorite haunts mentioned in "Tales From Margaritaville." It seemed like a natural second location for Margaritaville.

Author's Collection

"They opened the club just before the jazz festival this year," says Zachary Richard. "They're sold out every night that I know of, so I figure they're doing something right. I'm just happy there's another club in New Orleans downtown, because that's really been hurting for a long time."

Along with New Orleans music, Margaritaville serves Caribbean cuisine, and was favorably reviewed in Joe Simmer's June 1983 "Food for Thought" column in New Orleans' *Offbeat.* "Housed in the former Storyville club, Margaritaville strikes one as a big airy urban beach-house—doors opening to both Decatur Street and French Market Place, according a pleasant crossbreeze, vinyl tablecloths stapled to the underside of the tables to prevent them from moving around, and very sparse decor (less Jimmy Buffett presence than I had anticipated).

"The highlight of the island offerings here is the side order of Peas and Rice. In the Caribbean, beans (usually field peas or crowder peas) are served mixed with rice rather than having the beans served on top of the rice. The dish here was quite good, well seasoned yet not overly peppered, and served piping hot. It's the bargain of the menu—$2.95 and almost a meal in itself."

Buffett continued his conquest of the Crescent City as his Chameleon Caravan swung through the South. One of the tour's biggest blowouts was the Primo Parrothead Party in New Orleans on June 12 at Tad Gormley Stadium, City Park, which Buffett fondly recalled storming to see the Beatles back in 1964. It was a mini-festival with four music stages, arts, crafts, Caribbean food, and the music of Margaritaville label acts

Author's Collection

(Opposite) Parrot Head cooler at the Primo Parrothead Party, New Orleans, 1993.

Photo: Syndey Byrd

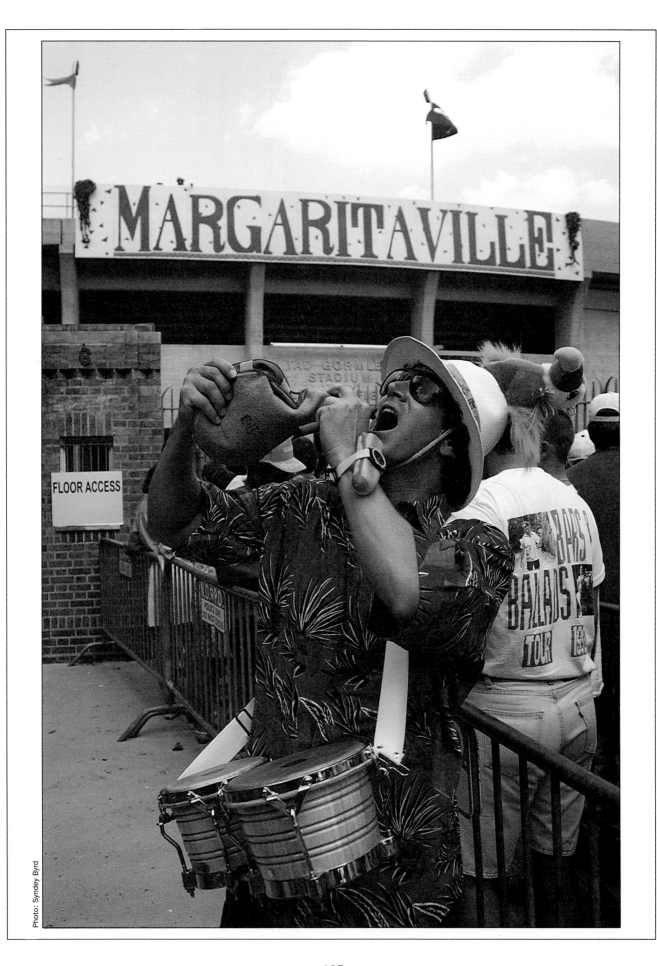

Evangeline and The Iguanas as well as veterans Little Richard (making his first New Orleans appearance in over twenty years) and ex-Doobie Brother Michael McDonald. "I've been going to Jazzfest for damn near as many years as it's been going on," Buffett told *Times-Picayune* reporter Scott Aiges. "I've had so much fun as a consumer of Jazzfest, I thought, 'Why not put a little of Jazzfest into the Jimmy Buffett show and see what happens?'" Buffett hoped a handful of mini-festivals at select locations "a couple of dozen times a year" might become the norm in place of the annual summer tour. "It's really laying the groundwork for the future," he told Aiges. "If it works, it's perfect for me because then I can cut back. I always still want to perform, but I don't want to perform at the schedule I have for the past twenty-five years...."

Sheila Stroup reviewed the Saturday bacchanal for Monday's *Times-Picayune*. PARROT HEADS CAN PARTY affirmed the headline. "The guy was wearing green stuff on his head. He was smoking a cigarette and exhaling into a plastic tube that wound around under the greenery and emerged at the point on top. And he was trying to give a logical explanation for why his brain appeared to be smouldering. 'I'm a volcano,' he said. Oh. Cool.

"The thing was, he didn't really stand out in the crowd milling around Tad Gormley Stadium warming up for the first annual Jimmy Buffett Parrothead Party Saturday afternoon. Fans wore cheeseburgers and margaritas and shark fins on their heads—all in honor of Buffett songs, of course. And parrots were everywhere—on shorts and earrings and hats. A hundred men (including my doctor) were wearing identical red tropical parrot shirts.

"Earlier in the week, when I asked my son if he was going to the eight-and-a-half-hour concert, he rolled his eyes. 'Right, Mom,' he said. 'It's gonna be ninety-five degrees and a bunch of people your age.' The kid was almost right. The temperature might have been ninety-nine. There were a bunch of people there—about 27,500—most of us old enough to remember when it was okay to

Courtesy Chris Robinson

Chris Robinson, proprietor of The Big Kahuna Chartering Service, Key West, 1991: "My hair's still halfway down my back and I can still boogie with the best of 'em if I want to."

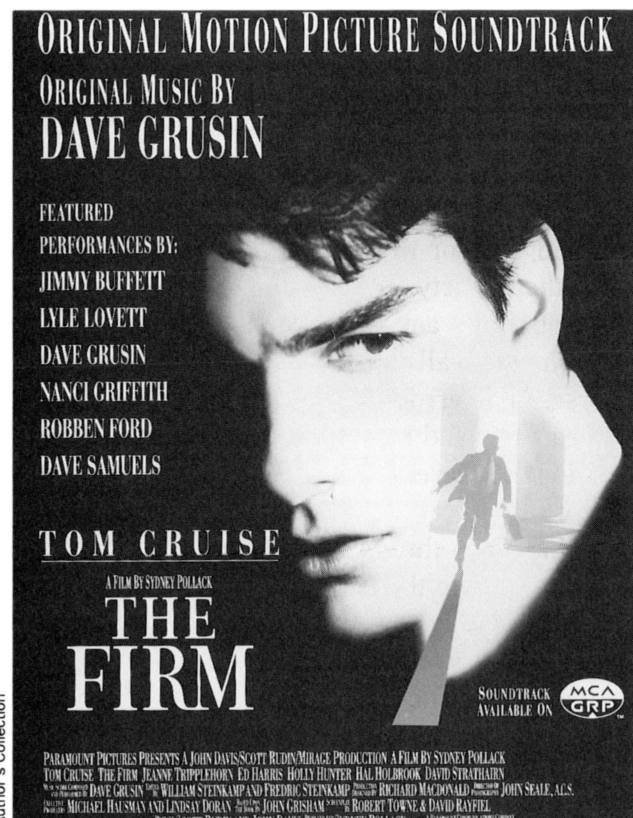

Author's Collection

The summer '93 Tom Cruise blockbuster, *The Firm,* was one of several films in which Buffett has had songs. Will a movie of *Joe Merchant* be next?

get a suntan....

"The party kicked off at three in the afternoon and ended just before midnight. There were performances by The Iguanas and Evangeline, plus parrotheads second-lining around the field behind the Young Olympia Brass Band, plus mountains of cheeseburgers in paradise (with lettuce and tomato) cooked up by the Artists Against Hunger and Homelessness.

"It included 27,500 people standing up, swaying, dancing for the whole two-hour Jimmy Buffett concert.... The biggest complaint of the day was that the beer lines were too long. (Nobody worried about forking over $3 a beer, especially after the first few.) 'We didn't quite expect it to be such a heavy beer-drinking crowd,' stadium manager Russell Doussan said. 'We'll take care of that next year.'"

Buffett's 1993 Chameleon Caravan Tour would go on to stage Primo Parrothead Parties in Atlanta and Buckeye Lake, Ohio. (A note to philologists: Parrot Head, separate as two words in Buffett's *Parrot Head Handbook,* was combined as Parrothead in the advertising for his New Orleans mini-festival, yet it remains Parrot Head in MCA's 1993 Buffett press release. So what gives?)

On tour, Buffett vowed a new album, *Quietly Making Noise,* would be recorded in October '93. He hasn't had an album of fresh material out since 1989's *Off to See the Lizard.* If Buffett follows his old marketing strategy, he'll release the new album sometime between December and March. If he follows the more recent strategy, he'll wait until the '94 summer tour. By then we should know more about the screen adaptation of *Where Is Joe Merchant?,* which Buffett may coproduce and Paramount may distribute. Given Buffett's history with much-talked-about-but-never-made movies, we'll safely hedge our bets. There may be a *Joe Merchant* movie, we hear.

While a successful movie would be a major (and long-longed-for) conquest for Buffett, it would surely not be his last "new frontier." There

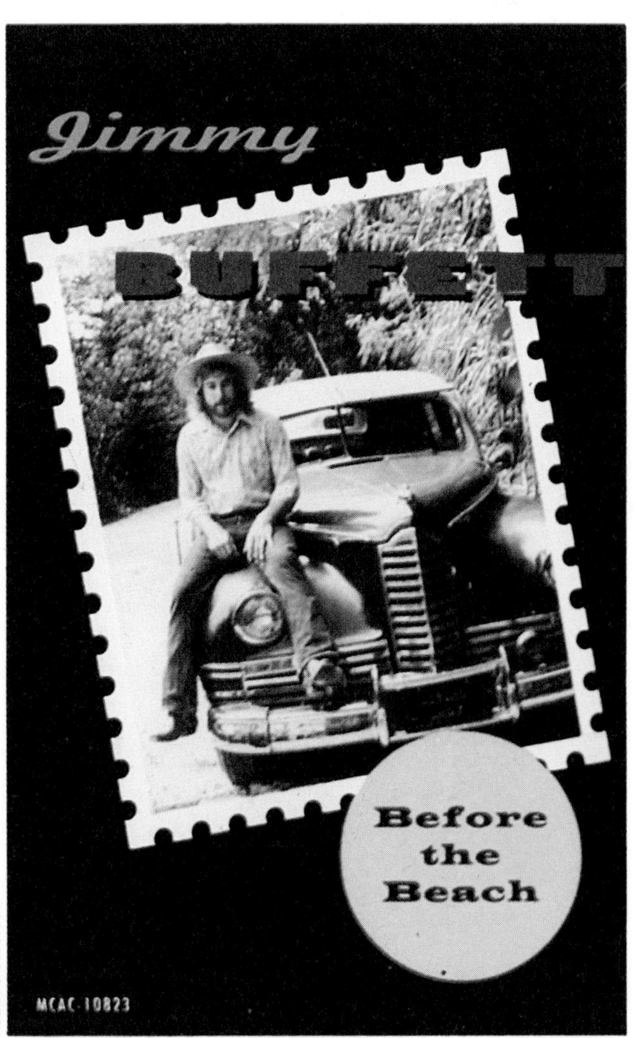

Author's Collection

Old recordings, new packaging went out to greet Parrot Heads for the Chameleon Caravan Tour. Buffett's ill-starred Barnaby label recordings got a better reception twenty-three years later.

are always new angles, and as long as there are Parrot Heads, Buffett will explore them. "You gotta be calculating," he told *High Times* back in 1976. "You gotta bust your ass if you want to do anything. For me, it's like I can't just be a sensitive artist and still be out here surviving. I've also gotta be a businessman.... If you're going to go up there and try to make it, you're not out there totally for aesthetic value. Let's face it—you're out there to secure your future, too, and anybody that says they're not is totally false. I couldn't say that the money doesn't mean anything to me."

Imagine a Parrot Head cable network, hawking Buffetabilia between Tahitian and Caribbean travelogues, old episodes of *Adventures in Paradise,* and Buffett music videos. It would probably be a great success. Jimmy Buffett's greatest creation is not his songs, though he's written some fine ones, nor his novels, nor his someday-to-be- seen screenplays. Jimmy Buffett's greatest creation is Jimmy Buffett, the millionaire beach bum so many of us so happily envy and emulate. "How would you like to be remembered in history?" Buffett was asked in a 1986 issue of *Mix.* He replied: "My epitaph is going to read: 'Now we can get some work done.'"

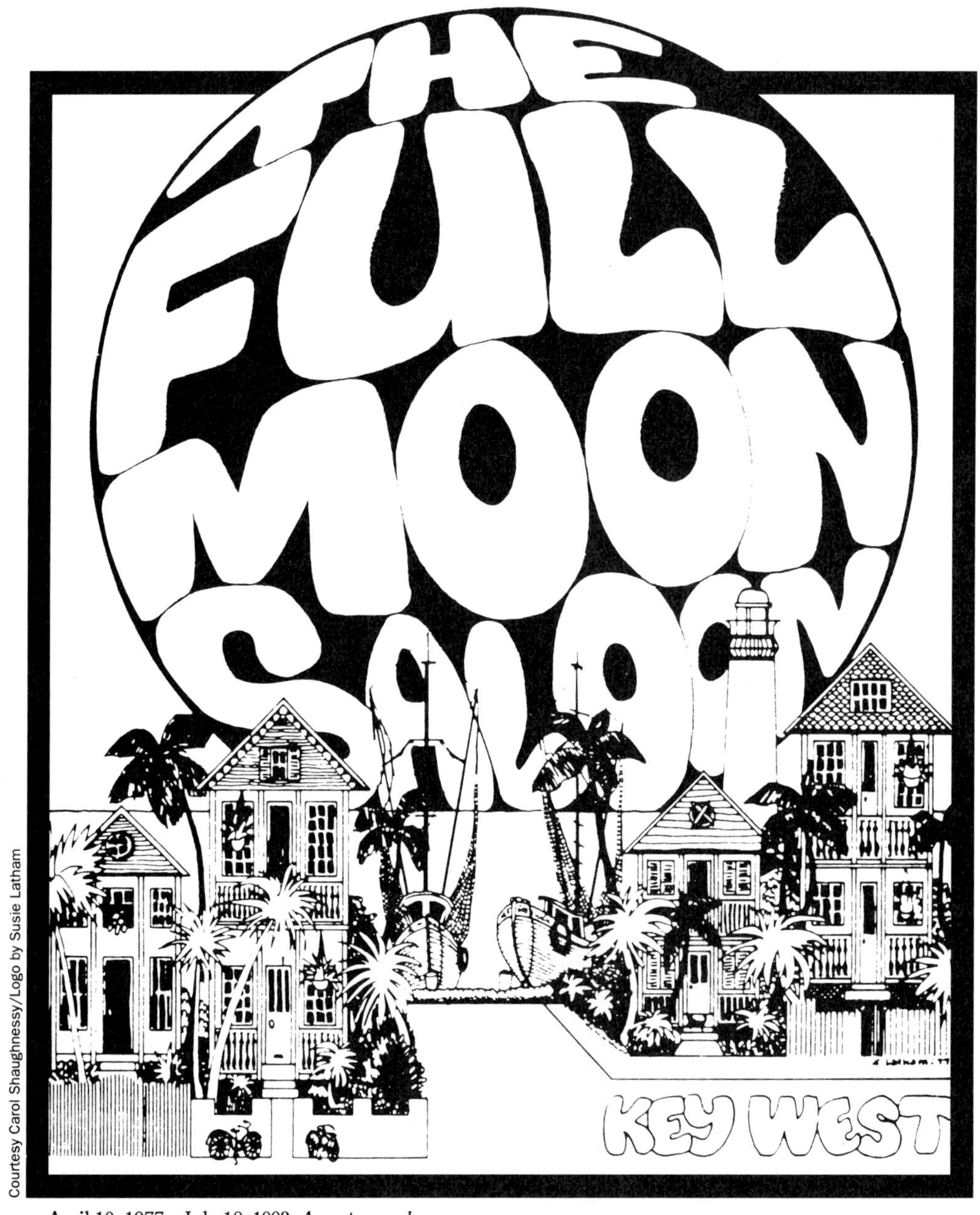

Courtesy Carol Shaughnessy/Logo by Susie Latham

April 10, 1977—July 18, 1993. *Ave atque vale.*

Parrot Heads put Buffett's adult fiction on the New York Times Bestseller list. He still longs to conquer "Holywood!"

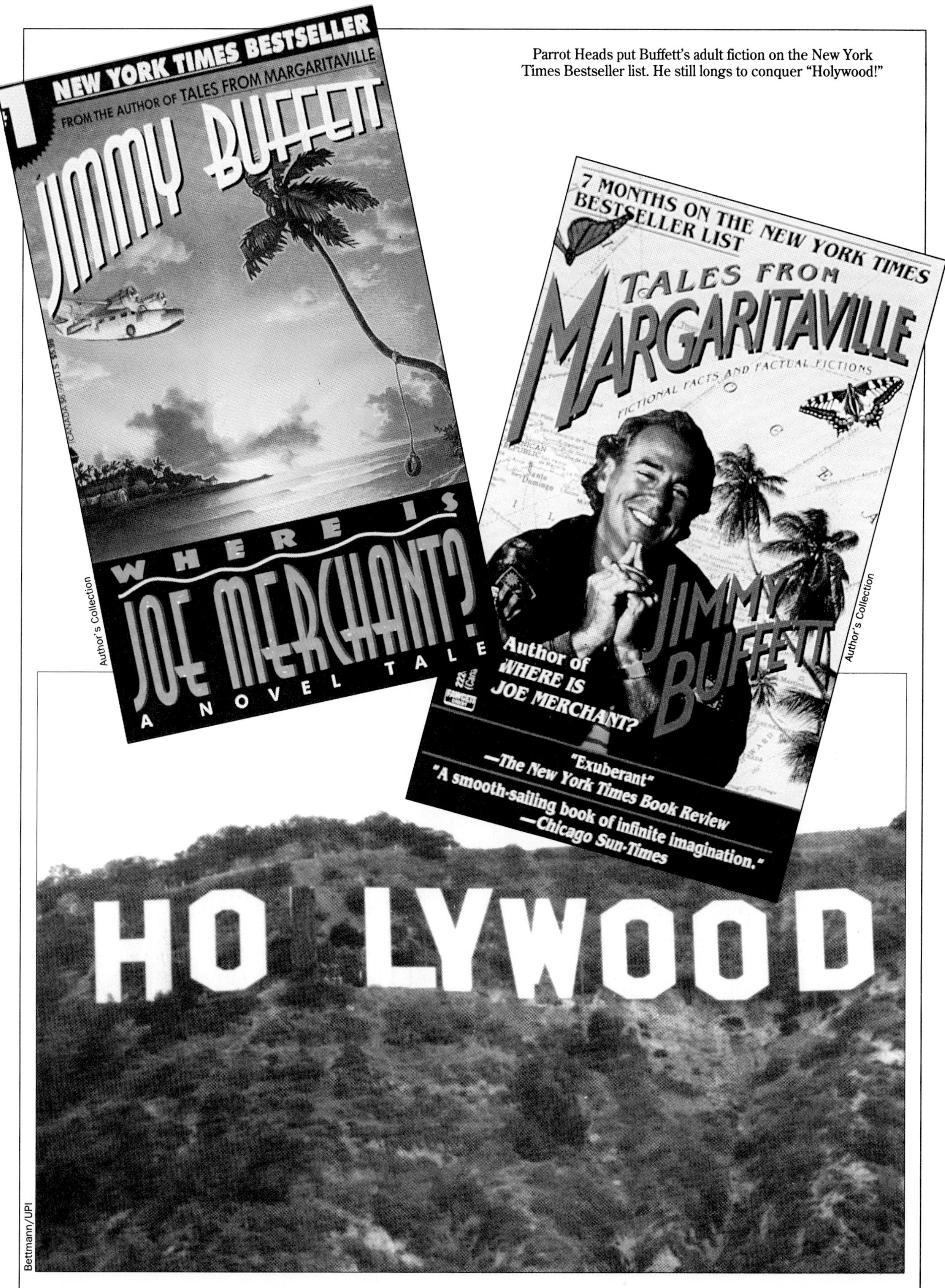

Author's Collection

Author's Collection

Bettmann/UPI

Wings Over the Water

My name is Frank Bama," Buffett writes at the beginning of *Where Is Joe Merchant?* "and I fly boats." Bama, the hero of Buffett's novel, is an obvious alter ego for the author. "He's always been into seaplanes," says Buffett's Key West pal Dink Bruce. And you can trace Buffett's fascination with flying back to his fifties childhood and the *Sky King* television series mentioned in "Pencil Thin Mustache." (Sky King's plane was named *The Songbird.*) But Buffett's seaplane fixation really became omnipresent in the early nineties. It was onstage as an elaborate prop (the Margaritaville Clipper was a takeoff on Boeing's Yankee Clipper), it was in his children's book, *Trouble Dolls,* and, as evidence of his adventurous good life, in the pages of his *Parrot Head Handbook* in a testimonial entitled "Why I Love My Seaplane." But most of all, it was evident in his novel, *Where Is Joe Merchant?*

Bama's Grumman Goose is practically one of the characters in *Joe Merchant.* The Goose appeared in 1936, a general utility amphibian which saw extensive transport and rescue service during World War II in the United States Navy and Army Air Corps. (The British Royal Air Force and the Royal Canadian Air Force also used the Goose.) With obvious pride, Buffett announced in the January 1993 *Coconut Telegraph* that he has just bought a Grumman Widgeon. This is a smaller version of the Goose, introduced in 1940. When the United States entered WW II, the Widgeon saw service as a Coast Guard patrol craft (one actually sank a U-boat). The two-to-three-passenger amphibian was used by the Navy for transport and training, and, as a communications aircraft, by the RAF in the West Indies.

Buffett's first seaplane was nothing as venerable and rare as the twin-engine Grummans. His first flying boat was a single-engine Lake Renegade. "He got his first seaplane when I was working for him," recalls Carol Shaughnessy. "A pilot from the company came down to teach him to fly the plane. He must have been down for six to eight weeks, teaching Jimmy to fly. Jimmy just loved it."

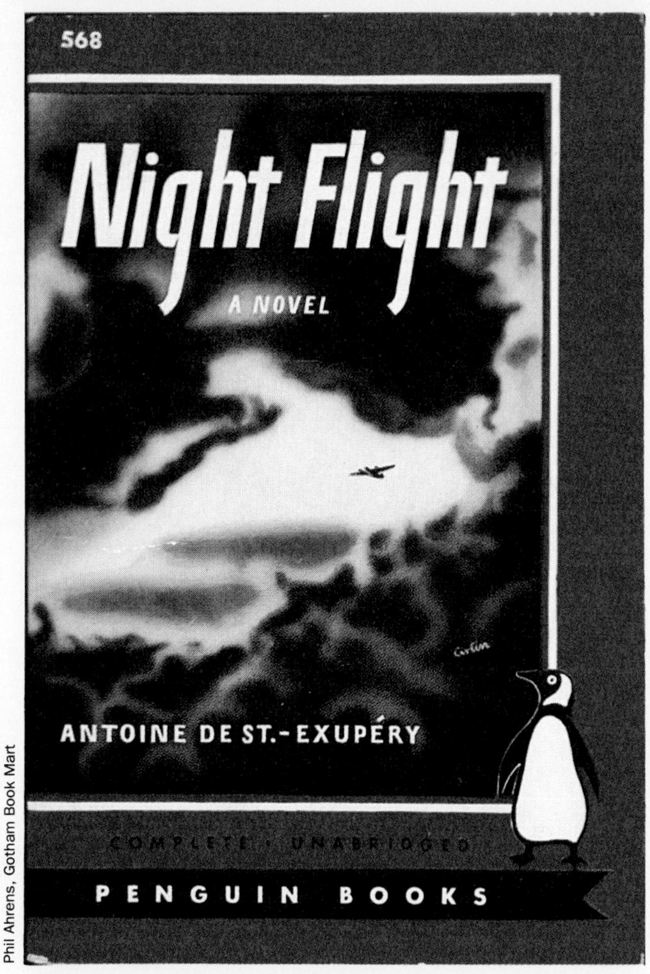

568
Night Flight
A NOVEL
ANTOINE DE ST.-EXUPÉRY
PENGUIN BOOKS

Phil Ahrens, Gotham Book Mart

Antoine de Saint-Exupéry's 1932 novel about flying the mail over the Andes won the Prix Femina, which compared him with Joseph Conrad—"the one writing of the oceans of the skies, the other of the oceans of salt water."

Zachary Richard recalls a flying voyage with Buffett from about 1987. "My wife and I flew out with Buffett to the Chandler Islands off the Mississippi Gulf Coast. I think this may have been one of his first seaplanes. I forget what this one was called, and he's probably got a few more since then, but this one had the propellor facing backwards, so it took off pretty dramatically. A vertical! He did all the pilot stuff, he was writing down and checking all the instruments and talking to the tower and doing all this shit. I don't know anything about driving a plane. I was pretty impressed. Most of my musician friends can hardly drive a car, let alone fly a plane."

In 1986, Buffett told *Los Angeles Herald*

Stan King Collection

LINDY

by Russ J. Hird

Stan King Collection

Stan King Collection

Charles Lindbergh. One of the few men to make history by his own choice. And then the deluge of extravagance accorded the heroes of the 1920s: the least of it (at top) a five cent cigar. (Above) The Charles Lindbergh-designed Hour Angle watch, manufactured by Longines in 1930, Pat. No. 1923305, worn on the wrist or leg over flying gear.

Examiner reporter Todd Everett about earning his wings: "Naval aviation always fascinated me, from the time I was a kid growing up on the Gulf Coast. Pensacola [Naval Air Station] had more sports cars per capita than anywhere else in the area, 'cause all the fliers had them. They were the coolest guys in the world to us.

"All my roommates went on and became pilots in the Navy. I flew little Cessnas myself when I was in school, and when I was about to get drafted I took the test to enter Pensacola and passed it. But then I failed the physical, so I didn't do anything.

"One of the commanders at the Navy base in Key West is a harmonica player who'd jam with me when I was in town. He invited me onto an aircraft carrier about a year and a half ago. I watched the planes take off and land, and I even got to drive the ship for a while. It's just like steering a boat, but it's *big.*

"Before they let me into a jet, I had to go to the naval aviation survival school in Norfolk, Virginia, and pass the four-day course before I could fly.... And when the Air Force heard that I had flown with the navy, they let me fly an F-15 in Atlanta, halfway through the last tour. I took a camera up, so now I have a video of it.

"It turns out there are a lot of Parrot Heads who are fighter pilots. So I want America to feel safe, knowing that the wings of the Parrot Heads are out there."

Amphibious aviation in America began in 1908 when Glenn Curtiss fitted canoe-like floats to his *June Bug,* then renamed the Loon. Curtiss's Loon skimmed nicely, but would not become airborne. Nearly three years and forty different floats later,

Stan King Collection

Anne Morrow and Charles Lindbergh leaving the Potomac on the second leg of their 7,000-mile flight to Tokyo, 1931. Mrs. Lindbergh is just visible in the rear cockpit of their low-winged, pontooned Ryan monoplane.

Harris Lewine Collection

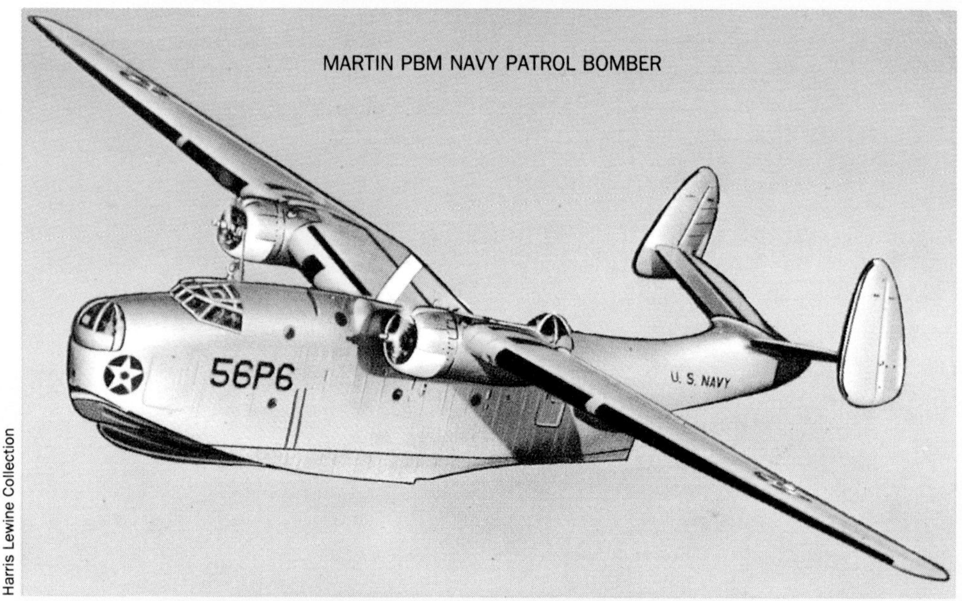

Harris Lewine Collection

Harris Lewine Collection

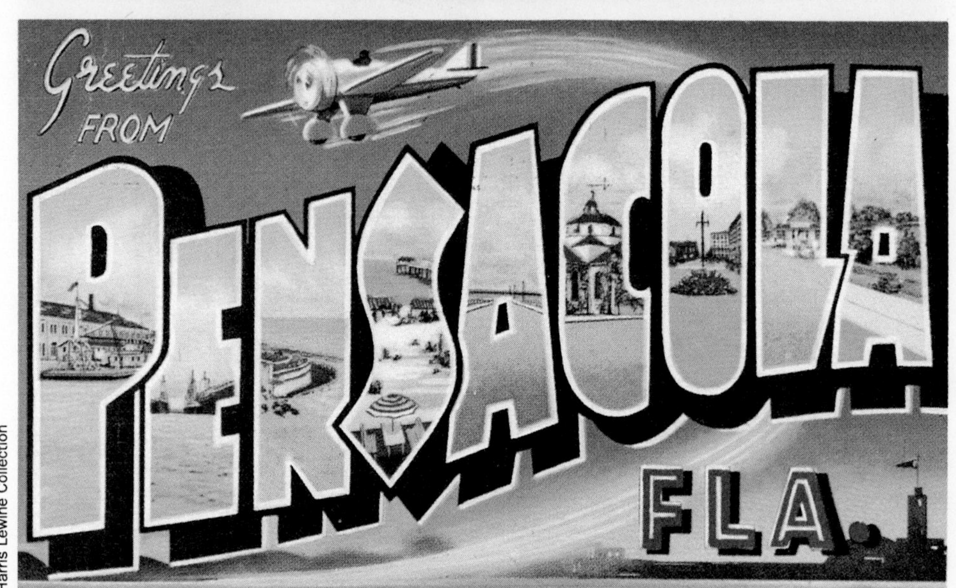

Curtiss successfully flew his "hydro-terra-aeroplane," and the U.S. Navy hired Curtiss to build what would be the first military seaplane, the A-1 Triad. Its 1911 maiden voyage lasted only five minutes (the craft soared to a lofty twenty-five feet), but the Navy was sufficiently impressed to order a second *Triad.* In 1914, Curtiss designed the H-4 America flying boat, which saw wartime service in Britain's Royal Naval Air Service in World War I. Britain made effective use of amphibious planes during World War I, but such crafts were to play a far greater role in World War II.

In *Joe Merchant,* Frank Bama tells us that his father was a World War II PBY pilot in the Pacific. The Consolidated PBY Catalina had its debut in 1935 and became one of the "stars" of the Pacific theater. Ironically, it was a slow and cumbersome behemoth (its wingspan was 104 feet) deemed obsolete when the United States entered World War II. But it was the only flying boat in production and, despite its vulnerability to attack, flew millions of wartime miles both as transport and a bomber.

As for *Merchant's* author, he is "muchly into flying," says Buffett's Key West crony Vic Latham. "It has a calming effect on him." Certainly the romance of the lone pilot charting his destiny by the stars is a balm to Buffett, expressed in the extensive quote from Antoine de Saint-Exupéry's classic *Wind, Sand and Stars* at the beginning of *Joe Merchant.* "Lindbergh had the right idea years ago," Buffett wrote in his *Parrot Head Handbook.* "Fly alone and be in charge of your own destiny. I wonder what he would think of my compact disc player mounted next to my navigation radios."

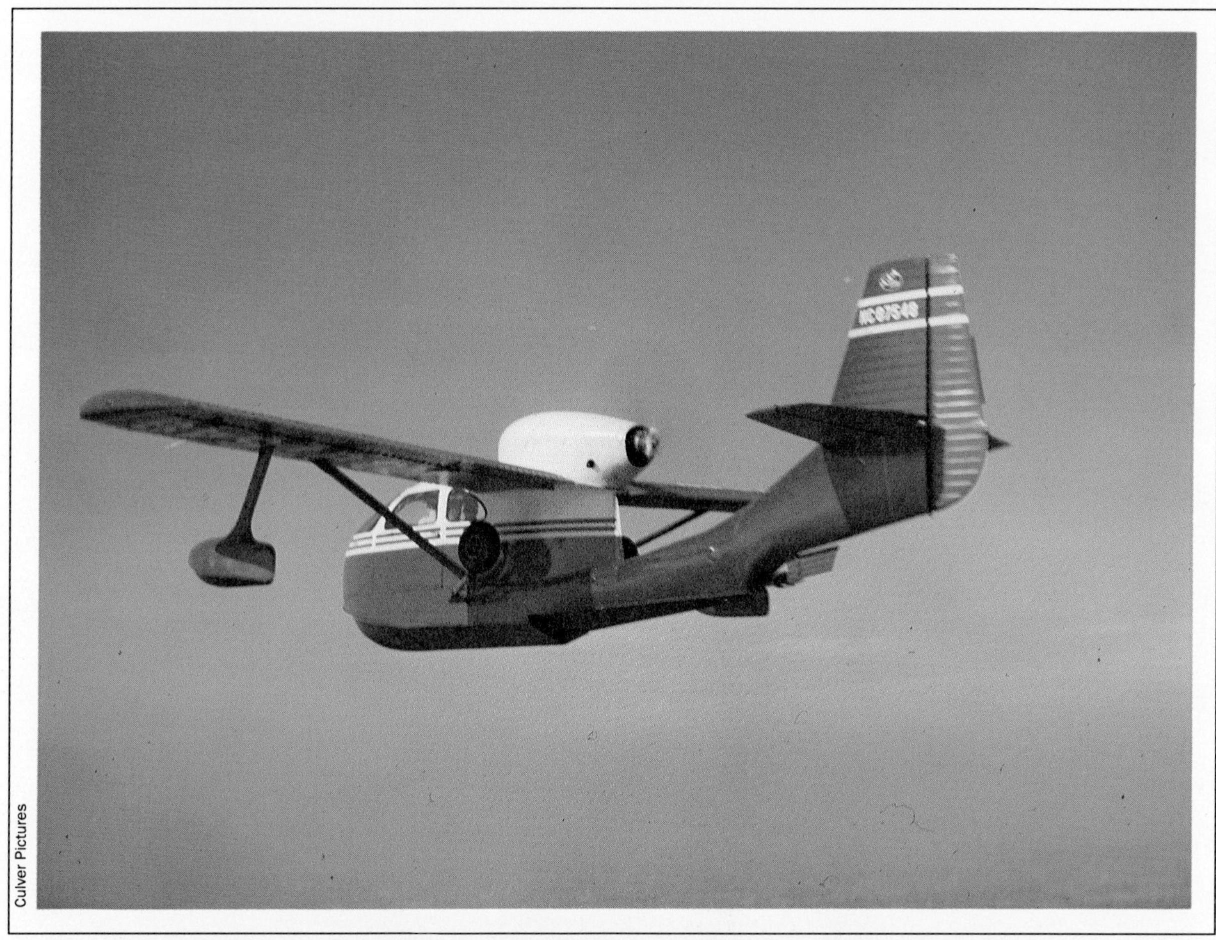

Culver Pictures

The Lake Renegade seaplane, Jimmy Buffett's favorite flying machine.

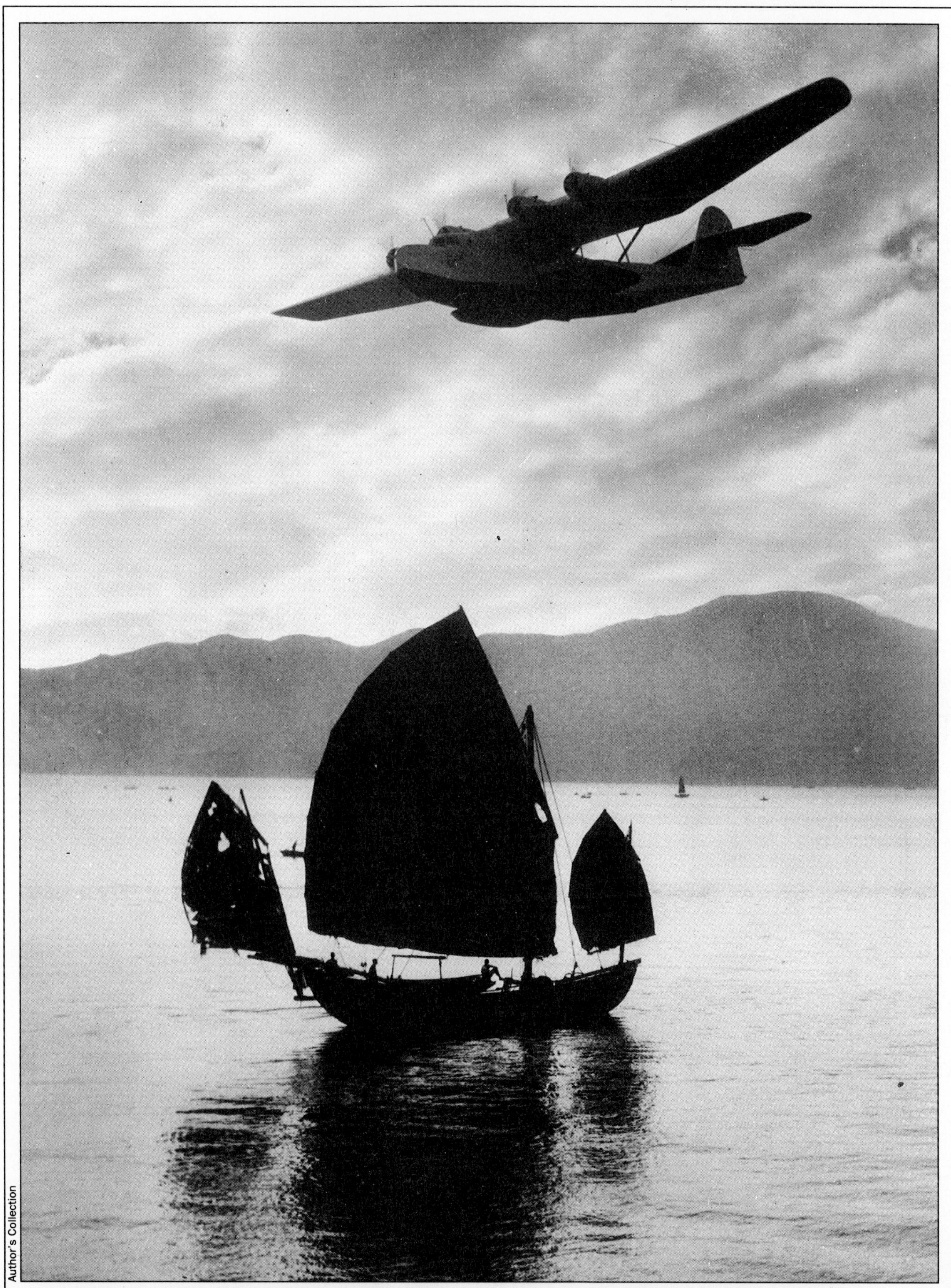

Author's Collection

Frank Bama flew boats and Herve Villechaize shouted ..."The plane! The plane!" on the television show *Fantasy Island.* They both would have shouted for the real China Clipper over Hong Kong.

Sacher Nature Collection